Second Student Research Workshop 2011

(RANLPStud 2011)

Associated with the 8th International Conference on Recent Advances in Natural Language Processing (RANLP 2011)

Hissar, Bulgaria
13 September 2011

ISBN: 978-1-62276-512-6

Printed from e-media with permission by:

Curran Associates, Inc.
57 Morehouse Lane
Red Hook, NY 12571

Some format issues inherent in the e-media version may also appear in this print version.

Printed by Curran Associates, Inc. (2012)

Association for Computational Linguistics
209 N. Eighth Street
Stroudsburg, Pennsylvania 18360

Phone: 1-570-476-8006
Fax: 1-570-476-0860

acl@aclweb.org

Additional copies of this publication are available from:

Curran Associates, Inc.
57 Morehouse Lane
Red Hook, NY 12571 USA
Phone: 845-758-0400
Fax: 845-758-2634
Email: curran@proceedings.com
Web: www.proceedings.com

Preface

The Recent Advances in Natural Language Processing (RANLP) conference, already in its eight year and ranked among the most influential NLP conferences, has always been a meeting venue for scientists coming from all over the world. Since 2009, we decided to give arena to the younger and less experienced members of the NLP community to share their results with an international audience. For this reason, further to the first successful and highly competitive Student Research Workshop associated with the conference RANLP 2009, we are pleased to announce the second edition of the workshop which is held during the main RANLP 2011 conference days on 13 September 2011.

The aim of the workshop is to provide an excellent opportunity for students at all levels (Bachelor, Master, and Ph.D.) to present their work in progress or completed projects to an international research audience and receive feedback from senior researchers. We have received 31 high quality submissions, among which 6 papers have been accepted as regular oral papers, and 18 as posters. Each submission has been reviewed by at least 2 reviewers, who are experts in their field, in order to supply detailed and helpful comments. The papers' topics cover a broad selection of resarch areas, such as:

- Annotation;
- BioMedical NLP;
- Coreference Resolution;
- Corpus Linguistics;
- Discourse Processing;
- Information Extraction;
- Machine Translation;
- Ontologies;
- Opinion Mining;
- Natural Language Generation;
- Parsing;
- Part-of-Speech Tagging;
- Question Answering;
- Text Classification;
- Text Segmentation;
- Text Summarization;
- Textual Entailment;
- Word Sense Disambiguation.

We are also glad to admit that our authors comprise a very international group with students coming from: Brazil, Bulgaria, France, Germany, Hungary, India, Iran, Romania, Russia, Spain, Serbia, Sweden, United Kingdom and United States.

We would like to thank the authors for submitting their articles to the Student Workshop and the members of the Programme Committee for their efforts to provide exhaustive reviews and for reacting in time. We are especially grateful to the RANLP Chairs Prof. Galia Angelova and Prof. Ruslan Mitkov for their indispensable support and encouragement during the Workshop organisation.

We hope that all the participants will receive invaluable feedback about their work. This year the conference and the workshop will take place in a new location (Hissar, Bulgaria), so we wish you to enjoy this new location and the Workshop!

Irina Temnikova, Ivelina Nikolova and Natalia Konstantinova
Organisers of the Student Workshop, held in conjunction with
The International Conference RANLP-11

Organizers:

Irina Temnikova (University of Wolverhampton, UK)
Ivelina Nikolova (Bulgarian Academy of Sciences, Bulgaria)
Natalia Konstantinova (University of Wolverhampton, UK)

Programme Committee:

Alexandra Balahur (University of Alicante, Spain)
Chris Biemann (Technical University Darmstadt, Germany)
Kevin Bretonnel Cohen (University of Colorado School of Medicine, USA)
Iustin Dornescu (University of Wolverhampton, UK)
Atefeh Farzindar (NLP Technologies Inc., Canada)
Darja Fišer (University of Ljubljana, Slovenia)
Najeh Hajlaoui (University of Wolverhampton, UK)
Laura Hasler (University of Strathclyde, UK)
Iustina Ilisei (University of Wolverhampton, UK)
Diana Inkpen (University of Ottawa, Canada)
Sobha Lalitha Devi (AU-KBC Research Centre, India)
Nikola Ljubešić (University of Zagreb, Croatia)
Wolfgang Maier (University of Düsseldorf, Germany)
Preslav Nakov (National University of Singapore, Singapore)
Constantin Orasan (University of Wolverhampton, UK)
Petya Osenova (Bulgarian Academy of Sciences, Bulgaria)
George Paltoglou (University of Wolverhampton, UK)
Ivandre Paraboni (University of Sao Paulo, Brazil)
Marta Recasens (University of Barcelona, Spain)
Georg Rehm (DFKI, Berlin, Germany)
Miguel Rios Gaona (University of Wolverhampton, UK)
Raphaël Rubino (University of Avignon, France)
Sebastian Rudolph (Karlsruher Institut für Technologie, Germany)
Doaa Samy (University of Cairo, Egypt)
Luis Sarmento (University of Porto, Portugal)
Thamar Solorio (University of Alabama at Birmingham, USA)
Lucia Specia (University of Wolverhampton, UK)
Asher Stern (Bar-Ilan University, Israel)
Ang Sun (New York University, USA)
Cristina Toledo (University of Málaga, Spain)
Yoshimasa Tsuruoka (Japan Advanced Institute of Science and Technology, Japan)
Cristina Vertan (University of Hamburg, Germany)
Pinar Wennerberg (Bayer, Germany)
Wajdi Zaghouani (University of Pennsylvania, USA)
Torsten Zesch (Technical University Darmstadt, Germany)

Table of Contents

Workshop Programme

Tuesday, 13 September, 2011

10:00–10:05 Opening

PLOVDIV hall: Oral Presentations

10:05–10:25 *Domain-Dependent Detection of Light Verb Constructions*
István T. Nagy, Gábor Berend, György Móra and Veronika Vincze

10:25–10:45 *A Weighted Lexicon of French Event Names*
Béatrice Arnulphy

11:00–11:30 Coffee Break and Student Posters (Lobby)

HISSAR hall: Oral Presentations

11:30–11:50 *Towards a Better Exploitation of the Brown 'Family' Corpora in Diachronic Studies of British and American English Language Varieties*
Sanja Štajner

11:50–12:10 *Projecting Farsi POS Data To Tag Pashto*
Mohammad Khan, Eric Baucom, Anthony Meyer and Lwin Moe

12:10–12:30 *Enriching Phrase-Based Statistical Machine Translation with POS Information*
Miriam Kaeshammer and Dominikus Wetzel

12:30–12:50 *Inter-domain Opinion Phrase Extraction Based on Feature Augmentation*
Gábor Berend, István T. Nagy, György Móra and Veronika Vincze

Lobby: Poster Presentations

15:40–16:20

ArbTE: Arabic Textual Entailment
Maytham Alabbas

RDFa Editor for Ontological Annotation
Melania Duma

Extracting Protein-Protein Interactions with Language Modelling
Ali Reza Ebadat

Experiments with Small-size Corpora in CBMT
Monica Gavrila and Natalia Elita

Question Parsing for QA in Spanish
Iria Gayo

Tuesday, 13 September, 2011 (continued)

Domain-Dependent Detection of Light Verb Constructions

István Nagy T.[1], **Gábor Berend**[1], **György Móra**[1] and **Veronika Vincze**[1,2]
[1]Department of Informatics, University of Szeged
{nistvan,berendg,gymora}@inf.u-szeged.hu
[2]Hungarian Academy of Sciences, Research Group on Artificial Intelligence
vinczev@inf.u-szeged.hu

Abstract

In this paper, we show how our methods developed for identifying light verb constructions can be adapted to different domains and different types of texts. We both experiment with rule-based methods and machine learning approaches. Our results indicate that existing solutions for detecting light verb constructions can be successfully applied to other domains as well and we conclude that even a little amount of annotated target data can notably contribute to performance if a bigger corpus from another domain is also exploited when training.

1 Introduction

Multiword expressions (MWEs) are lexical units that consist of more than one orthographical word, i.e. a lexical unit that contains spaces (Sag et al., 2002; Kim, 2008; Calzolari et al., 2002). They may exhibit peculiar semantic and syntactic features, thus, their NLP treatment is not without problems. Thus, they need to be handled with care in several NLP applications, e.g. in machine translation it must be known that they form one unit hence their parts should not be translated separately. For this, multiword expressions should be identified first.

There are several methods developed for identifying several types of MWEs, however, different kinds of multiword expressions require different solutions. Furthermore, there might be domain-related differences in the frequency of a specific MWE type. In this paper, we show how our methods developed for identifying light verb constructions can be adapted to different domains and different types of texts, namely, Wikipedia articles and texts from various topics. Our results suggest that with simple modifications, competitive results can be achieved on the target domain with both rule-based and machine learning approaches.

The structure of the paper is as follows. First, the characteristics of light verb constructions are presented, then related work is discussed. Our rule-based and machine learning approaches to detecting light verb constructions are presented and our results are analyzed in detail. The paper ends with a conclusion and some ideas on future work are also offered.

2 The Characteristics of Light Verb Constructions

Light verb constructions (LVCs) consist of a nominal and a verbal component where the noun is usually taken in one of its literal senses but the verbal component (also called *light verb*) usually loses its original sense to some extent (e.g. *to take a decision, to take sg into consideration*).

In the Wikipedia database used for evaluation (see 4.1) 8.5% of the sentences contain a light verb construction, thus, they are not so frequent in language use. However, they are syntactically flexible: the nominal component and the verb may not be adjacent (in e.g. passive sentences), which hinders their identification. Their proper treatment is especially important in information (event) extraction, where verbal elements play a central role and extracted events may differ if the verbal and the nominal component are not regarded as one complex predicate.

Light verb constructions deserve special attention in NLP applications for several reasons (Vincze and Csirik, 2010). First, their meaning is not totally compositional, that is, it cannot be computed on the basis of the meanings of the verb and the noun and the way they are related to each other. Thus, the result of translating the parts of the MWE can hardly be considered as the proper translation of the original expression. Second, light verb constructions (e.g. *make a mistake*) often share their syntactic pattern with other constructions such as literal verb + noun combinations (e.g. *make a cake*) or idioms (e.g. *make a meal*), thus, their identification cannot be based on solely syntactic patterns. Third, since the syntactic and the semantic head of the construction are not the same (the syntactic head being the verb and the semantic head being the noun), they require special treatment when parsing. It can be argued that they form a complex verb similar to phrasal or prepositional verbs.

3 Related Work

Light verb constructions have been paid special attention in NLP literature. Sag et al. (2002) classify them as a subtype of lexicalized phrases and flexible expressions. They are usually distinguished from productive or literal verb + noun constructions on the one hand and idiomatic verb + noun expressions on the other hand: Fazly and Stevenson (2007) use statistical measures in order to classify subtypes of verb + noun combinations.

There are several solutions developed for identifying different types of MWEs in different domains. Bonin et al. (2010) use contrastive filtering in order to identify multiword terminology in scientific, Wikipedia and legal texts: the extracted term candidates are ranked according to their belonging to the general language or the sublanguage of the domain.

The tool `mwetoolkit` (Ramisch et al., 2010a) is designed to identify several types of MWEs in different domains, which is illustrated through the example of identifying English compound nouns in the Genia and Europarl corpora and in general texts (Ramisch et al., 2010b; Ramisch et al., 2010c).

Some hybrid systems make use of both statistical and linguistic information as well, that is, rules based on syntactic or semantic regularities are also incorporated into the system (Bannard, 2007; Cook et al., 2007; Al-Haj and Wintner, 2010). This results in better coverage of multiword expressions.

Rule-based domain adaptation techniques are employed in multi-domain named entity recognition as well, and their usability is demonstrated in news stories, broadcast news and informal texts (Chiticariu et al., 2010). They show that domain-specific rules on the classification of ambiguous named entities (e.g. city names as locations or sports clubs) have positive influence on the results.

4 Experiments

For the automatic identification of light verb constructions in corpora, we implemented several rule-based methods and machine learning approaches, which we describe below in detail.

4.1 Corpora Used for Evaluation

We evaluate our approaches on a Wikipedia based corpus, in which several types of multiword expressions (including light verb constructions) and named entities were marked. Two annotators worked on the texts, and 15 articles were annotated by both of them. Differences in annotation were later resolved. As for light verb constructions, the agreement rates between the two annotators were 0.707 (F-measure), 0.698 (Kappa) and 0.5467 (Jaccard), respectively. The corpus contains 368 occurrences of light verb constructions and can be downloaded under the Creative Commons license at `http://www.inf.u-szeged.hu/rgai/mwe`. This dataset proved to be the source domain for the identification of light verb constructions.

Light verb constructions were first identified in the Wikipedia corpus and methods were adapted to the English part of a parallel corpus in which we annotated light verb constructions (14,261 sentence alignment units in size containing 1100 occurrences of light verb constructions). The parallel corpus consists of texts from magazines, novels[1], language books and texts on the European Union are also included. In this corpus, different syntactic forms of light verb constructions are annotated:

- verb + noun combinations: *give advice*
- participles: *photos taken*
- nominal forms: *service provider*
- split constructions (i.e. the verb and the noun are not adjacent): *a decision has rarely been made*

The average agreement rate between annotators was 0.7603 (F-measure). The corpus is available under the Creative Commons license at `http://www.inf.u-szeged.hu/rgai/mwe`.

Data on the corpora are shown in Table 1.

4.2 Rule-Based Methods for Identifying Light Verb Constructions

In our investigations, we applied similar methods to those described in Vincze et al. (2011).

[1]Not all of the literary texts have been annotated for light verb constructions in the corpus, which made us possible to study the characteristics of the domain and the corpus without having access to the test dataset.

Corpus	Sentence	Token	LVC
Wikipedia	4,350	114,570	368
Parallel	14,262	298,948	1,100

Table 1: Frequency of light verb constructions in different corpora

The POS-rule method meant that each n-gram for which the pre-defined patterns (e.g. `VB.?(NN|NNS)`) could be applied was accepted as a light verb construction. For POS-tagging, we used the Stanford POS-tagger (Toutanova and Manning, 2000). Since the methods to follow rely on morphological information (i.e. it is required to know which element is a noun), matching the POS-rules is a prerequisite to apply those methods for identifying LVCs.

The 'Suffix' method exploited the fact that many nominal components in light verb constructions are derived from verbs. Thus, in this case only constructions that matched our POS-rules and contained nouns ending in certain derivational suffixes were allowed.

The 'Most frequent verb' (MFV) method relied on the fact that the most common verbs function typically as light verbs (e.g. *do*, *make*, *take* etc.) Thus, the 12 most frequent verbs typical of light verb constructions were collected and constructions that matched our POS-rules and where the stem of the verbal component was among those of the most frequent ones were accepted.

The 'Stem' method pays attention to the stem of the noun. The nominal component is typically derived from a verbal stem (*make a decision*) or coincides with a verb (*have a walk*). In this case, we accepted only candidates that had a nominal component whose stem was of verbal nature, i.e. coincided with a stem of a verb.

Syntactic information can also be exploited in identifying LVCs. Typically, the syntactic relation between the verb and the nominal component in a light verb construction is `dobj` or `partmod` (using the Stanford parser (Klein and Manning, 2003)) – if it is a prepositional light verb construction, the relation between the verb and the preposition is `prep`. The 'Syntax' method accepts candidates among whose members the above syntactic relations hold.

We combined the above methods to identify light verb constructions in our databases (the union of candidates yielded by the methods is denoted by $\cup$ while the intersection is denoted by $\cap$ in the respective tables). In order to use the same dataset for evaluating rule based and machine learning methods, we randomly separated the target domain into 70% as training set (used in machine learning approaches) and 30% as test set. As the target domain contained several different topics, we separated all documents into training and test parts. We evaluated our various models in this resulting test set.

4.3 Machine Learning Approaches for Identifying Light Verb Constructions

In addition to the above-described approach, we defined another method for automatically identifying LVCs. The Conditional Random Fields (CRF) classifier was used (MALLET implementations (McCallum, 2002)). The basic feature set includes the following categories (Szarvas et al., 2006):

orthographical features: capitalization, word length, bit information about the word form (contains a digit or not, has uppercase character inside the word, etc.), character level bi/trigrams;

dictionaries of first names, company types, denominators of locations; noun compounds collected from English Wikipedia;

frequency information: frequency of the token, the ratio of the token's capitalized and lowercase occurrences, the ratio of capitalized and sentence beginning frequencies of the token which was derived from the Gigaword dataset[2];

shallow linguistic information: part of speech;

contextual information: sentence position, trigger words (the most frequent and unambiguous tokens in a window around the word under investigation) from the training database, the word between quotes, etc.

Some of the above presented LVC specific methods were added to this basic feature set for identifying LVCs. We extended dictionaries with the most frequent verbs like the 'MFV' feature from the rule based methods and a dictionary of the stems of nouns was also added. We extended the orthographical features with the 'Suffix' feature too. As syntax can play a very important role in identifying light verb constructions, we had to extend the shallow linguistic information features with syntactic information.

[2]Linguistic Data Consortium (LDC), catalogId: LDC2003T05

5 Results

We first developed our methods for LVC identification for the source corpus. The Wikipedia dataset is smaller in size and contains simpler annotation, therefore it was selected as the source domain (containing 4350 sentences and not being annotated for subtypes of light verb constructions).

5.1 Rule-Based Approaches

Results on the rule-based identification of light verb constructions can be seen in Table 2. In the case of the source domain, the recall of the baseline (POS-rules) is high, however, its precision is low (i.e. not all of the candidates defined by the POS patterns are light verb constructions). The 'Most frequent verb' (MFV) feature proves to be the most useful: the verbal component of the light verb construction is lexically much more restricted than the noun, which is exploited by this feature. The other two features put some constraints on the nominal component, which is typically of verbal nature in light verb constructions: 'Suffix' simply requires the lemma of the noun to end in a given n-gram (without exploiting further grammatical information) whereas 'Stem' allows nouns derived from verbs. When combining a verbal and a nominal feature, union results in high recall (the combinations typical verb + non-deverbal noun or atypical verb + deverbal noun are also found) while intersection yields high precision (typical verb + deverbal noun combinations are found only).

Methods developed for the source domain were also evaluated on the target domain without any modification (T w/o ADAPT column). Overall results are lower than in the case of the source domain, which is especially true for the 'MFV' method: while it performed best on the source domain (41.94%), it considerably declines on the target domain, reaching only 24.67%. The intersection of a verbal and a nominal feature, namely, 'MFV' and 'Stem' yields the best result on the target domain.

Techniques for identifying light verb constructions were also adapted to the other domain. The parallel corpus contained annotation for nominal and participial occurrences of light verb constructions. However, the number of nominal occurrences was negligible (58 out of 1100) hence we aimed at identifying only verbal and participial occurrences in the corpus. For this reason, POS-rules and syntactic rules were extended to treat postmodifiers as well (participial instances of light verb constructions typically occurred as postmodifiers, e.g. *photos taken*).

Since the best method on the Wikipedia corpus (i.e. 'MFV') could not reach such an outstanding result on the parallel corpus, we conducted an analysis of data on the unannotated parts of the parallel corpus. It was revealed that *have* and *go* mostly occurred in non light verb senses in these types of texts. *Have* usually denotes possession as in *have a son* vs. *have a walk* while *go* typically refers to physical movement instead of an abstract change of state (*go home* vs. *go on strike*). The reason for this might be that it is primarily everyday topics that can be found in magazines or novels rather than official or scientific topics, where it is less probable that possession or movement are described. Thus, a new list of typical light verbs was created which did not contain *have* and *go* but included *pay* and *catch* as they seemed to occur quite often in the unannotated parts of the corpus and in this way, an equal number of light verb candidates was used in the different scenarios.

The T+ADAPT column of Table 2 shows the results of domain adaptation. As for the individual features, 'MFV' proves to be the most successful on its own, thus, the above mentioned changes in the verb list are beneficial. Although the feature 'Suffix' was not modified, it performs better after adaptation, which suggests that there might be more deverbal nominal components with the given endings in the PART class of the target domain, which could not be identified without extended POS-rules. In the light of this, it is perhaps not surprising that its combination with 'MFV' also reaches better results than on the source domain. The intersection of 'MFV' and 'Stem' performs best after adaptation as well. Adaptation techniques add 1.5% to the F-measure on average, however, this value is 6.17% in the case of 'MFV'.

The added value of syntax was also investigated for LVC detection in both the source and the target domains. As represented in Table 3, syntax clearly helps in identifying light verb constructions: on average, it adds 2.58% and 2.45% to the F-measure on the source and the target domains, respectively. On the adapted model, syntactic information adds another 1.39% to performance, thus, adaptation techniques and syntactic features together notably contribute to performance (3.84% on average). The best result on the

Method	SOURCE			T w/o ADAPT			T+ADAPT		
POS-rules	7.02	76.63	12.86	4.28	73.33	8.09	4.28	73.33	8.09
Suffix	9.62	16.3	12.1	9.83	14.58	11.74	9.92	15.42	12.07
MFV	33.83	55.16	**41.94**	16.25	51.25	24.67	22.48	49.17	30.85
Stem	8.56	50.54	14.64	6.55	57.08	11.75	6.55	57.08	11.75
Suffix ∩ MFV	44.05	10.05	16.37	32.35	9.17	14.28	**48.94**	9.58	16.03
Suffix ∪ MFV	19.82	61.41	29.97	13.01	56.67	21.17	15.51	55.0	24.2
Suffix ∩ Stem	10.35	11.14	11.1	11.59	11.25	11.42	11.6	12.08	11.84
Suffix ∪ Stem	8.87	57.61	15.37	6.55	60.42	11.82	6.55	60.42	11.82
MFV ∩ Stem	39.53	36.96	38.2	24.08	40.83	**30.29**	30.72	39.17	**34.43**
MFV ∪ Stem	10.42	68.75	18.09	6.64	67.5	12.09	6.97	67.08	12.63
Suffix ∩ MFV ∩ Stem	**47.37**	7.34	12.7	**40.0**	7.5	12.63	51.35	7.92	13.72
Suffix ∪ MFV ∪ Stem	10.16	**72.28**	17.82	6.53	**69.17**	11.94	6.8	**68.75**	12.39

Table 2: Results of rule-based methods for light verb constructions in terms of precision, recall and F-measure. SOURCE: source domain, T: target domain, ADAPT: adaptation techniques, POS-rules: matching of POS-patterns, Suffix: the noun ends in a given suffix, MFV: the verb is among the 12 most frequent light verbs, Stem: the noun is deverbal.

Corpus	Precision	Recall	F-measure
Wikipedia	60.40	41.85	49.44
Parallel	63.60	39.52	48.75

Table 4: Results of leave-one-out approaches in terms of Precision, Recall and F-measure.

source domain, again, is yielded by the 'MFV' method, which is about 30% above the baseline. On the target domain, it is still the intersection of 'MFV' and 'Stem' that performs best, however, 'MFV' also achieves a good result.

5.2 CRF-Based Approaches

To identify light verb constructions we used the manually annotated corpora (Wikipedia and Parallel) to train CRF classification models (they were evaluated in a leave-one-document-out scheme). Results are shown in Table 4. However, as in the case of the rule-based approach, LVC specific features were adapted to the target corpus. In this way, for instance, the MFV dictionary did not contain *have* and *go* but *pay* and *catch* instead. In the case of the 'Stem' feature, we used domain specific dictionaries. Furthermore, when we trained on the Parallel corpus, we extended the syntax feature rules with `partmod`. On both of the two corpora the CRF based approach can achieve better results than rule-based methods.

For machine learning based domain adaptation we extended our LVC feature set as described in Daumé III (2007). In this way, we extended the above presented basic CRF feature set with domain dependent LVC specific features and with their union. So, some LVC specific features ('MFV' and 'Stem') are represented three times: Wikipedia based, Parallel based and their union, while for the syntax feature, we only used the parallel based one.

As the Wikipedia set was the source domain, we used it as the training set with the above presented extended features, and we extended this training set with randomly selected sentences from the training set of the target domain. We extended the source training set with 10%, 20%, 25%, 33% and 50% of the target domain training sentences in a step-by-step fashion. As Table 5 shows, we evaluated the model trained with the source domain specific feature set (BASE) and the domain adapted trained model (ADAPT) too.

As the results show, the addition of even a little amount of target data has beneficial effects on performance in both the BASE and the ADAPT settings. Obviously, the more target data are available, the better results are achieved. Interestingly, the addition of target data affects precision in a positive way (adding only 10% of parallel data improves precision by about 11%) and recall in a negative way, however, its general effect is that the F-measure improves. Results can be enhanced by applying the domain adapted model. Compared to the base settings, with this feature representation, the F-measure improves 1.515% on average, again primarily due to the higher precision, which

Method	SOURCE+SYNT			T w/o ADAPT + SYNT			T+ADAPT+SYNT		
POS-rules	9.35	72.55	16.56	5.93	69.17	10.92	5.93	69.17	10.92
Suffix	11.52	15.22	13.11	12.1	14.17	13.05	12.1	14.17	13.05
MFV	40.21	51.9	**45.31**	19.54	49.17	27.96	28.28	45.83	34.97
Stem	11.07	47.55	17.96	9.0	54.17	15.43	9.0	54.17	15.43
Suffix ∩ MFV	11.42	54.35	18.88	34.92	9.17	14.52	52.5	8.75	15.0
Suffix ∪ MFV	23.99	57.88	33.92	15.82	54.17	24.48	19.52	51.25	28.27
Suffix ∩ Stem	12.28	11.14	11.68	15.17	11.25	12.92	15.17	11.25	12.92
Suffix ∪ Stem	11.46	54.35	18.93	8.85	57.08	15.32	8.85	57.08	15.32
MFV ∩ Stem	46.55	34.78	39.81	27.81	39.17	**32.53**	37.18	36.25	**36.7**
MFV ∪ Stem	13.36	64.67	22.15	9.0	64.17	15.79	9.56	63.75	16.63
Suffix ∩ MFV ∩ Stem	**50.0**	6.79	11.96	**45.0**	7.5	12.86	**56.67**	7.08	12.59
Suffix ∪ MFV ∪ Stem	13.04	**68.2**	21.89	8.77	**65.42**	15.46	9.21	**65.0**	16.14

Table 3: Results of rule-based methods enhanced by syntactic features for light verb constructions in terms of precision, recall and F-measure. SOURCE: source domain, T: target domain, ADAPT: adaptation techniques, SYNT: syntactic rules, POS-rules: matching of POS-patterns, Suffix: the noun ends in a given suffix, MFV: the verb is among the 12 most frequent light verbs, Stem: the noun is deverbal.

clearly indicates that the domain adaptation techniques applied are optimized for precision in the case of this particular setting and datasets. The advantage of applying both domain-adapted features and adding some target data to the training dataset can be further emphasized if we compare the results achieved without any target data and with the basic feature set (34.88% F-score) and with the 50% of target data added and the adapted feature set (44.65%), thus, an improvement of almost 10% can be observed.

6 Discussion

As the results of the leave-one-out approaches indicate, it is not a trivial task to identify light verb constructions. Sometimes it is very difficult to decide whether an expression is a LVC or not since semantic information is also taken into consideration when defining light verb constructions (i.e. the verb does not totally preserve its original meaning). Furthermore, the identification of light verb constructions requires morphological, lexical or syntactic features such as the stem of the noun, the lemma of the verb or the dependency relation between the noun and the verb.

For identifying light verb constructions we examined rule-based methods and machine learning based methods too. Rule-based methods were transformed into LVC specific features in machine learning. With the extended feature set the CRF models can achieve better results than the rule-based methods in both corpora.

We also investigated how our rule-based methods and machine learning approaches developed for identifying light verb constructions can be adapted to different domains. For adaptation, characteristics of the corpora must be considered: in our case, the topics of texts determined the modifications in our methods and the implementation of new methods. Our adapted methods achieved better results on the target domains than the original ones in both rule-based and machine learning settings.

The importance of domain-specific annotated data is also underlined by our machine learning experiments. Simple cross-training (i.e. training on Wiki and testing on Parallel) yields relatively poor results but adding some Parallel data to the training dataset efficiently improves results (especially precision).

If rule-based methods and machine learning approaches are contrasted, it can be seen that machine learning settings almost always outperform rule-based methods, the only exception being when there are no Parallel data used in training. Thus suggests that if no annotated target data are available, it might be slightly more fruitful to apply rule-based methods, however, if there are annotated target data and a larger corpus from another domain, domain adaptation techniques and machine learning may be successfully applied. In our settings, even about 1000 annotated sentences from the target domain can considerably improve performance if large outdomain data are also ex-

Method	BASE			ADAPT		
Wiki	29.79	42.08	34.88	31.04	43.33	36.18
Wiki + 10%	40.44	37.91	39.14	42.72	37.91	40.18
Wiki + 20%	40.09	38.75	39.40	43.60	38.33	40.79
Wiki + 25%	41.96	39.16	40.51	47.37	37.5	41.86
Wiki + 33%	45.78	38.41	41.79	46.44	40.83	43.46
Wiki + 50%	47.89	37.91	42.32	49.24	40.83	44.65

Table 5: Results of machine learning approach for light verb constructions in terms of precision, recall and F-measure. BASE: source domain specific feature set trained model, ADAPT: domain adapted trained model.

ploited.

7 Conclusion

In this paper, we focused on the identification of light verb constructions in different domains, namely, Wikipedia articles and general texts of miscellaneous topics. We solved this problem with rule-based methods and machine learning approaches too. Our results show that identifying light verb constructions is a very hard task. Our rule-based methods and results were exploited in the machine learning approaches. We developed our methods for the source domain and then we adapted the characteristics to the target domain. Our results indicate that with simple modifications and little effort, our initial methods can be successfully adapted to the target domain as well. On the other hand, even a little amount of annotated target data can considerably contribute to performance if a bigger corpus from another domain is also exploited when training. As future work, we aim at experimenting on more domains and corpora and we would like to investigate other ways of domain adaptation and machine learning techniques for identifying light verb constructions.

Acknowledgments

This work was supported by the Project "TÁMOP-4.2.1/B-09/1/KONV-2010-0005 – Creating the Center of Excellence at the University of Szeged", supported by the European Union and co-financed by the European Regional Development Fund and by the project BELAMI financed by the National Innovation Office of the Hungarian government.

References

Hassan Al-Haj and Shuly Wintner. 2010. Identifying multi-word expressions by leveraging morphological and syntactic idiosyncrasy. In *Proceedings of Coling 2010*, Beijing, China.

Colin Bannard. 2007. A measure of syntactic flexibility for automatically identifying multiword expressions in corpora. In *Proceedings of the Workshop on a Broader Perspective on Multiword Expressions*, MWE '07, pages 1–8, Morristown, NJ, USA. ACL.

Francesca Bonin, Felice Dell'Orletta, Giulia Venturi, and Simonetta Montemagni. 2010. Contrastive filtering of domain-specific multi-word terms from different types of corpora. In *Proceedings of the 2010 Workshop on Multiword Expressions: from Theory to Applications*, pages 77–80, Beijing, China, August. Coling 2010 Organizing Committee.

Nicoletta Calzolari, Charles Fillmore, Ralph Grishman, Nancy Ide, Alessandro Lenci, Catherine MacLeod, and Antonio Zampolli. 2002. Towards best practice for multiword expressions in computational lexicons. In *Proceedings of LREC-2002*, pages 1934–1940, Las Palmas.

Laura Chiticariu, Rajasekar Krishnamurthy, Yunyao Li, Frederick Reiss, and Shivakumar Vaithyanathan. 2010. Domain adaptation of rule-based annotators for named-entity recognition tasks. In *Proceedings of EMNLP 2010*, pages 1002–1012, Stroudsburg, PA, USA. ACL.

Paul Cook, Afsaneh Fazly, and Suzanne Stevenson. 2007. Pulling their weight: exploiting syntactic forms for the automatic identification of idiomatic expressions in context. In *Proceedings of the Workshop on a Broader Perspective on Multiword Expressions*, pages 41–48, Morristown, NJ, USA. ACL.

Hal Daumé III. 2007. Frustratingly easy domain adaptation. In *Proceedings of the 45th Annual Meeting of the Association of Computational Linguistics*, pages 256–263, Prague, Czech Republic, June. Association for Computational Linguistics.

Afsaneh Fazly and Suzanne Stevenson. 2007. Distinguishing Subtypes of Multiword Expressions Using Linguistically-Motivated Statistical Measures. In *Proceedings of the Workshop on A Broader Perspective on Multiword Expressions*, pages 9–16,

Prague, Czech Republic. Association for Computational Linguistics.

Su Nam Kim. 2008. *Statistical Modeling of Multiword Expressions*. Ph.D. thesis, University of Melbourne, Melbourne.

Dan Klein and Christopher D. Manning. 2003. Accurate unlexicalized parsing. In *Proceedings of the 41st Annual Meeting on Association for Computational Linguistics*, ACL '03, pages 423–430, Stroudsburg, PA, USA. Association for Computational Linguistics.

Andrew Kachites McCallum. 2002. Mallet: A machine learning for language toolkit. http://mallet.cs.umass.edu.

Carlos Ramisch, Aline Villavicencio, and Christian Boitet. 2010a. Multiword Expressions in the wild? The mwetoolkit comes in handy. In *Coling 2010: Demonstrations*, Beijing, China.

Carlos Ramisch, Aline Villavicencio, and Christian Boitet. 2010b. mwetoolkit: a framework for multiword expression identification. In Nicoletta Calzolari, Khalid Choukri, Bente Maegaard, Joseph Mariani, Jan Odjik, Stelios Piperidis, and Daniel Tapias, editors, *Proceedings of LREC'10*, Valletta, Malta. ELRA.

Carlos Ramisch, Aline Villavicencio, and Christian Boitet. 2010c. Web-based and combined language models: a case study on noun compound identification. In *Coling 2010: Posters*, Beijing, China.

Ivan A. Sag, Timothy Baldwin, Francis Bond, Ann Copestake, and Dan Flickinger. 2002. Multiword Expressions: A Pain in the Neck for NLP. In *Proceedings of CICLing-2002*, pages 1–15, Mexico City, Mexico.

György Szarvas, Richárd Farkas, and András Kocsor. 2006. A Multilingual Named Entity Recognition System Using Boosting and C4.5 Decision Tree Learning Algorithms. In *Discovery Science*, pages 267–278.

Kristina Toutanova and Christopher D. Manning. 2000. Enriching the knowledge sources used in a maximum entropy part-of-speech tagger. In *Proceedings of EMNLP 2000*, pages 63–70, Stroudsburg, PA, USA. Association for Computational Lingustics.

Veronika Vincze and János Csirik. 2010. Hungarian corpus of light verb constructions. In *Proceedings of Coling 2010*, Beijing, China.

Veronika Vincze, István Nagy T., and Gábor Berend. 2011. Detecting noun compounds and light verb constructions: a contrastive study. In *Proceedings of the Workshop on Multiword Expressions: from Parsing and Generation to the Real World*, pages 116–121, Portland, Oregon, USA, June. Association for Computational Linguistics.

A Weighted Lexicon of French Event Names

Béatrice Arnulphy
LIMSI-CNRS & Univ. Paris Sud 11
Orsay, France
{firstname.lastname}@limsi.fr

Abstract

This paper describes a study in the purpose of annotation of event names in French texts. It presents a theoretical study about the notion of Event and defines the types of event names under study. It then presents related works about Events in NLP. Afterwards, we first use manually supervised lexicons that provide lists of nouns representing events, and demonstrate the limitations of lexicons in the task of event recognition. Further experiments are presented to propose an automatic method for building a weighted lexicon of event names.[1]

1 Introduction

Information extraction consists in a surface analysis of text dedicated to a specific application. Within this general purpose, detection of event descriptions is often an important clue. However, events are, in open-domain information extraction, less studied than general named entities like location and person names. Furthermore, other fields in NLP are concerned by the recognition of events.

Verbs *vs.* nouns. Most events are expressed in texts by verbs and nouns. (Vendler, 1967) described the events verbal forms in a formal way while (Pustejovsky et al., 2005) used natural language processing application to process this study. Verbs are also more frequent and easier than nouns to identify and to link to other temporal information than nouns, such as temporal expressions and signals. However, (especially in newswire articles and in all languages) verbs often express less meaningful events, especially in newswire articles, whatever the language observed is: the most frequent verbs in texts are common words like *say*, *accept*, *look*. Verbs are used to talk about "common" events, while important events are frequently nominalized. For this reason, studies on events in the humanities, like sociology and particularly linguistics, mainly focus on nominal events.

[1] This work has been partially founded by OSEO under the Quaero program

Name of Events. An event is what happens, it corresponds to a change of state. It can be either recurring or unique, predicted or not. It may last a moment or be instantaneous. It can also occur indifferently in the past, the present or the future.

The name given to an event can be formed either from deverbal nouns, from nouns that intrinsically denote events, or words taking their eventness in context. These constructions are detailed in Section 2. For each of those three classes, we observed that using resources is a first approach that give results we have to refine in context; context must be used to decide whether nouns or noun phrases are events.

Objectives. Existing lexicons provide lists of nouns that can be considered as events in context. Indeed, almost all nouns are highly dependent on context to assign an event characteristic. In this paper, our aim is to present the interest to use lexicons in event recognition, and their limits. We then propose a lexicon of event nouns providing quantitative information concerning the "eventness" of the words. Such a lexicon would help disambiguation of noun class in context.

This paper is organized as follows: Section 2 introduces the notion of events and presents our vision of the construction of events names. Section 3 deals with events in NLP. In Section 4, we focus on the resources that we created or used: our manually-annotated corpus (used for evaluation), as well as existing lexicons and extraction rules that we identified. Section 5 is dedicated to our experiments, leading to the automatic elaboration of a weighted lexicon, presented in Section 6.

2 Events and their Names

Events have been studied for years in several fields and in different ways. Here is an overview of works dealing with the general definition of events. We also present our observation about the formation of their names.

Event Entity There are some definitions of the event in philosophy, history, linguistics and also in media theory. The last two are of particular interest for our own work.

In the 70's, an important reflexion was conducted about the notion of **mediatical** event. Following Davidson's ideas of 1970 about Mental Events (Davidson, 1980), these works focus on "what makes the event" and how medias create it. More recently, Neveu and Quéré (1996) presents the notion of event, as a simple occurrence, unplanned, not repeatable, happened in a recent or distant past. We disagree with this definition and we consider planned or unplanned events, such as those taking place in the past, present or future. However, there is no information about the nominalization of event descriptions.

In **linguistics**, a few researches try to deal with the problem of events in its globality. Velde (2000) refers to the general notion of "triad" I-here-now, and notices that if persons and locations are considered as proper names, then "proper names of time" should exist as well. Moreover, location names and dates can, by the mean of metonymy, take an eventive reading. It is the case for the toponym *Tchernobyl* (Lecolle, 2004) that designates the nuclear explosion which happened in the city of Tchernobyl in 1986; or for the hemeronym *September-11* (Calabrese Steimberg, 2008) which names the terrorist attack on New York in 2001. We are interested in the detection of such metonymical event names.

How are they constructed? In the humanities, studies about events in humanities usually deal with one case among others. We do not consider events in the same way. This is why according to their studies and our corpus analysis we propose a description of the lexical construction of names of events.

We organize event names into three types, according to their construction:

- Events supported by **deverbal nouns**, derived from event verbs or verb phrases by a process of nominalization. For example, the verb *to assign* is nominalized into *assignment*. In all languages, this nominalization is often ambiguous (here, *assignment* can be the act of assigning something, but also the result of this action).
- Names introduced by **nouns that intrinsically denote events**, as *festival* or *match*. Once again, a disambiguation is needed: in French, *salon* can be either a lounge or an exhibition show – *salon de l'automobile* "motor exhibition").
- Nouns or noun phrases that become **events in specific contexts**, often by metonymy, as some location names (*Tchernobyl* designates the 1986 nuclear accident) or dates (*September-11* stands for the 2001 attacks).

In the litterature, we can find clues of definitions of the event, a challenge is to deal with them in a NLP approach.

3 Events in NLP

In NLP, the definition of events seems to be quite *ad hoc* to the application they are meant to.

Events in temporal extraction. TimeML (Pustejovsky et al., 2003) is a specification language for events and temporal expressions, originally developed to improve the performance of question answering systems. In TimeML, it is considered that an event is "a cover term for situations that happen or occur". Their qualities are punctuality or duration, and can describe states. In our own work, we consider all kinds of events, proper names or not, taking place in the past, the present or the future. We do not consider states (even if they can also be nominalized) and we focus only on nominalization of events, not on verbs or predicative clauses, which are the main interest of TimeML.

Events in Named Entity studies. The task of Named Entity recognition generally focuses on classical notions of location, organisation, person or date (*e.g.* the MUC campaigns). Events Named Entitiy are rarely considered, and only in a very specific, task-oriented type definition. However, events expressed by noun phrases have many common points with "traditional" named entities; in particular, applications are nearly the same (information extraction, relationship extraction, summarization, technology watch, etc.). Nevertheless, some aspects are different, for example event phrases are more subject to variations, and they are more frequently composed of several words with an internal structure (head, modifiers and arguments).

Only few named entity evaluation campaigns considered events in their frameworks. In the event extraction project **ACE** (Automatic Content Extraction) in (2005), the classification of events is detailed and precise, but concerns only a very limited number of domains. For example, the category "life" is composed of "be-born", "die", "be-injured", etc. Specific arguments are related to particular events, such as the origin and destination for transportation. The objective of ACE is to detect thematic events, and the classification, precise but incomplete, is coherent from this point of view. We do not have the same objectives. In our work, we are interested in all mentions of nouns describing events without any thematical predefined class. In the continuation of MUC (Grishman and Sundheim, 1996) and ACE, SemEval[2] paid interest to events, but only in semantic role labelling approach and detection of eventive verbs in Chinese news.

French **ESTER** campaigns provide a very different classification of events as named entities: the aim is to produce an open-domain named entity tagging. For this reason, event typology is quite simple: *historical and unique* events on the one hand, *repetitive* events on the other hand. This typology is quite close to our point of view on events.

Nominal Event Extraction. Only a few researches have been fully dedicated to automatic extraction of nominal events. We described here some works that follow a comparable approach as ours, where clues can be used on various languages.

Evita (Saurí et al., 2005) is an application recognizing verbal and nominal events in natural language English texts. This work was achieved in a TimeML way. Disambiguation of nouns that have both eventive and non-eventive interpretations is based on a statistical module, using a lexical lookup in WordNet and the use of a Bayesian Classifier trained on SemCor.

Also for English, following the ACE definition of events, Creswell et al. (2006) created a classifier that labels NPs as events or non-events for English. They worked on seed term lexicons from WordNet and the British National Corpus.

Eberle et al. (2009) present a tool using cues for the disambiguation of readings of German *ung*-nominalizations within their sentential context.

[2]http://semeval2.fbk.eu/semeval2.ph

Russo et al. (2011) focused on the eventive reading of deverbals in Italian, using syntagmatic and collocational cues.

Dealing with the classification of deverbals (result, event, underspecified or lexicalized nouns), Peris et al. (2010) focus on Spanish. Several lexicons, as well as automatically or manually extracted features, are evaluated in a machine learning model. Using lexicons turned out to perform under a simple baseline (which is "all instances are *result*").

4 Resources

In this section, we introduce the resources we used or developed to carry through the study proposed in this paper: corpora, trigger lexicons, extraction rules.

4.1 Corpora

Two types of corpora (one annotated and one text-only) have been used in this study.

Manually-Annotated Corpus. We annotated a corpus of 192 French newspaper articles from *Le Monde* and *L'Est Républicain*, for a total of 48K words and 1,844 nominal events. Our corpus is as large as those in other languages in term of number of tagged nouns.[3]

Among our annotated corpus, 109 documents are common with FR-TimeBank, the French manually TimeML-annotated corpus (Bittar, 2010). The annotations given in FR-TimeBank and ours are different, but seem quite similar according to the good inter-annotator agreement (kappa=0.704).

We wrote a quite detailed document describing annotation guidelines: it details a typology of events, as well as instructions for deciding whether a noun or a noun phrase is an event or not. In this paper, we only focus on the heads of the noun phrases. Based upon this definition, the two annotators obtained a good agreement (kappa=0.808). This score proves that guidelines are well defined.

In the whole manually-annotated corpus, there are 1,844 annotated events, among them 725 different occurrences of head nouns. 269 of these eventive nouns occur only once. Among the nouns

[3]For a comparison purpose : 3,695 event nouns in IT-TimeBank (Russo et al., 2011), 1,579 in the English corpus from (Creswell et al., 2006), 663 in the French FR-TimeBank (Bittar, 2010). TimeBank (Pustejovsky et al., 2003) contains 7,571 events in total, but the number of nouns among them is not specified.

that appear more than once in the corpus, only 31% denote events every time they occur (100% time event: disparition "disappearance", démission "resignation").

Non-annotated corpus. For an experimental purpose (see below Section 6), we also used a simple text corpus of 120,246 newswire articles from *Le Monde* (two years).

4.2 Lexicons

Two existing lexicons have been used for our experiments: VerbAction (Tanguy and Hathout, 2002) and Bittar's alternative lexicon (Bittar, 2010).

VerbAction: a Deverbal Noun Lexicon. VerbAction lexicon contains a list of French verbs of action (*e.g. fêter* "to celebrate") together with the deverbal nouns derived from these verbs (*la fête* "the feast/celebration"). However, deverbals' eventive reading can be ambiguous, mainly because they can also refer to the result of the action. The *VerbAction* lexicon contains 9,393 noun-verb lemma pairs and 9,200 unique nominal lemmas. It was built by manually validating a list of candidate couples automatically composed from lexicographical resources and from the Web.

The Alternative Noun Lexicon of Bittar. This lexicon contains 804 complementary event nouns[4]. These nouns are not deverbals (*e.g. anniversaire* "birthday" and *grève* "strike"). They have at least only one eventive reading, and can be ambiguous, as for deverbals: they may denote the event or the object of the process, as it is the case for *apéro* "aperitif/cocktail" and *feu* "fire". Some of these nouns describe a state and do not match our definition of events, *e.g. absence* "non-attendance". Lots of these nouns (like *anticoagulothérapie* "anticoagulation therapy" belong to specific language registers. This lexicon has been used for TimeML manual annotation in French.

4.3 Extraction Rules

Beside these reflections concerning lists of nouns having an eventive reading, we achieved a study concerning several contextual clues that can be used for nominal event extraction.

Trigger Verbs: *VB Rules*. In (Arnulphy et al., 2010), we focused on French verbs introducing event names in at least one of their arguments. The NPs related to these verbs were manually annotated by three experts, by validating or not the eventive reading of nouns in context. The study showed which verbs are meaningful for event extraction and in which configuration it would be useful to use them. Two types of verbs are considered.

The first consideration is for the verbs which explicitly introduce events, such as *avoir lieu/se tenir* "to take place", or:

(1) *Le **sommet du G8** est organisé à Deauville.*
(The **G8 Summit** is organized in Deauville)

The second type of verbs shows a relation of cause or consequence. The point of view is that a causal action or event provokes another event. It is the case of *entraîner* "to lead to/to entail" or *provoquer* "to provoke".

(2) *La **crise économique** entraînera la **famine** dans de nombreux pays sous-développés.*
(The **economic crisis** will lead to **famine** in many underdeveloped countries)

(3) *Le **feu** provoqué par l'**attaque-suicide**, n'était pas encore éteint que [...]*
(The **fire** provoked by the **suicide attack**, was not extinguish yet that [...])

In sentence 2, syntactical subject and object of *entraîner* are both events. The "famine" is the evential consequence of the event "economic crisis". In 3, the verb *provoke* introduces the *fire* as an event, being a consequence of the agent *suicide attack*.

According to this former study, only a few verbs were quite always meaningful for event extraction, but these ones had a good precision. For example, five verbs have an eventive subject in 90 to 100% of the cases (*avoir lieu* "to take place" or *se traduire par* "to lead to"). Others introduce an event in argument position, such as *organiser* "to organize" in more than 94% of its occurrences (*cf.* Table 1). We called this list of verbs *VB90*.

Temporal Indications: *IT Rules*. Events are anchored to time, and this is why they are often used with temporal prepositions and in temporal context.

These prepositions can indicate the occurrence of an event (*à l'occasion de* "at the time/moment of"), a referential use of the event (*avant/après*

[4] We are thankful to André Bittar for providing us this list.

Lemma	Translation	Rate of events
Subject Position		
avoir lieu	to take place	100%
se produire	to happen	94%
s'expliquer par	to be the consequence of	92%
avoir pour origine	to originate from	100%
être entraîné	to be driven by	100%
Argument Position		
organiser	to organize	94%
déclencher	to trigger	100%
conduire à	to lead to	93%
assister à	to attend	93%
donner lieu à	to give rise to	100%

Table 1: Examples of *VB90*, verbs that lead to an eventive reading of their subject or argument in more than 90% of the cases.

"before/after" or *la veille / le lendemain de* "the day before/after"), an internal moment of the event (*à l'issue de* "at the close of").

However, few of these prepositions are unambiguously temporal triggers. Some like *avant*, *après*, *au commencement de* can be either temporal or locative, while *à l'occasion de* or *la veille* have only a temporal interpretation.

Using these temporal markers (Table 2) is then a good way to extract event noun phrases. We call *IT rules* the rules using them in order to extract events.

Temporal indicator	Translation
à la suite de	following (only temporal)
lors de	during
à l'occasion de	on the occasion of
au moment de	at the moment of
au lendemain de	at the day after

Table 2: Examples of temporal indicators used as event triggers.

VB and IT rules will be used in next sections to build our weighted lexicon.

5 Experiments

This set of experiments concerns the whole manually-annotated corpus.

XIP (Aït-Mokhtar et al., 2002) is a robust parser for French and English which provides dependency relations and named entity recognition. Syntactic relations, as well as "classical" named entities like persons or locations, are identified, but events are not. XIP is a product from XRCE (Xerox Research Centre Europe), distributed with encrypted grammars that cannot be changed by the users. However, it is possible to add resources and grammar rules to the existing ones in order to enrich the representation. The experiments described below are performed by this means.

Considering the resources described in this paper, two distinct runs can be performed:

1. Using the French lexicons *VerbAction* and *Bittar*, described in Section 4.2, in order to evaluate the performance of a system using only these lists of nouns for event extraction.

2. Using the clues introduced in Section 4.3, *i.e.* triggers verbs (*VB rules*) and temporal indicators (*IT rules*) in order to extract events independently from lexicons.

These experiments have been evaluated in terms of precision, recall and f-measure. Precision is defined as the observed probability for a hypothesized element to be correct, recall is the observed probability for a referenced element to have been found and F-measure is the weighted harmonic mean of precision and recall.

5.1 Existing Lexicons

VerbAction and Bittar's lexicons are used to annotate the corpus. Results obtained by applying these lexicons on our corpus are presented in Table 3. They show that *VerbAction* obtained a precision of 48.7%, confirming that deverbals have more non-event than event reading. The recall is 66.8%; even if the lexicon does not contain *all* deverbal nouns, it is large enough (9,200 words) and we can conclude that about one third of the events do not come from a deverbalization.

Adding the nouns from *Bittar*'s lexicon increases the recall (from 66.8% to 84.1%) without affecting the precision (48.7% to 48.3%). However 15% of events are still missed, and the precision stays quite low.

5.2 Verbs and Temporal Clues.

We automatically annotated a noun as an event if XIP indicated that this noun was subject or argument of a verb from the *VB90* list. On the

	Precision	Recall	F-measure
VerbAction	**48.7%**	**66.8%**	0.56
VA + Bittar	**48.3%**	**84.1%**	0.61

Table 3: Results with VerbAction and Bittar lexicons on the whole manually-annotated corpus.

other hand, nouns introduced by a temporal context identified by the *IT rules* (*during*, *the day before*, etc.) were also marked as events.

	Precision	Recall	F-measure
IT	81.2%	6.1%	0.11
VB90	**84.0%**	**1.1%**	0.02
VB90 + IT	**81.6%**	**7.2%**	0.13

Table 4: Results with XIP rules on the whole corpus.

As expected, and contrary to the approach exclusively based on lexicon, our extraction rules obtained a good precision and a very bad recall (Table 4). As we already mentionned, the implemented rules are focused on precise event designations.

5.3 Combination of Lexicons and Rules.

When combining lexicons and rules, recall increases of 1.8 points (from 84.1% to 85.9%), precision decreases from 48.3% to 48%.

6 A Weighted Lexicon for Event Nominals

The experiments described in the previous section show that our rules lead to a quite good precision (higher than 80%). For this reason, they can be used in order to automatically build a lexicon. As the recall is low, the rules should be applied on a large corpus. We used the non-annotated corpus presented in Section 4.1 (120,246 articles from *Le Monde*).

This method allows the extraction of a list of eventive nouns, but also, and more interestingly, it provides information about the level of ambiguity (eventive or non-eventive reading) of each word in the corpus. Otherwise, we are able to predict how eventive the word is expected to be.

6.1 Building the Lexicon

This prediction is achieved as follows: after applying the rules on the corpus, we calculate a ratio for each noun extracted as an event at least twice. This ratio $r(w)$ is the number of occurrences of the word w that are tagged by the rules, divided by the total number of its occurrences $t(w)$, then ratio $r(w) = e(w)/t(w)$.

As the recall of the rules is low, r is obviously not a rate or a probability of the eventive reading of this word. However, a relative comparison with other ratios allows us to estimate how ambiguous the noun is in a given corpus. This value is then interesting for noun classification. This interest is illustrated by examples given in Table 5.

Potential triggers French	English	Nb. detected / total occurrences	**Ratio**
chute	fall	434 / 2620	**0.166**
clôture	closing	63 / 470	**0.134**
élection	election	1243 / 9713	**0.128**
bousculade	jostle	12/115	**0.104**
crise	crisis	286 / 6185	**0.046**
tension	tension	16 / 1595	**0.001**
subvention	subvention	2 / 867	**0.002**
Anschluss	Anschluss	3 / 4	**0.750**
méchoui	mechoui	3 / 5	**0.600**
krach	krach	20 / 169	**0.118**
RTT	~ day off	14 / 166	**0.084**
demi-finale	semifinal	35 / 553	**0.063**
cessez-le-feu	cease-fire	15 / 440	**0.034**
accès	access	9 / 2828	**0.003**
11 septembre	September-11	12 / 4354	**0.003**

Table 5: Examples of trigger words extracted by the extraction rules.

Many of these words can be found in lexicons *VerbAction* or *Bittar* (first part of the list), while others are not (second part). Nouns that are non-ambiguous in their eventive reading have a quite high ratio (higher than the average recall described in previous section). It is the case of *fall*, *election* or *krach*. On the other hand, highly ambiguous words like *tension*, *subvention* or *access* get a low ratio. The date *September 11* is also in this latter case, but dates are very rare in these results, and this one has by far the best rate. The French *clôture*, that can be translated as *fencing* or *closing*, seems almost not ambiguous in newswire articles.

These rules helped us to discover 305 new names of events that were not present in the trigger lexicons, such as those shown in Table 5, but also *tollé* "hue and cry", *mise en sourdine* "soften" or *couac* "false note".

6.2 Evaluation

We evaluated our weighted lexicon by comparing its performances in event extraction with the two standard lexicons.

Direct Application of Lexicon In a first evaluation experiment, we applied this new weighted lexicon on our annotated corpus (see Section 4.1), as done for VerbAction and Bittar in Section 5. To observe the evolution of performances, we tested different "slices" of the lexicon, according to the ratios obtained: all words with a ratio higher than 10%, then all those with a ratio greater than 8%, 6%, etc. The results are presented in the Table 6.

Words of ratio >	Precision	Recall	F-measure
10%	84.1%	16.6%	0.28
8%	83.6%	24.3%	0.38
6%	79.8%	31.5%	0.45
1%	56.3%	71.0%	0.63
0.5%	43.4%	80.1%	0.56

Table 6: Results when applying "slices" of ratio on the corpus.

Precision and recall evolve in an opposite way: when the lexicon is less selective, the recall increases and the precision decreases. The best F-measure (for 1% ratio) is 0.63, a value similar to the F-measure of the VerbAction and Bittar's lexicons combined (0.61).

Machine-Learning Evaluation As a second evaluation of the automatically-built weighted lexicon, we added the word ratios as a feature in the rule-based classifier J48, an implementation of C4.5 algorithm (Quinlan, 1993), as implemented in the software Weka (Hall et al., 2009).

Our corpus has been splitted into a test set (49 documents) and development set (143 documents, which is small but sufficient for our study). We implemented three very basic models, allowing us to show the trade-off introduced by the ratios, without any suspicion of side effect due to other features:

- M_l uses only the two standard lexicons VerbAction and Bittar.
- M_r uses only the ratios, as a real value.
- M_{rl} uses both existing and ratio lexicons. When a word is not in the ratio lexicon, this word is given ratio 1 if in standard lexicons and 0 otherwise.

Results are given at Table 7. Using only our automatic ratio lexicon M_r leads to similar results than using standard, manually validated lexicons M_l. Combining all information leads to a small improvement of precision and recall.

	M_l	M_r	M_{rl}
Precision	0.51	0.49	**0.54**
Recall	0.86	0.89	**0.89**
F-measure	0.64	0.63	**0.67**

Table 7: Comparison of models using standard lexicons (M_l), ratio lexicon (M_r) and both (M_{rl}).

Discussion Those results show that our weighted lexicon, automatically built and without any manual validation, leads to obtain comparable results than manually-validated lexicons. Combining all of them improves both precision and recall.

Creating this weighted lexicon requires the implementation of language-specific rules, but these rules seem quite easy to adapt to another language, provided that a syntactic parser exists for this language. Building such a lexicon is then much less time-consuming than validating an entire lexicon.

Moreover, if applied on much larger and diverse corpora, this method should make possible the detection of more metonymic events, as *September-11*, in order to build a knowledge base of event candidates.

7 Conclusion

We presented in this article several experiments aiming at studying the use of event names in French texts, as well as an automatic method for building a weighted lexicon of event names.

We first defined the object we are dealing with: what is, from our point of view, an event. Then, we noticed that the existing lexicons which can be used in an event extraction perspective are not sufficient for a wide coverage. Some words are not intrinsically events, but take theirs eventness in the context. These words cannot be found in such lexicons.

We applied our rules based on verbs and temporal clues, which provide events in more than 80% of cases, that allows us to construct a new weighted lexicon. Our experiments show that the lexicon is as precise as manually-validated lists, and that weights can be used to improve the classification of nouns.

Because some words take an evential meaning

at a given moment (*eg. le nuage islandais* – literally "Icelandic cloud" – refers to the blast of the Eyjafjöll volcano from march to october 2010), we are now working on a new lexicon which would consider the date of the apparition of an event name.

We are also working on a weighted lexicon in English.

References

2005. ACE (Automatic Content Extraction) - English Annotation Guidelines for Events, Version 5.4.3 2005.07.01. Technical report, Linguistic Data Consortium.

Salah Aït-Mokhtar, Jean-Pierre Chanod, and Claude Roux. 2002. Robustness beyond Shallowness: Incremental Deep Parsing. *Natural Language Engineering*, 8.

Béatrice Arnulphy, Xavier Tannier, and Anne Vilnat. 2010. Les entités nommées événement et les verbes de cause-conséquence. In *Actes de TALN 2010*.

André Bittar. 2010. *Building a TimeBank for French: A Reference Corpus Annotated According to the ISO-TimeML Standard*. Ph.D. thesis.

Laura Calabrese Steimberg. 2008. Les héméronymes. Ces évènements qui font date, ces dates qui deviennent évènements. *Mots. Les langages du politique*, 3.

Cassandre Creswell, Matthew J. Beal, John Chen, Thomas L. Cornell, Lars Nilsson, and Rohini K. Srihari. 2006. Automatically extracting nominal mentions of events with a bootstrapped probabilistic classifier. In *Proceedings of the COLING-ACL '06*.

Donald Davidson, 1980. *Essays on Actions and Events*, chapter 11 "Mental Events" (1970). Psychology as Philosophy. Calendron Press.

Kurt Eberle, Gertrud Faaß, and Ulrich Heid. 2009. Corpus-based identification and disambiguation of reading indicators for German nominalizations. In *Proceedings of Corpus Linguistics 2009*.

Ralph Grishman and Beth Sundheim. 1996. Message Understanding Conference: A Brief History. In *Proceedings of COLING 1996*.

Mark Hall, Eibe Frank, Geoffrey Holmes, Bernhard Pfahringer, Peter Reutemann, and Ian H. Witten. 2009. The WEKA Data Mining Software: An Update. *SIGKDD Explorations*.

Michelle Lecolle. 2004. Toponymes en jeu : Diversité et mixage des emplois métonymiques de toponymes. In *Studii si cercetari filologice 3 / 2004. Université de Pitesti, Roumanie*.

Erik Neveu and Louis Quéré. 1996. Présentation. *Réseaux*, 14(75).

Aina Peris, Mariona Taulé, Gemma Boleda, and Horacio Rodriguez. 2010. ADN-classifier: Automatically assigning denotation types to nominalizations. In *Proceedings of LREC'2010*.

James Pustejovsky, José Castaño, Robert Ingria, Roser Saurí, Robert Gaizauskas, Andrea Setzer, and Graham Katz. 2003. TimeML: Robust Specification of Event and Temporal Expressions in Text. In *Proceedingd of IWCS-5*.

James Pustejovsky, Robert Knippen, Jessica Littman, and Roser Saurí. 2005. Temporal and Event Information in Natural Language Text. *Language Resources and Evaluation*, 39(2-3).

R. Quinlan. 1993. *C4.5: Programs for Machine Learning*. Morgan Kaufman Publishers.

Irene Russo, Tommaso Caselli, and Francesco Rubino. 2011. Recognizing deverbal events in context. In *Proceedings of CICLing 2011, poster session*. Springer.

Roser Saurí, Robert Knippen, Marc Verhagen, and James Pustejovsky. 2005. Evita: A Robust Event Recognizer for QA Systems. In *Proceedings of HLT/EMNLP*.

Ludovic Tanguy and Nabil Hathout. 2002. Webaffix : un outil d'acquisition morphologique dérivationnelle à partir du Web. In *Actes de TALN 2002*.

Danièle Van De Velde. 2000. Existe-t-il des noms propres de temps ? *Lexique*, 15.

Zeno Vendler, 1967. *Facts and events*, chapter Verbs and Times, pages 97–121. Cornell University Press.

Towards a Better Exploitation of the Brown 'Family' Corpora in Diachronic Studies of British and American English Language Varieties

Sanja Štajner
University of Wolverhampton, UK
S.Stajner@wlv.ac.uk

Abstract

Since the 1990s, the Brown 'family' corpora have been widely used for various diachronic studies of 20th century English language. However, the existing methodologies failed to exploit its full potential as they only used the four main text categories. In this paper, we present the results of two experiments on diachronic changes of the Coleman-Liau readability Index (CLI) in British and American English in the period 1961–1991/2. The first experiment used all fifteen fine-grained text genres, while the second only used the four main text categories. The comparison of the results of these two experiments demonstrated the importance of using all fifteen fine-grained text genres for obtaining a better understanding of how language changes.

1 Introduction

The Brown University corpus of written American English[1] was published in 1964 with the aim of standardising the future parallel corpora of British English or American English of other periods (Francis, 1965 in Leech and Smith, 2005). Following this idea, the LOB corpus[2] of written British English was compiled as the first corpus to match the Brown corpus, in respect of the year of sampling (1961) and its representation of different text types (Leech and Smith, 2005). This provided the possibility for a synchronic comparison between two major English language varieties – British and American. In the 1990s, the emergence of the FLOB[3] and Frown[4] corpora, representing written British English in 1991 and American English in 1992, respectively, added a diachronic component. It created the opportunity to use the Brown 'family' corpora in diachronic studies of 20th century written English texts in these two regional language varieties. As they are publicly available as part of the ICAME Corpus Collection[5] and cover fifteen different text genres over the four main text categories (Press, Prose, Learned and Fiction), the Brown 'family' corpora have been widely used in various diachronic studies throughout the linguistic community.

Readability formulas provide assistance to a writer in producing comprehensible text and maintaining a consistent reading level throughout a document (McCallum and Peterson, 1982). They were initially designed for educational purposes with the aim of defining the appropriate reading levels for primary and secondary school text books (McCallum and Peterson, 1982). The most commonly used variables in a readability formula are the measures of sentence and word difficulty (Klare 1968; 1974 in McCallum and Peterson, 1982). In a survey on the most commonly used readability formulas of that period (McCallum and Peterson, 1982), special attention was given to the Coleman-Liau Index (Coleman and Liau, 1975) and Automated Readability Index (Smith and Kincaid, 1970), as these formulas are simpler to compute. Unlike most of readability formulas which use the number of syllables per word, these two formulas use the number of characters per word as a measure of word difficulty. Therefore, we decided to use one of these – Coleman-Liau Index, as a measure of text readability. The result of this formula is the U.S. grade level necessary to comprehend the given text.

The primary focus of this study was to highlight possibly misleading interpretations of the results in diachronic studies when using only the four main text categories, instead of all fifteen fine-grained text genres of the Brown 'family' corpora. In order to achieve this, we conducted two experi-

[1] http://khnt.aksis.uib.no/icame/manuals/brown
[2] http://khnt.aksis.uib.no/icame/manuals/lob
[3] http://khnt.aksis.uib.no/icame/manuals/flob
[4] http://khnt.aksis.uib.no/icame/manuals/frown

[5] http://www.hit.uib.no/icame

ments – first using all fifteen fine-grained text genres and then using only the four main text categories (Section 4). Both experiments were based on the investigation of diachronic changes of the Coleman-Liau Index in British and American English in the period 1961–1991/2. The results of those experiments are compared in Section 5. The main conclusions and suggestions for future exploitation of the Brown 'family' corpora in diachronic studies are given in Section 6.

2 Related Work

The four corpora – LOB, FLOB, Brown and Frown, were used for investigating the trends of change in various lexical, grammatical and syntactic features by Mair and Hundt (1995), Mair (1997; 2002), Mair, Hundt, Leech and Smith (2002), Smith (2002; 2003a; 2003b), Leech (2003; 2004), Leech and Smith (2006), Mair and Leech (2006). Mair, Hundt, Leech and Smith (2002) demonstrated the possibilities of these corpora in the investigation of diachronic changes of POS frequencies. Leech and Smith (2006) and Mair and Leech (2006) further exploited the corpora by investigating diachronic changes of core modals, semi-modals, passive, *wh-* and *that* relativisation, personal pronouns, nouns, *of-* and *s-* genitive constructions. More recent studies (Leech and Smith, 2009; Leech, Mair, Hundt and Smith, 2009) expanded the time-span for diachronic studies in British English by using the Lancaster1931 corpus together with the LOB and FLOB corpora.

All these studies shared the same methodology:

(1) They used the POS tagged versions of the Brown and Frown corpora and the manually post-edited versions of the LOB and FLOB corpora.

(2) The experiments were conducted first on the whole corpora and later separately on each of the four major subdivisions of the corpora: Press, General Prose, Learned and Fiction.

(3) The log likelihood test was applied as a measure of statistical significance of the results.

Although the Brown 'family' corpora provided an opportunity for separate investigation of diachronic trends across all fifteen fine-grained text genres, none of the above mentioned diachronic studies utilised this trait. They only differentiated between texts across the four main text categories and made the hypotheses about the trends of language change accordingly.

There are numerous readability studies of different texts genres and comparisons among them. However, to our best knowledge, there have been no diachronic studies of text readability. For this reason, we decided to use the Coleman-Liau Index as an initial experiment to trace the diachronic changes of text readability in 20th century English language.

3 Corpora

The Brown 'family' corpora is comprised of two corpora of American English:

- The Brown University corpus of written American English (**Brown**)
- The Freiburg - Brown Corpus of American English (**Frown**),

and two corpora of British English:

- The Lancaster-Oslo/Bergen Corpus (**LOB**)
- The Freiburg-LOB Corpus of British English (**FLOB**),

while the fifth corpus to join the 'family' – Lancaster1931 (BLOB) is still not publicly available.

All five corpora are mutually comparable (Leech and Smith, 2005) and contain texts published in the years 1931±3 (Lancaster1931), 1961 (LOB and Brown), 1991 (FLOB) and 1992 (Frown). Each corpus consists of approximately one million words – 500 texts of about 2000 running words each, selected at a random point in the original source. The sampling range covers 15 text genres, which can be grouped into four more generalised categories:

- **Press**
  - Press: Reportage (A)
  - Press: Editorial (B)
  - Press: Review (C)
- **General Prose**
  - Religion (D)
  - Skills, Trades and Hobbies (E)
  - Popular Lore (F)
  - Belles Lettres, Biographies, Essays (G)
- **Learned**
  - Miscellaneous (H)
  - Science (J)

- **Fiction**
  - General Fiction (K)
  - Mystery and Detective Fiction (L)
  - Science Fiction (M)
  - Adventure and Western (N)
  - Romance and Love Story (P)
  - Humour (R)

The distribution of the texts for each genre and corpus is given in Table 1. As the LOB and FLOB corpora share exactly the same text distribution across all fifteen genres, they are presented in the same column – '(F)LOB'.

Genre	(F)LOB	Brown	Frown
A	44	44	44
B	27	27	27
C	17	17	17
D	17	17	17
E	38	36	36
F	44	48	48
G	77	75	75
H	30	35	30
J	80	80	80
K	29	29	29
L	24	24	24
M	6	6	6
N	29	30	29
P	29	29	29
R	9	9	9

Table 1: Text distribution in the corpora.

It can be noticed that the number of texts varies significantly among genres belonging to the same broad text categories. For example, in the Press category (A–C), the number of texts in each of the genres A, B and C is 44, 27 and 17, respectively. Therefore, it is reasonable to expect that the trend of change in genre A (Press: Reportage) will have the greatest impact on the overall trend of change in the whole Press category. This could lead to a failure to observe the changes present in some of the genres with a smaller number of texts. More importantly, different directions of changes (increase and decrease) in two genres of the same broad text category might lead to the overall perception of no change in that category. Neglecting the changes present in those genres could result in misleading conclusions and hypotheses regarding the way language changes.

4 Methodology

As the primary focus of this study was to compare the conclusions which can be drawn from the results obtained from two different approaches, we conducted two separate experiments:

- **Experiment I** – Investigation of diachronic changes of CLI in the period 1961–1991/2 across all fifteen text genres (A–R)
- **Experiment II** – Investigation of diachronic changes of CLI in the period 1961–1991/2 across the four main text categories (Press, Prose, Learned and Fiction)

Both experiments were conducted separately for each of the English language varieties (British and American), using the Brown 'family' corpora (LOB, FLOB, Brown and Frown).

4.1 Sentence Splitting and Tokenisation

The Brown and LOB corpora are available in their POS tagged and tokenised versions with sentence boundaries, while the Frown and FLOB corpora do not contain markers for sentence and word boundaries. In order to achieve a higher consistency for sentence splitting and tokenisation and offer a fairer comparison of the results among the corpora, we used the raw text versions of all four corpora and parsed them with the state-of-the-art Connexor's Machinese Syntax parser[6].

The parser tokenises contractions and hyphenated words in the following manner: the verb and its negation (e.g. *isn't*) are treated as two separate tokens (*is* and *not*), while *'s* is treated in two different ways, depending on its role in the sentence. In cases where *'s* represent a genitive form, *'s* and its antecedent noun are treated as one token. In other cases where *'s* represent a contracted form of the verb *be (is)* or *have (has)*, *'s* is treated as a separate token. E.g. In the sentence *"That's a Tory doctor's reaction to the new health charges..."* (LOB: A01), *That's* is treated as two separate tokens – *that* and *is*, while the *doctor's* is treated as one token *doctor's*. Hyphenated words, e.g. *30-year-old, built-in, type-recorder* (LOB: A10) are treated as one token. All punctuation marks are treated as separate tokens.

4.2 Feature Extraction

The Coleman-Liau Index (CLI) was calculated separately for each of the 500 texts in each of the

[6] www.connexor.eu

corpora, using the following formula:

$$CLI = 5.89\frac{c}{w} - 29.5\frac{s}{w} - 15.8 \quad (1)$$

where *c*, *w* and *s* represent, respectively, the total number of characters, words and sentences in the text. The number of characters, words and sentences were calculated using the parser's output. Sentences were counted as the number of sentence tags (<s>) in the parser's output, words – as the number of word tags (<text>) excluding those which contained only punctuation marks, and characters – as the number of characters inside the word tags counted as words.

4.3 Statistical Significance

First we examined whether the data follow the normal distribution, using the Kolmogorov-Smirnov Z test. The results of this test demonstrated that the distribution of the CLI is not significantly different from the normal distribution (at a 0.05 level of significance), in each language variety, year, category and genre. Therefore, we used the two-tailed t-test as a measure of statistical significance of the change.

5 Results and Discussion

The results of the experiments on diachronic changes of CLI are given separately for British and American English in Sub-sections 5.1 and 5.2, respectively. Trends of change are compared between these two language varieties in Sub-section 5.3.

Table 2 (Sub-section 5.1) presents the results of the two experiments for British English, while Table 3 (Sub-section 5.2) presents the results of the same experiments for American English. The tables contain the results of both experiments in two consecutive columns – 'Exp. I' and 'Exp. II', thus enabling their direct comparison. For each of the experiments, results are presented in two columns – 'change' and 'p'.

Column 'change' presents the absolute change of CLI over the period 1961-1991/2. Both – starting (1961) and ending (1991/2) values were calculated as an arithmetic mean of the feature value in all texts of the relevant text genre/category and corpus. The direction of change is indicated by the sign '+' for increase and '−' for decrease.

Column 'p' represents the p-value of the two-tailed t-test. Statistically significant changes at a 0.05 level of significance ($p < 0.05$) are shown in bold.

5.1 Diachronic Changes of CLI in British English

The results of the experiments on diachronic changes of the Coleman-Liau Index (CLI) in British English are presented in Table 2.

Genre	Exp. I		Exp. II	
	change	p	change	p
A	+0.54	0.063		
B	+0.09	0.762	**+0.44**	**0.038**
C	+0.74	0.061		
D	**+2.35**	**0.001**		
E	**+1.04**	**0.002**	**+1.21**	**0.000**
F	**+1.26**	**0.002**		
G	**+1.01**	**0.000**		
H	**+1.10**	**0.009**	**+1.35**	**0.000**
J	**+1.44**	**0.000**		
K	−0.49	0.210		
L	−0.25	0.573		
M	+0.01	0.994	+0.19	0.143
N	**+1.17**	**0.006**		
P	+0.52	0.072		
R	−0.62	0.267		

Table 2: CLI in British English (1961–1991).

On the basis of the results of the second experiment (Exp. II, Table 2), it could be concluded that the change of CLI in the period 1961–1991 were significant in the Press, Prose and Learned text categories and not in the Fiction category. However, the results of the first experiment (Exp. I, Table 2) lead to different conclusions regarding the trend of change of CLI in the Press and Fiction text categories. In the Fiction category, the results of the first experiment (Exp. I, Table 2) indicate a statistically significant change of CLI in genre N (Adventure and Western). This change was not reflected in the second experiment (Exp. II, Table 2) probably due to the following two reasons: (1) a high heterogeneity of the results in the category, i.e. different directions of change among genres belonging to this text category (genres K–R, Exp. I, Table 2) and (2) unbalanced distribution of texts among the genres inside this text category (genres K–R, Table 1, Section 3). In the Press category, the results of the first experiment (Exp. I, Table 2) indicate that the changes of CLI in the period 1961–1991 were not statistically significant in any of the three genres (A–C) inside this category. It is interesting to notice that the p-value of the t-test in genres A and C (0.063 and 0.061, respectively) is very close to the chosen critical value (0.05). Most probably, the results of the second experiment in the Press category (Exp. II, Table 2) reflect the cumulative effect of those changes in genres A and C, which were not reported as statistically significant in the first experiment (Exp. I, Table 2).

Furthermore, the results of the first experiment in the Prose and Fiction categories (Exp. I, Table 2) revealed two interesting phenomena, that the genres inside the same broad text category manifest: (1) different trends of change (genres K–R in the Fiction category) and (2) different intensities of change (genres D–G in the Prose category). In the Fiction category, CLI had a statistically significant increase in genre N (Adventure and Western), in genre M (Science Fiction) CLI stayed unchanged ($p > 0.99$), while in genres K (General Fiction) and R (Humour) the results indicated a possible decrease of CLI during the same period 1961–1991. The high heterogeneity of the results among different genres in the Fiction category raises a question: "is it possible to talk about a general trend of change in a text category if different genres inside that text category manifest different trends of change?" In the Prose category, CLI had a statistically significant increase over the observed period in all four genres (D–F), but the intensity of the increase was significantly higher in genre D (+2.35) than in the other three genres (+1.04, +1.26 and +1.01). These two phenomena, though important for obtaining a better understanding of the way text readability changes in British English, could be overlooked by using only the results of the second experiment (Exp. II, Table 2).

A general conclusion based on the results of the first experiment is that all genres which manifested a statistically significant change of CLI (genres D–J and N) had the same direction of change – an increase. This could be interpreted as a tendency in these genres to make texts more complex, using longer words and sentences.

5.2 Diachronic Changes of CLI in American English

The results of both experiments investigating diachronic changes of the Coleman-Liau Index (CLI) in American English are presented in Table 3.

Genre	Exp. I		Exp. II	
	change	p	change	p
A	+0.22	0.501	+0.36	0.093
B	**+0.71**	**0.049**		
C	+0.19	0.506		
D	**+2.01**	**0.015**	**+0.99**	**0.000**
E	+0.31	0.558		
F	**+1.46**	**0.000**		
G	**+0.77**	**0.013**		
H	+0.80	0.152	**+0.98**	**0.037**
J	**+1.05**	**0.001**		
K	−0.56	0.209	−0.31	0.280
L	+0.27	0.445		
M	−0.96	0.412		
N	+0.20	0.606		
P	−0.44	0.248		
R	−1.80	0.069		

Table 3: CLI in American English (1961–1992).

Similarly as in the case of British English (Sub-section 5.1), the results of the second experiment in American English (Exp. II, Table 3) could lead to potentially incorrect conclusions regarding the change of CLI in the Press, Prose and Learned text categories. They indicate that in the Press category there had been no statistically significant changes of CLI in the observed period, while the results of the first experiment (Exp. I, Table 3) clearly demonstrate a statistically significant increase of CLI in one genre of this category – genre B (Press: Editorial). This result, important for obtaining a better understanding of the way text readability was changing in the Press category of American English, could be overlooked by using only the results of the second experiment (Exp. II, Table 3).

The difference between the conclusions made about the changes of CLI in the Prose and Learned category, based on the results of the first and second experiment, is more subtle. If we assume that the trend of change for a broad text category should correspond to the trend which is the most common among its genres, the results of the first and second experiment in the Prose category (Table 3) are consistent. However, the phenomenon that the genres inside the same broad text category manifest different intensities of change (already discussed in Sub-section 5.1) could be overlooked if we relied solely upon the results of the second experiment (Exp. II, Table 3). The results of the first experiment (Exp. I, Table 3) demonstrated that all three genres (D, F and G), which manifested a statistically significant increase of CLI in the Prose category, exhibited significantly different intensities of that change (+2.01, +1.46 and +0.77, respectively).

The result of the second experiment (Exp. II, Table 3) suggests that CLI had a statistically significant increase in the Learned category over the period 1961–1992. However, the results of the first experiment (Exp. I, Table 3) demonstrate that CLI had a statistically significant increase only in genre J (Science), while the results of the t-test in genre H (Miscellaneous) do not allow us to be certain about the behaviour of CLI in this genre. As the Learned category is comprised of only these two genres (J and H), the result of the second experiment misleadingly creates the impression that the increase of CLI was present in the whole category. This result is probably a reflection of the unequal distribution of texts between these two genres – 80 texts in J genre and 30 (35) texts in H genre (Table 1, Section 3).

5.3 Comparison of Diachronic Changes between British and American English

The fact that the British and American part of the Brown 'family' corpora are mutually comparable (Leech and Smith, 2005) allows us to compare the trends of change between these two English language varieties in both experiments.

The results of both experiments (Table 2 and Table 3) lead to a central conclusion that all statistically significant changes of CLI in the period 1961–1991/2 had the same trend of change – an increase, in both English language varieties. However, those changes were not present in the same genres and text categories across the two language varieties. The differences are noticeable even at the level of the four main text categories, where CLI manifested a statistically significant increase in the Press category only in British (Exp. II, Table 2) and not American English (Exp. II, Table 3). The results of the first experiment revealed some additional differences in the behaviour of CLI between British and American English. Genre B (Press: Editorial) had a statistically significant increase only in American English (Exp. I, Table 3), while genres E (Skills, Trades and Hobbies), H (Miscellaneous) and N (Adventure and Western) had a statistically significant increase only in British English (Exp. I, Table 2).

The comparison of the results between British and American English in the Press category emphasised the importance of carefully choosing the granularity of genres in diachronic studies. The results of the first and second experiment in the Press category led to the opposite conclusions. The results of the second experiment suggested an increase of CLI only in British English (Exp. II, Table 2), while the results of the first experiment demonstrated an increase of CLI only in genre B of American English (Exp. I, Table 3) and no statistically significant changes of CLI in any of the three genres of the Press category in British English (Exp. I, Table 2).

6 Conclusions

The results presented in this study indicated that in all genres of the Prose and Learned text categories and one genre (N – Adventure and Western) of the Fiction category in British English, a tendency existed to render texts more complex, using longer words and sentences. Furthermore, the results demonstrated that different genres inside the same broad text category do not follow the same trend of change. In the Fiction category of British English, genre N (Adventure and Western) manifested a statistically significant increase of CLI between 1961 and 1991, while in genre M (Science Fiction) texts from both years – 1961 and 1991 had approximately the same value of CLI, thus indicating a stable text complexity in terms of sentence and word length in the observed period. They also demonstrated that different genres inside the same text category, even if they follow the same trend of change, differ by the intensity of those changes. In the Prose category, genre D (Religion) exhibited a significantly higher intensity of increase than the other three genres of the same category – E (Skills, Trades and Hobbies), F (Popular Lore) and G (Belles Lettres, Biographies, Essays).

According to the results of the first experiment, several genres – B (Press: Editorial), D (Religion), F (Popular Lore), G (Belles Lettres, Biographies, Essays) and J (Science) of American English demonstrated a statistically significant increase of CLI between 1961 and 1992. Similarly as in the case of British English, all three genres of the Prose category in American English which manifested a statistically significant increase of CLI, differed by the intensity of those changes.

Most importantly, the comparison between the results of the two experiments – using all fifteen fine-grained text genres and then using only the four broad text categories, revealed the potential pitfalls of hypothesising about the trends of diachronic change solely based on the results of the second approach. It also pointed out two types of misleading results. The first type would indicate that there were no significant changes in the observed broad text category, while after closer scrutiny some of the genres of that category did actually demonstrate significant changes. Those changes in the fine-grained text genres are probably masked by a high heterogeneity of changes or unbalanced distribution of texts among different genres in the relevant category. Therefore, they will not be reflected in the results of the examination of the whole broad text category. The second type of misleading result would indicate a specific trend/direction of change in the whole observed text category, while after closer examination, different genres in that category actually demonstrated different trends of change. We would expect that the general trend of change in the broad text category is determined by the trend which is most common among its genres. However, as the distribution of texts is unbalanced, what we actually see reflected is the trend of the genre(s) with the greatest amount of texts.

Acknowledgements

I would like to express my gratitude to my supervisor Prof. Ruslan Mitkov for his guidance and support. This project was supported by the European Commission, Education & Training, Erasmus Mundus: EMMC 2008-0083, Erasmus Mundus Masters in NLP & HLT.

References

Laurie Bauer. 1994. *Watching English change: and introduction to the study of linguistic change in standard English in the twentieth century.* London: Longman.

Meri Coleman and T. L. Liau. 1975. A computer readability formula designed for machine scoring. *Journal of Applied Psychology*, 60 (2): 283–284.

David Denison. 1994. A Corpus of Late Modern English Prose. In: M. Kytö et al. eds. *Corpora Across the Centuries*: 7–16 Amsterdam: Rodopi.

Nelson W. Francis. 1965. A standard corpus of edited present-day American English. *College English*, 26: 267–273.

George R. Klare. 1968. The Role of Word Frequency in Readability. *Elementary English*, 45: 12–22.

George R. Klare. 1974. Assessing Readability. *Reading Research Quarterly*, 1: 62–102.

Geoffrey Leech. 2003. Modality on the move: the English modal auxiliaries 1961-1992. In: R. Facchinetti, M. Krug and F. Palmer, eds. *Modality in contemporary English.* Berlin/New York: Mouton de Gruyter, 223–240.

Geoffrey Leech. 2004. Recent grammatical change in English: data, description, theory. In: K. Aijmer and B. Altenberg, eds. *Advances in Corpus Linguistics: Papers from the 23rd International Conference on English Language Research on Computerized Corpora (ICAME 23) Göteborg 22-26 May 2002.* Amsterdam: Rodopi, 61–81.

Geoffrey Leech and Nicholas Smith. 2005. Extending the possibilities of corpus-based research on English in the twentieth century: a prequel to LOB and FLOB. *ICAME Journal*, 29: 83–98.

Geoffrey Leech and Nicholas Smith. 2006. Recent grammatical change in written English 1961–1992: some preliminary findings of a comparison of American with British English. In: A. Renouf and A. Kehoe, eds. *The Changing Face of Corpus Linguistics.* Amsterdam: Rodopi, 186–204.

Geoffrey Leech and Nicholas Smith. 2009. Change and constancy in linguistic change: How grammatical usage in written English evolved in the period 1931-1991. In: A. Renouf and A. Kehoe, eds. *Corpus Linguistics: Refinements and Reassessments.* Amsterdam/New York, 173–200.

Geoffrey Leech, Marianne Hundt, Christian Mair and Nicholas Smith. 2009. *Change in Contemporary English: A Grammatical Study.* Cambridge: Cambridge University Press.

Christian Mair and Marianne Hundt. 1995. Why is the progressive becoming more frequent in English? A corpus-based investigation of language change in progress. *Zeitschrift für Anglistik und Amerikanistik*, 43: 111–122.

Christian Mair. 1997. The spread of the going-to-future in written English: a corpus-based investigation into language change in progress. In: R. Hickey and St. Puppel, eds. *Language history and linguistic modelling: a festschrift for Jacek Fisiak on his 60th birthday.* Berlin: Mouton de Gruyter, 1536–1543.

Christian Mair. 2002. Three changing patterns of verb complementation in Late Modern English: a real-time study based on matching text corpora. *English Language and Linguistics*, 6: 105–131.

Christian Mair, Marianne Hundt, Geoffrey Leech and Nicholas Smith. 2002. Short term diachronic shifts in part-of-speech frequencies: a comparison of the tagged LOB and F-LOB corpora. *International Journal of Corpus Linguistics*, 7: 245–264.

Christian Mair and Geoffrey Leech. 2006. Current change in English syntax. In: B. Aarts and A. MacMahon, eds. *The Handbook of English Linguistics*. Oxford: Blackwell, Ch.14.

Douglas R. McCallum and James L. Peterson. 1982. Computer-based readability indexes. *In Proceedings of the ACM '82 Conference*: 44–48. New York, NY.

Edgar A. Smith and Peter J. Kincaid. 1970. Derivation and Validation of the Automated Readability Index for Use with Technical Materials. *Human Factors: The Journal of the Human Factors and Ergonomics Society*, 12(5): 457–464.

Nicholas Smith. 2002. Ever moving on? The progressive in recent British English. In: P. Peters, P. Collins and A. Smith, eds. *New frontiers of corpus research: papers from the twenty first International Conference on English Language Research on Computerized Corpora, Sydney 2000.* Amsterdam: Rodopi, 317–330.

Nicholas Smith. 2003a. A quirky progressive? A corpus-based exploration of the will + be + -ing construction in recent and present day British English. In: D. Archer, P. Rayson, A. Wilson and T. McEnery, eds. *Proceedings of the Corpus Linguistics 2003 Conference*: 714–723. Lancaster University: UCREL Technical Papers.

Nicholas Smith. 2003b. Changes in the modals and semi-modals of strong obligation and epistemic necessity in recent British English. In: R. Facchinetti, M. Krug and F. Palmer, eds. *Modality in contemporary English.* Berlin/New York: Mouton de Gruyter, 241–266.

Projecting Farsi POS Data To Tag Pashto

Mohammad Khan, Eric Baucom, Anthony Meyer, Lwin Moe
Indiana University
{khanms,eabaucom,antmeyer,lwinmoe}@indiana.edu

Abstract

We present our findings on projecting part of speech (POS) information from a well resourced language, Farsi, to help tag a lower resourced language, Pashto, following Feldman and Hana (2010). We make a series of modifications to both tag transition and lexical emission parameter files generated from a hidden Markov model tagger, TnT, trained on the source language (Farsi). Changes to the emission parameters are immediately effective, whereas changes made to the transition information are most effective when we introduce a custom tagset. We reach our best results of 70.84% when we employ all emission and transition modifications to the Farsi corpus with the custom tagset.

1 Introduction

State-of-the-art work in computational linguistics typically requires heavy investment in language-specific resources. Large-scale resources, in the form of corpora with part of speech (POS), syntactic, or semantic annotation schemes, are used in nearly all statistically driven natural language processing applications. For global languages like English, these resources are already present in at least some form, but, for less commonly taught languages like Pashto, they are not.

Work has already been done exploring how to rapidly develop resources for less commonly taught languages. Feldman and Hana (2010) present a method utilizing Hidden Markov Model (HMM) POS tagging information from a well resourced language (Czech) to help tag a lower resourced language (Russian). They perform various modifications on the two kinds of parameter files generated by the HMM, lexical and transition, in order to make a closer fit between the source and target languages. Following the same basic approach, we perform various syntactic transformations, or "Pashtifications", on the training input in order to improve the tag transition information from the source language, and also develop a tagset that is suitable to both source and target. To improve lexical emission information from the source language, we use "cognate" analysis (employing minimum edit distance), rudimentary morphological analysis (based on suffixes and focusing on verbs), along with enrichment of the source lexicon (by adding closed class words of the target language).

We perform a series of experiments involving different combinations of these strategies and evaluate on a small hand-tagged test set. The aim of this project is to rapidly develop a resource for a lower-resourced language using as little language-specific information as possible. In theory, this could be performed without any in-depth knowledge of the target language, though in our case we did have a native Pashto speaker to assist in tagging our gold standard for evaluation.

The rest of the paper is structured as follows: we begin by discussing related work in section 2; then in section 3 we give some background on Pashto morphosyntax; next we discuss the corpora and tagsets used in our experiments (section 4), followed by the experiments and results themselves (section 6); finally, we offer conclusions and discuss future work in section 7.

2 Related Work

2.1 POS Tagging for Low-resourced Languages

Feldman and Hana (2010) provide the basic approach that we followed in our method. They use annotated corpora from comparatively well resourced languages to provide information about morphological/POS tagging in related, under-resourced languages. In their HMM model for POS tagging, they use transitional probabilities from the source language (with or without modifications) along with lexical emission probabilities for the target language derived through various means.

For their transition probabilities that they derived from Czech, Feldman and Hana (2010) introduced some "Russifications" to the Czech training data to make it more similar to Russian syntax (target language). Most of the changes from the source involved changing a particle to an affix, or vice versa.

For lexical emission probabilities, Feldman and Hana (2010) combine different methods to obtain the best results. They obtained "cognates" from source languages by looking at Levenshtein distance and used the gold POS tags to count word and tag maximum likelihood estimate (MLE) frequencies. They also used a morphological analyzer, developed by hand with the help of language experts, to inform the lexical probabilities.

2.2 Pashto POS Tagging

Rabbi et al. (2009) present a rule-based POS tagger for Pashto. Their method is to manually tag a lexicon and then use that lexicon and Pashto specific rules to tag unknown tokens. They reach an accuracy of 88% with 100 000 tagged words in the lexicon and 120 Pashto specific rules. This approach achieves good results but requires a very large manually tagged lexicon and a large manually created set of language specific rules in order to do so. Operating within a resource-light paradigm, our aim is to reach comparable results using less time and effort.

3 Pashto Morphology and Syntax

Pashto has a rich morphology. It uses three forms of affixation: prefixes, infixes, and suffixes. The morphology represents gender, number, case, tense, and aspect. There is also ambiguity among the morphemes. For example, the suffix *-wo* is used as an oblique plural marker for nouns and adjectives, and as a past tense maker in one class of verbs.

Verbs are ergative in Pashto, i.e. they agree with the subjects in present imperfective cases, while in the past tense, the verb agrees with the object regardless of the aspect. Pashto has "subject object verb" word order, but that order is relatively flexible if compared to English. There are two types of verbs in Pashto: compound verbs and non-compound verbs. Compound verbs are derived by adding a light verb (similar to "be," "do," etc.) to a noun or adjective. Non-compound verbs, which are less common, are not derived. For example, the word for "sharpening" is *terə kawəl* ("sharp"+"do"), while the word for "to go" *tləl* is not derived from a noun or adjective. Compound verbs are written as one or two words depending on the phonotactic properties of the compounding elements.

As compared to Farsi, noun-noun compounding is relatively less common in Pashto. In spoken Farsi, such nouns end with an audible vowel affix known as the *harf-e-izafat*, but this suffix is not actually written in Farsi text. Such compounding is formed by using prepositions in front of the first noun in Pashto. For example "computer table" is formed from *də campuʈər mez* meaning "of computer table" in Pashto. Pashto uses postpositions as well. For example, the phrase for "in the stream" is formed as *pə wyalə ke* ("the stream in").

Adjectives that modify a noun precede the modified nouns, and the intensifiers precede the adjectives, as in English.

4 Corpora and Tagsets

4.1 Farsi

Farsi is a sister language of Pashto spoken in the same geographical area. It is also the official language of Iran. Farsi has a large lexical similarity with Pashto. It shares a large number of cognates and borrowed terms (from Arabic). The syntaxes of the two languages do differ to some extent. However, Farsi is the only language we found that is close enough to Pashto and has enough resources to be useful in our task.[1] We therefore used Farsi as the source language in our experiments.

The Bijankhan Corpus[2] (Oroumchian et al., 2006) is a freely available Farsi corpus. This corpus was manually tagged for POS at the University of Tehran in Iran. The corpus is a collection of 4 300 articles from the daily news and other common texts. It has 2.6 million tokens. The tagset used to tag the corpus consists of 550 different POS tags and is described further in section 4.3.

4.2 Pashto

Test corpora We use two different corpora for testing and development. The first corpus is a hand-tagged corpus of spoken Pashto, which consists of dialogues between an English speaker and a Pashto speaker mediated by an interpreter. The

[1] Urdu is another close language but, compared to Farsi, is not as resource rich.

[2] http://ece.ut.ac.ir/dbrg/bijankhan/

spoken corpus consists of 708 tokens and is based on news data. We hand-annotated 375 tokens of news articles.

Web corpus In order to improve our lexical emission probabilities in the tagger, we needed to conduct both morphological and cognate analysis. A large amount of raw text in our target language, Pashto, was needed for the two processes. Since we could not find any such resource that was both readily available and in the appropriate domain, we decided to obtain our own corpus from the web.

We used `BootCaT` (Baroni and Bernardini, 2004) with appropriate seeds (such as words containing one or more of eight Pashto-specific characters, unique closed class words, etc.) to find Pashto websites. We then used `wget` to obtain a web-corpus of 473 MBs (text only) in size. We then extracted a Pashto lexicon of more than a million words. This lexicon was used in the morphological analysis and cognate detection.

4.3 Tagsets

4.3.1 The BijanKhan Corpus Tagset

The Bijankhan tagset, containing 550 tags, has a hierarchical structure, with most full tags comprising three or more tiers. The first tier specifies the coarse, primary word class; the second tier specifies either a word subclass or a piece of morphological information; and the third tier often expresses information of a semantic nature. For example, the tag `N_SING_LOC` means that the word in question is 1. a noun, 2. singular, and 3. a location of some kind (e.g. Bloomington). Note that delimiter between the tiers is the underscore symbol ("_"). In other tags, the third and fourth tiers express some grammatical or morphological, rather than semantic, nuance, as in `N_SING_CN_GEN` where the fourth-tier subtag `GEN` indicates *harf-e-izafat*, which is also used as a genitive marker in Farsi.

Because the original, or "extended" BijanKhan tagset of 550 tags can become impractical for NLP purposes and lead to data sparsity issues, Amiri et al. (2007) devise a systematic, if somewhat simplistic, method for dramatically reducing the tagset size. Their method essentially consists of the following steps: 1. for any tag with of three or more tiers, they eliminate any subtag past the second tier; 2. for two-tier tags, they remove the second tier if it is used rarely; and 3. they discard any whole tag that occurs rarely. They use this method to derive a tagset of just 40 tags.

4.3.2 Reducing the Extended Tagset

In our experiments, we used two tagsets. First, we used the reduced tagset of Amiri et al. (2007), rather than trying to work with full 550-tag tagset. Preliminary experiments then showed that this tagset did not provide enough morphosyntactic information and resulted in low accuracies. The problem in our case lay in our cross-lingual application of Amiri et al.'s (2007) tagset. The morphological and syntactic differences between Farsi and Pashto are such that much information pertinent to Pashto is destroyed by Amiri et al.'s (2007) simplistic tagset-reduction technique. The more nuanced information found in the extended tags' third and fourth tiers is often necessary for relating Farsi morphosyntactic categories and POS-tag sequences to those of Pashto. For instance, the tag `N_SING_LOC_GEN` (followed by another noun tag) is indicative of the Farsi noun-noun compound construction, i.e. N_1N_2. The equivalent Pashto expression requires the explicit use of the preposition *də* "of" (a stand-alone word), in addition to the reversal of the ordering of the two nouns, so that N_1N_2 (Farsi) $\rightarrow$ *də* N_2N_1 (Pashto). Several of our Pashtification rules involve noun phrases of this type, but their application is nearly impossible without access to the original extended tags.

We therefore decided to build our own tagset. We mapped the original extended tags to a reduced tagset of our own design, dubbing it the Pashto Extended Reduced Tagset (PERT). By starting with the extended tags from the Farsi corpus, we can provide the Pashtification rules with the fine-grained information they require. We also ensure that the final set of reduced tags is equally applicable to both Farsi and Pashto. Our goal was to remain as close to the original Farsi tagset nomenclature and design as possible. Our reduced tagset consists of the 39 tags presented in table 1. In the design of this tagset we could not include all the necessary categories for Pashto. For example, such important categories as gender, case, and aspect are missing, which could be a third tier of information added to an existing category. We could not add these because Farsi does not possess such grammatical categories. Similarly, we did not want to have categories such as `NP` for Pashto because its nonstandard orthography makes this category especially problematic, but needed to have

ADJ	Adjective
ADJ_INO	Participle
ADJ_ORD	Cardinal numbers
ADJ_SUP	Superlative adjective
ADV	Adverb
ADV_EXM	Adverb of examples
ADV_I	Interrogative adverb
ADV_LOC	Adverb of location
ADV_NEGG	Adverb of negation
ADV_NI	Negative interrogative adverb
ADV_TIME	Temporal adverb
AR	Arabic (foreign language)
CON	Conjunction
DET	Determiner
IF	Conditional if
MORP_SING	Singular morpheme
MORP_PL	Plural morpheme
QUA	Quantifier
MS	Mathematics symbol
N_PL	Plural noun
N_SING	Singular noun
NN	Numeric date
NP	Noun phrase
OH	Addressee
OHH	Addresser
P	Preposition
PP	Det. + Preposition
PRO	Pronoun
PS	Whole phrase
V_PRS	Present tense verb
MOD	Modal
V_PA	Past tense verb
V_IMP	Imperative verb
CL	Clitic
P_POS	Postposition
V_SUB	Subjunctive verb
INF	Infinitive
NEGG	Negation particle
DELM	Delimiter (e.g. commas, period)

Table 1: Pashto Extended Reduced Tagset (PERT)

them to stay consistent with Farsi tagset, a language with a more standardized orthographic convention. The syntactic distribution of the subcategories of adverbs vary from one subcategory to another in both languages. We therefore chose six subcategories of adverbs whose inclusion results in better transition probabilities.

5 Cross-language Projection

We now discuss the modifications made to the parameter files generated by TnT (Brants, 2000), our HMM POS tagger, after being trained on Farsi. The tag transition parameter file was modified via "Pashtification" in order to more closely model the POS tag sequences and morphosyntactic structure of Pashto. We discuss these modifications in section 5.1. The lexical emission parameter file was modified directly by adding closed class words and their POS tags and by adding other Pashto words with hypothesized POS tags based on analyses of our development corpora. We discuss these modifications in section 5.2.

5.1 Pashtification

To improve the transition probabilities obtained from the source language, we performed various syntactic modifications, or "Pashtifications", on the Farsi corpus. The changes were based on systematic syntactic differences between Pashto and Farsi, but did not require extensive Pashto knowledge.

One of our "Pashtifications" involved inserting Pashto prepositions into long noun-noun compounds in the Farsi corpus. Contrary to Pashto, Farsi allows intensive noun-noun compounding where the component nouns are joined by *harf-e-izafat* (spoken preposition). *Harf-e-izafat* is not written in Farsi and has multiple grammatical functions including genitive marking. But, as shown in section 3, the linking prepositions are made explicit in the Pashto orthography, so we inserted the Pashto linking prepositions into the original Farsi corpus.

We applied 47 "Pashtification" rules, most of which were related to verbs. Below is a synopsis.

Preposition insertion. Insert a preposition in the noun-noun chain whenever two or more nouns are tagged with a genitive subcategory.

Adjective-Noun inversion. As discussed earlier, adjectives precede nouns in Pashto, but follow their modified nouns in Farsi.

Indefinite article insertion. Indefinite articles are suffixed in Farsi adjectives or nouns. Pashto, on the other hand, uses a separate word before the noun or adjective. We applied a rule that makes this change by adding a determiner category before the noun or adjective.

Clitic insertion. Farsi uses personal affixes attached to nouns and adjectives to describe possession or belonging, such as "his book." Pashto, on the other hand, uses a clitic. We inserted Pashto clitics after the nouns tagged with the personal affixes.

Present tense verb rules. Verbs that are formed from an adjective or a noun root are marked as adjectivized or nominalized verbs in the Farsi corpus. Sometimes these verbs are written as two separate words in Farsi, yet they are tagged as one word. In Pashto, this type of construction almost always occurs as two separate words. For example, for an adjective followed by a present tense verb, we changed the one V_PRS_ADJ tag to two tags of ADJ and V_PRS. The same rule was applied to the verbs tagged as verb present, adverb, noun, and pronoun. Also, in Farsi negation is inflected in verbs almost all the time while it is not the case with Pashto. Negative verbs were changed to negation plus verb in Pashto.

Past tense verb rules. We made similar changes to past tense verbs. Some participle plus verb constructions are treated simply as past tense in Farsi. These were tagged with a specific tag (`V_PA_NAR_POS`). We changed these to `ADJ_INO` (tag for participle) plus present as two different tags.

Auxiliary rules. The category `AUX` is extremely ambiguous in the BijanKhan corpus. It sometimes refers to a main verb in the matrix clause, or it refers to a modal such as *bayad* ("must"). We included several rules and new categories to exclude the need for an `AUX` category. Pashto does not use any auxiliary verbs other than for constructing participles. Participles are marked as `ADJ_INO` (accusative adjectives) in the BijanKhan corpus. Often the adjective and the verbal part are combined as one token despite the orthography showing two separate words. We used the subcategory portion of `AUX` tags to change the auxiliaries to present, past, or subjunctive categories if the auxiliary needed to be translated to a verb.

Imperative verb. Like other verbs, imperatives in Farsi are written with the negation inserted. In Pashto, the negation is not part of the verb. We applied a rule that separates the two.

***Ra* exclusion.** Farsi uses a direct object marker *ra* which we changed to `P_POST` (postposition). The Farsi accusative marker occurs in the same syntactic location as a `P_POST` in Pashto.

5.2 Lexical Modifications

5.2.1 Cognate Analysis

Farsi and Pashto share many "cognates", an umbrella term we are using to describe both true linguistic cognates (where the words share a common ancestor) and loan words (borrowed from the same language, in this case usually Arabic). We exploited this lexical similarity to improve our tagger by assuming that words we determined to be cognates would share similar tag distributions.

We used a normalized Levenshtein distance to detect cognates in Farsi and Pashto. Levenshtein distance is a measure of similarity between two strings (Levenshtein, 1966), so the intuition is that if words are spelled similarly, they will have similar meanings, or, crucially for our application, they will have the same POS tag distribution.

We first obtained a table listing all the edit distance scores of all possible word-word combinations between the Farsi corpus and our Pashto lexicon obtained from the web-based corpus. In order to avoid favoring shorter words, which have shorter edit distances by virtue of having fewer letters to permute, we normalized the score with the lengths of words in question. We chose the maximum length of the two words in consideration, and used that length to divide the Levenshtein distance to get the normalized score:

$$normalized\_score = \frac{Levenshtein\_distance}{maximum\_word\_length}$$

If the normalized score was below a certain threshold, then we added the Pashto version of the word to the lexicon, which was used by our tagger, along with the tag distribution from the Farsi word. If the Pashto word was similar to more than one Farsi words, we combined the tag distribution of all the Farsi words. If the word was already present in the lexicon, we simply used its tag distribution. For example, if Pashto word p is similar to Farsi word f, whose tag distribution is "`ADJ` 10, `ADV` 5", we added p with the tag distribution of f to our lexicon. If a Pashto word x already existed in our lexicon, the tag distribution of the Farsi cognate was the same, because the Pashto lexicon was originally generated from the Farsi corpus.

We ran a series of experiments, evaluating on our hand-tagged test set, to determine the optimal threshold to use for deciding which Farsi and Pashto words were cognates. We first ran three experiments with 0.3, 0.5 and 0.8 as our threshold values. We found that 0.3 gave us the best results. We then ran another series of experiments with these values—0.24, 0.25, 0.26, 0.27, 0.28, 0.29, 0.30, 0.31, and 0.32. We finally chose the best value, 0.28, from the experiments.

5.2.2 Morphological Analysis

We also modified the original lexical emission file from Farsi by including information from a morphological analysis of our Pashto web corpus. The morphological analysis proceeded as follows: we developed a short list of affixes that typically occur with various parts of speech categories in Pashto; we then looped through our Pashto web corpus and checked whether the current word appeared with any of the affixes anywhere else in the web corpus; if the word did occur with those affixes above a certain threshold, we could then assume with a measure of confidence that that word should be tagged as indicated by the suffix.

An example in English: imagine our suffixes are {`-ed`, `-ing`, `-s`} and our current word in the corpus is "work". We now check to see if "worked", etc., occur elsewhere in the corpus. If the threshold is met, we then alter the entry for the word plus suffix in the tagging lexicon, hopefully improving the lexical information for tagging.

5.2.3 Lexical Enrichment

To further improve the lexicon for the tagger, we added a set of closed class words. We chose the 200 most frequent words from the Bijankhan corpus for translation into Pashto. Our cognate detector was able to detect 91 of those. We therefore only had to translate 109 Farsi words into Pashto. We replaced these Farsi words with their Pashto equivalents. Not all the closed class elements were included in the two hundred frequent words—we therefore added 24 of the most common prepositions, postpositions, pronouns, and conjunctions to the training lexicon. We also included most (42) forms of light verbs. We believe that such language information does not constitute an intensive language resource. It can be obtained from any Pashto grammar resource in approximately 3-4 hours.

6 Experiments and Results

We performed two sets of experiments, in which we used two different tagsets (discussed in section 4.3.2). In the first set of experiments (section 6.1), we used the Amiri et al. (2007) tagset. In the second set of experiments (section 6.2), we used our custom tagset PERT.

6.1 Experiments with Amiri et al. (2007) Tagset

We ran a series of experiments combining different amounts and levels of information to see which provided the most help in tagging our Pashto test corpus using the Amiri et al. (2007) tagset. As a baseline, we determined that the most common tag in our test corpus was `N_SING`, the singular noun, and labeled every word with it. This naive approach was 16.62% accurate, meaning 16.62% of the words in the test corpus were singular nouns according to the gold standard.

PERT baseline	25.89%
all Pashtifications	37.60%
translate frequent F words to P	51.77%
closed-class words added	61.85%
morphological analysis	68.66%
cognate analysis	**70.84%**

Table 3: Results with PERT

Our biggest improvement over this baseline came from enriching the lexicon with closed class Pashto words (table 2, row 2). Other modifications like adding information from the morphological and cognate analyses did help, but not to the same degree.

The columns in table 2 correspond to different modifications made to the lexical information: "plain Farsi" is the lexicon obtained directly from Farsi, "+Cogs" includes information from the cognate analysis, "+MA" includes information from the morphological analysis, and "+Cogs MA" includes both types of information. The rows indicate whether the Farsi lexicon was enriched with Pashto vocabulary or not.

Across all trials, both cognate and morphological analysis information improved results, with the cognate information being more useful. The contribution of these lexical modifications has a greater effect in the experiments without the addition of Pashto closed class words where the Pashto-impoverished lexicons are introduced to at least some Pashto. The jump from adding basic closed class lexical information alone is substantial: from 16.91% to 62.65%, using an otherwise plain Farsi lexicon and plain Farsi transitions. The best results of 66.32% are achieved with a combination of closed class, cognate, and morphological analysis information. "Pashtifications" were not tested with this tagset due to poor preliminary performance.

6.2 Experiments with PERT

In order to test our "Pashtifications", we ran experiments using PERT as well. The results are presented in table 3. Each row in the table represents one level of enhancement; with each level, more modifications are used to enhance the tagger's performance. Each level is also built upon the previous level, and thus includes the previous

Modifications	plain Farsi	+Cogs	+MA	+Cogs MA
plain Farsi	16.91%	22.50%	20.15%	24.56%
enriched	62.65%	65.88%	63.82%	**66.32**%

Table 2: Results using Amiri et al. (2007) tagset with different levels of modification to the lexicon.

level's performance boost.

Looking at table 3, we can see that merely changing the tagset to PERT for our baseline gets a performance boost of nearly 10 percentage points (cf. table 2). Seen in row 2, the application of the "Pashtification" rules results in a nearly 12 point accuracy boost to 37.60%. Rows 3-4 show the tagger's performance after successive levels of lexical enrichment. In row 3, the 109 most frequent words in the Farsi corpus have been translated into Pashto, leading to a 10 point increase in accuracy. In row 4, the lexicon is further enhanced through the direct addition of Pashto closed-class words and light verbs to the lexicon which results in a further boost to 61.85%. The addition of morphological analysis in row 5 brings the tagger's accuracy to nearly 68.66%. Finally, the addition of cognate detection takes the accuracy to our maximum accuracy of 70.84%. This accuracy is over 4 points higher than that achieved by the Amiri et al. (2007) tagset experiments (without Pashtifications).

The experiments with the two different tagsets shows that the level of detail captured by the choice in tagset can have a meaningful effect on the results, especially for any syntactic alterations. Indeed, implementing our Pashtification rules required a level of granularity that we were able to provide with PERT. Also, seen in the experiments with either tagset, the inclusion of the closed class elements (lexical enrichment) is key to achieving maximum results.

7 Conclusions and Future Work

We have presented a method of using the POS tagging information from Farsi, a relatively well-resourced language, to help automatically tag Pashto, a relatively lower-resourced language. We used a Hidden Markov Model trigram tagger, TnT, to generate the parameter files which we then modified through various means. Our modifications to the HMM parameter files proved very effective in boosting the tagger's performance on our hand-tagged Pashto test set, with lexical modifications (particularly closed class words) providing the largest boost, and transition modifications contributing substantially with a customized tagset. Ultimately, we improved a 16.62% baseline to 70.84%, which is a respectable number given Pashto's morphological complexity.

In the future, we plan to work on three points to improve this approach. First, we plan to build a better morphological analyzer (MA). Pashto is a morphologically rich language and a robust MA can help tag parts of speech more successfully. Second, we plan to increase the size of our test set to 3000 tokens. Lastly, we will use our automatically tagged test data as additional training and investigate the effect of iterative bootstrapping on the tagger's performance.We can use our 473 MB Pashto web corpus for this purpose.

Acknowledgments

We would thank to thank Sandra Kübler for her guidance and helpful comments, along with the three anonymous reviewers.

References

H. Amiri, H. Hojjat, and F. Oroumchian. 2007. Investigation on a feasible corpus for Persian POS tagging. In *Proceedings of the 12th international CSI computer conference, Iran*.

M. Baroni and S. Bernardini. 2004. BootCaT: Bootstrapping corpora and terms from the web. In *Proceedings of LREC*.

Thorsten Brants. 2000. TnT–a statistical part-of-speech tagger. In *Proceedings of the 1st Conference of the North American Chapter of the Association for Computational Linguistics and the 6th Conference on Applied Natural Language Processing (ANLP/NAACL)*, pages 224–231, Seattle, WA.

A. Feldman and J. Hana. 2010. A resource-light approach to morphosyntactic tagging. In C. Mair, C. F. Meyer, and N. Oostdijk, editors, *Language and Computers 70: Studies in Practical Linguistics*. Rodopi Press, Amsterdam-New York.

A. Hardie. 2003. Developing a model for automated part-of-speech tagging in Urdu. In *Proceedings of Corpus Linguistics*, pages 298–307.

Vladimir I. Levenshtein. 1966. Binary codes capable of correcting deletions, insertions, and reversals. *Cybernetics and Control Theory*, 10(8):707–710.

F. Oroumchian, S. Tasharofi, H. Amiri, H. Hojjat, and F. Raja. 2006. Creating a feasible corpus for Persian POS tagging. Technical report, University of Wollongong in Dubai. No. TR3/06.

I. Rabbi, A. M. Khan, and R. Ali. 2009. Rule-based part of speech tagging for Pashto language. In *Conference on Language and Technology, Lahore, Pakistan*.

Z. Xiao, A. M. McEnery, Paul Baker, and Andrew Hardie. 2004. Developing Asian language corpora: standards and practice. In *Proceedings of the 4th Workshop on Asian Language Resources, Sanya, China*, pages 1–8.

Enriching Phrase-Based Statistical Machine Translation with POS Information

Miriam Kaeshammer and **Dominikus Wetzel**
Department of Computational Linguistics
Saarland University
Saarbrücken, Germany
{miriamk,dwetzel}@coli.uni-sb.de

Abstract

This work presents an extension to phrase-based statistical machine translation models which incorporates linguistic knowledge, namely part-of-speech information. Scores are added to the standard phrase table which represent how the phrases correspond to their translations on the part-of-speech level. We suggest two different kinds of scores. They are learned from a POS-tagged version of the parallel training corpus. The decoding strategy does not have to be modified. Our experiments show that our extended models achieve similar BLEU and NIST scores compared to the standard model. Additional manual investigation reveals local improvements in the translation quality.

1 Introduction

Currently, the most prominent paradigm in statistical machine translation (SMT) are phrase-based models (Koehn et al., 2003), in which text chunks (*phrases*) of one language are mapped to corresponding text chunks in another language. This standard approach works only with the surface forms of words and no linguistic information is used for establishing the mapping between phrases or generating the final translation. It has been shown, however, that integrating linguistic knowledge, e.g. part-of-speech (POS) or morphological information, in pre- or post-processing or directly into the translation model improves the translation quality (cf. Section 2).

Factored translation models (Koehn and Hoang, 2007) are one extension of the standard phrase-based approach, which allow to include rich linguistic knowledge into the translation model. Additional models for the specified factors are used, which makes decoding computationally more complex as the mapping between the factors can result in an explosion of translation options.

With this work, we explore a different approach to integrate linguistic knowledge, in particular POS information, into the phrase-based model. The standard phrase (translation) table is enriched with new scores which encode the correspondence on the POS level between the two phrases of a phrase pair; for example the probability of "translating" the POS sequence of one phrase into the POS sequence of the other phrase. We propose two methods to obtain such *POS scores*. These extra scores are additional feature functions in the log-linear framework for computing the best translation (Och and Ney, 2002). They supply further information about the phrase pairs under consideration during decoding, but do not increase the number of translation options.

The presented extension neither makes use of hand-crafted rules nor manually identified patterns. It can therefore be performed fully automatically. Furthermore, our approach is language-independent and does not rely on a specific POS tagger or tag set. Adaptation to other language pairs is hence straightforward.

This paper first describes related work and then introduces our extended translation model. Evaluation results are reported for experiments with a German-English system. We finally discuss our work and suggest possible further extensions.

2 Related Work

There are several strategies for improving the quality of standard phrase-based SMT by incorporating linguistic knowledge, in particular POS information.

One such approach is to modify the data in a pre-processing step. For example, Collins et al. (2005) parse the sentences of the source language and restructure the word order, such that it matches the target language word order more closely. Language-specific, manually devised rules are employed. Popović and Ney (2006) follow the same idea, but make use of manually defined patterns based on POS information: e.g. local adjective-noun reordering for Spanish and long-range reorderings of German verbs. Essentially, this strategy aims at facilitating and improving the word alignment. Another example along those lines is (Carpuat, 2009). Surface words in the training data are replaced with their lemma and POS tag. Once the improved alignment is obtained, the phrase extraction is based on the original training data, thus a different decoding strategy is not necessary. Another data-driven approach is presented in (Rottmann and Vogel, 2007), where word reordering rules based on POS tags are learned. A word lattice with all reorderings (including probabilities for each) is constructed and used by the decoder to make more informed decisions.

Another strategy is concerned with enhancing the system's output in a post-processing step. Koehn and Knight (2003) propose a method for noun phrases where feature-rich reranking is applied to a list of n-best translations.

Instead of the above pre- or post-processing steps, Koehn and Hoang (2007) present factored models which allow for a direct integration of linguistic information into the phrase-based translation model. Each surface word is now represented by a vector of linguistic factors. It is a general framework, exemplified on POS and morphological enrichment. In order to tackle the increasing translation options introduced by additional factors, the decoding strategy needs to be adapted: translation options are precomputed and early pruning is applied. Factored models including POS information (amongst others) are employed for example by Holmqvist et al. (2007) for German-English translation and Singh and Bandyopadhyay (2010) for the resource-poor language pair Manipuri-English.

3 Extended Translation Model

The general idea is to integrate POS information into the translation process by adding one or several *POS scores* to each phrase pair in the standard phrase table which represents the translation model and usually contains phrase translation probabilities, lexical weightings and a phrase penalty. The additional scores reflect how well the POS sequence which underlies one phrase of the pair corresponds to the POS sequence of the other phrase of the pair. Two concrete methods to calculate this correspondence will be described in Section 3.2. The new scores can be integrated into the log-linear framework as additional feature functions.

Figure 1 shows two phrase pairs from a German-English phrase table. In this particular case, the POS scores should encode the correspondence between `ART ADJA NN` from the German side and `DT JJ NNS VBN` (a) or `DT JJ NNS` (b) from the English side. Intuitively, `ART ADJA NN` corresponds better to `DT JJ NNS` than to `DT JJ NNS VBN`. Phrase pair (b) should therefore have higher POS scores.

The transition from the standard translation model to the extended one can be broken up into two major steps: (1) **POS-Mapping**, which is the task of mapping each phrase pair in the standard phrase table to its underlying pair of POS sequences (henceforth *POS phrase pair*), and (2) **POS-Scoring**, which refers to assigning POS scores to each phrase pair based on the previously determined POS phrase pair.

3.1 POS-Mapping

Obtaining the part-of-speech information for each phrase in the phrase table cannot be achieved by tagging the phrases with a regular POS tagger. They are usually written for and trained on full sentences. Phrases would therefore get assigned incorrect POS tags, since a phrase without its context and the same phrase occurring in an actual sentence are likely to be tagged with different POS sequences.

Since the phrase pairs in the phrase table originate from specific contexts in the parallel training corpus, we require a phrase to have the same POS sequence as it has in the context of its sentence. Consequently, our approach takes the following steps: First, both sides of the training corpus are POS-tagged. Secondly, the untagged phrases in the phrase table and their tagged counterparts in the corpus are associated with each other to establish a mapping from phrase pairs to POS phrase pairs. This procedure is consequently not called POS-Tagging, but rather POS-Mapping.

Our approach is to apply the same phrase extraction algorithm again that has been used to obtain the standard phrase table. Phrase pairs are ex-

(a)	die möglichen risiken	|||	the possible risks posed	|||	1.0	[...]	0.155567	0.000520715
(b)	die möglichen risiken	|||	the possible risks	|||	0.1	[...]	0.178425	0.0249141

Figure 1: Two phrase pairs, each with the first standard translation score and two new POS scores.

tracted from the POS-tagged parallel training corpus, thereby taking over the word alignments that have been established for the parallel sentences to extract standard phrase pairs before. In the resulting *word/POS phrase table*, a token is a combination of a word with a POS tag. For this to work, words and POS tags must be delimited by any special character other than a space. Thanks to the reused word alignments, the word/POS phrase table contains each phrase pair of the standard phrase table at least once. If a phrase pair occurs with several different POS sequences in the training data, the word/POS phrase table contains an entry for each of them.

By matching the standard phrase table against the word/POS phrase table, the POS phrase pair(s) for each standard phrase pair are obtained. The word/POS phrase table is hence used as the mapping element between phrase pairs and their corresponding POS phrase pairs. The result of this POS-Mapping step is a $1 : k$ (with $k \geq 1$) mapping from phrase pairs to POS phrase pairs. The POS phrase pairs are the basis for calculating the POS scores as explained in the following subsection.

An alternative approach to POS-Mapping would be a search for the phrases in the tagged sentences. This however requires elaborate techniques such as indexing.

3.2 POS-Scoring

We propose two different kinds of POS scores to encode the correspondence on the POS level between the two phrases of a phrase pair: *POS Phrase Translation (PPT)* and *POS Phrase Frequency (PPF)* scores.

PPT scores PPT scores encode how likely it is to "translate" one POS phrase into another POS phrase. The idea behind those scores and also the way how they are obtained is very similar to the scores in a standard phrase table, namely translation probabilities and lexical weightings. The difference is that the tokens that constitute the phrases are POS tags. Consequently, phrase pair extraction and phrase pair scoring (maximum likelihood estimation for translation probability and lexical weighting in both translation directions) is performed on a version of the parallel training corpus, in which each word is substituted by its POS tag. Again, as we did in Section 3.1 to obtain the word/POS phrase table, the word alignments that were established to extract the standard phrase pairs are reused.

In this way, a *POS phrase table* is trained which has four scores attached to each POS phrase pair. Those are the desired PPT scores. Due to the reused word-alignment, it contains all POS phrase pairs that also occur in the word/POS phrase table.

The standard phrase table is combined with the new PPT scores via the mapping from phrase pairs to POS phrase pairs introduced in Section 3.1. As this is a $1 : k$ mapping, it needs to be decided which of the k POS phrase pairs and corresponding scores to use. Currently, we decide for the POS phrase pair for which the sum of the scores is maximal and use the corresponding PPT scores $\hat{s}$:

$$\hat{s} = \operatorname*{argmax}_{s_k} \sum_{i=1}^{|s_k|} s_k(i) \qquad (1)$$

where k ranges over the POS phrase pairs which are mapped to the current phrase pair, s_k are the (four) PPT scores of the kth POS phrase pair and i is an index into these scores. This decision rule is a crucial point in the extended model where additional experiments using other techniques should be conducted.

From the four PPT scores in $\hat{s}$, several extended translation models have been derived which differ in the number of scores that are added to the standard phrase table: i. all 4 PPT scores, ii. only the phrase translation probabilities (PPT scores 1 and 3), iii. only the lexical weightings (PPT scores 2 and 4) and iv. only the inverse phrase translation probability (PPT score 1).

As an example, the last two scores on each line in Figure 1 are PPT scores (phrase translation probabilities) that have been obtained with the described method. Indeed both are higher for (b), which coincides with our expectation.

PPF score The PPF score encodes the raw frequency of POS phrase pairs; more specifically how often a POS phrase pair occurs in the word/POS phrase table (see Section 3.1). The intuition behind it is that POS phrase pairs which correspond to more than one distinct surface phrase pair are more reliable than POS phrase pairs that produce only one type of phrase pair. The latter could for example originate from a wrong alignment. This score abstracts away from directly counting the phrase pair occurrences in the parallel training corpus, which is information that is already incorporated in the standard phrase table scores.

To combine the obtained counts with the standard phrase table, we again use the $1:k$ mapping from phrase pairs to POS phrase pairs and select the maximum out of the k PPF scores. As an example, phrase pair (a) in Figure 1 receives a PPF score of 289, while phrase pair (b) has PPF score 9735, according to the most frequent underlying POS phrase pair.

We anticipate the issue that shorter phrase pairs get higher counts, since their corresponding POS sequences are more likely to occur in the word/POS phrase table. This seems to result in a bias towards selecting shorter phrases during decoding, which stands in contrast to a phrase penalty which favors longer phrases that is commonly employed in phrase-based translation systems. We assume that the tuning procedure will find weights for the feature functions such that those two complement each other.

4 Experiments

For our experiments we used the Moses phrase-based SMT toolkit (Koehn et al., 2007; Koehn, 2010) to train translation systems from German to English.

4.1 Data

As training data we used the German and English documents from the Europarl Corpus Release v5 (Koehn, 2005), excluding the standard portion (Q4/2000). The data was sentence-aligned, tokenized and lowercased by the provided scripts. Sentences longer than 40 tokens on either language side were removed with their translations from the training corpus, resulting in about 1.1 million sentence pairs. From the held-out data 3000 sentences for development and 2000 sentences for testing were randomly chosen.

To generate the POS-tagged version of the tokenized training data, we applied the OpenNLP 1.4 POS tagger[1] using the provided German and English models. Afterwards, the POS-tagged training corpus was lowercased.

For the language model, we used the English side of the complete training corpus containing the lowercased data (about 1.5 million sentences). The model was generated with the SRILM toolkit 1.5.8[2] using 3-grams and Kneser-Ney discounting.

4.2 Setup

We used the Moses training script with the standard parameters except for the alignment heuristic (`grow-diag-final-and`) together with GIZA++ (Och and Ney, 2003) to train the standard translation model. The obtained word alignment was used for phrase extraction and scoring in order to construct the word/POS phrase table and the POS phrase table.

We tuned our extended systems as well as the standard system with minimum error rate training (MERT) (Och, 2003). For the extended models, the tuning script that comes with Moses needs to be adapted slightly. Additional triples specifying initialization and randomization ranges for the weights of our additional feature functions have to be inserted. Because of the possibility that the MERT algorithm gets trapped in a local maximum, several tuning runs for the same model with the same development data were performed.

We skipped recasing and detokenization, since we are only interested in the effect of our extended model with respect to the baseline.

4.3 Results

Table 1 shows the automatic evaluation of the outcome of the conducted experiments. Our extended model with all four PPT scores (t1) achieved the best results, followed by the baseline (t2) in terms of BLEU and our PPF model according to NIST. However, the reported scores are similar and the differences in performance between the extended models and the baselines are insignificant.

For two models, we report the performance of the systems that were obtained with two independent tuning instances (t1 and t2) in Table 1. The varying scores indicate the importance of the tuning step.

[1] `http://opennlp.sourceforge.net/`
[2] `www.speech.sri.com/projects/srilm/`

		BLEU	NIST
Standard Model	Baseline (t1)	25.59	6.7329
	Baseline (t2)	25.83	6.7817
Extended Model	all 4 PPT scores (t1)	**25.88**	**6.8091**
	all 4 PPT scores (t2)	25.60	6.7835
	PPT scores 1 and 3	25.58	6.7651
	PPT scores 2 and 4	25.66	6.7758
	PPT score 1	25.61	6.7590
	PPF score	25.73	6.7882

Table 1: Performance of the models on the test set.

To sum up, according to the automatic evaluation, none of our extended models clearly outperforms the baseline. This could suggest on the one hand that the additional POS scores do not lead to better translation models. One the other hand, BLEU and NIST might just not be able to reflect our improvements in the translation models and quality. They are automatic metrics and we only provide one reference translation for each sentence in the development and test data. Consequently, further inspection of the translated data is necessary.

4.4 Manual Investigation

Out of the 2000 test sentences, our extended model with all four PPT scores (t1) provides the same translation as the baseline (t2) in 613 cases (470 for t2 of the extended model). To find out about the variations that occur in the translations which differ, we manually inspected some sample sentences. As follows, we will present and describe the examples in Figure 2. In (2a) – (2f) the translation of our extended model is better than the one provided by the baseline system.

The baseline translation in (2a) is neither understandable nor grammatical. Our model accomplishes to translate the two genitive constructions and provides a suitable translation for the verb, which is missing completely in the baseline. In (2b) the relative clause construction in the scope of the negation is missing in the baseline. This leads to a severe change in meaning. The sentence provided by the extended system, in contrast, is fully meaningful and understandable. Obviously, it is not perfect; for example, *philosophical sense* lacks a determiner.

The baseline system provides ungrammatical translations that are hardly understandable for the test sentences in (2c), (2d) and (2e). In (2c) *wie* is not translated as the interrogative pronoun, and in (2d) the infinitive verb is missing. Our extended system produces good translations for both sentences. The test sentence in (2e) is difficult for machine translation because the verb in the subordinate clause is omitted from the first part of the conjunction. In fact, both systems cannot handle it. However, the extended system at least achieves to put the right content words into the two parts of the coordination; only the verb in the first part is missing.

Example (2f) shows that our extended model helps at conveying the semantics of the source sentence. The translation given by the baseline is not completely wrong, but it fails at expressing the *possibility* of the conflict and also the *process* of getting into a conflict. The translation of our extended system (*which could come into conflict*) conveys both.

There are also sentences within the test set, on which the baseline system performs better than the extended model. In (2g), the translation given by our model lacks a conjugated verb. (2h) shows an instance of a wrongly translated pronoun by our extended system. The sentence is furthermore ungrammatical whereas the translation by the baseline system is acceptable.

The given examples have revealed that the differences in the translations provided by the baseline system and our extended system are generally local. Often only a small number of words is affected. However, even local changes lead to better translations as shown in the examples (2a) – (2f). It is left to quantify these results to check whether the extended translation model overall introduces more improvements or deteriorations.

The examples in Figure 2 also illustrate why BLEU and NIST do not show a difference between the extended system and the baseline: Even if a translation is acceptable, it is usually very different from the provided reference translation. The small improvements are consequently not reflected in the automatic score.

5 Discussion & Future Work

With our extended model, we are able to incorporate linguistic information into the otherwise pure statistical MT approach. We have realized our approach within the framework provided by Moses and its tools, but other phrase-based SMT systems could be extended in the same way. Once the scores encoding the additional information are calculated, almost no modification to existing code is necessary.

The presented method does not make use of any language-specific behavior or patterns, which leaves it open to any language combination, provided that there are POS taggers for the involved languages available. Since no hand-crafted rules need to be designed for the extension, our approach can be applied to new language pairs with only a minimum amount of time and effort. Moreover, any POS tagger with any POS tag set can be used in order to annotate the training data. It is also noteworthy that POS tagging is only needed during training and not during decoding.

The automatic evaluation represented in the BLEU/NIST scores showed only insignificant improvement for our extended system over the baseline. However, a manual investigation of the translated test data revealed qualitatively better translations. Some local phenomena seem to be handled better in the linguistically informed model. Certainly, in order to make reliable judgments, human evaluation of a representative set of translations is needed.

Tuning the weights of the feature functions is an essential step for obtaining a good translation system (cf. (Koehn, 2010)). The effect of different tuning instances on the translation output and thus BLEU/NIST can be seen in our experimental results in Table 1. Accordingly, it needs to be determined whether the MERT algorithm is still capable of finding good weights when more than the standard weights need to be tuned. A review of the literature did not clarify the impact of the number of weights on MERT tuning. Other tuning algorithms could be considered. Furthermore, MERT relies on automatic evaluation metrics. Because of their shortcomings (cf. (Callison-Burch et al., 2006)), the tuning approach might not exploit the full potential of the additionally encoded linguistic information. An improvement would be to include a human-based evaluation component in MERT (cf. (Zaidan and Callison-Burch, 2009)).

A very important further step would be to fully compare our approach to factored models (using POS information on the source and target side) (Koehn and Hoang, 2007) under the same experimental conditions as reported in this work. From a theoretical point of view, the main difference between our approach and the factored models is that the linguistic information is explicitly encoded in several phrase tables in the latter, while in the former it is implicit in the additional score(s) in just one phrase table. As mentioned before in Section 2, factored models have the shortcoming of a drastic rise of translation options during decoding. Our approach, in contrast, does not change the number of translation options. It rather provides more informed phrase pair selection criteria by means of the POS scores. The decoding strategy therefore does not need to be adapted.

Interestingly, Koehn and Hoang (2007) report only minor improvements in BLEU for their English-German system when using only the surface form and POS in the factored models. However, they report a greater improvement when also adding morphological information. This could suggest that POS information on its own is not informative enough to improve the BLEU score.

There are various ways to improve and extend the presented approach. One crucial point where we have made a rather ad hoc decision is the procedure in Equation 1. Ideally, one would want to use the POS scores that are optimal with respect to the translation result. Furthermore, this procedure should be improved such that it only considers the subset of POS scores that is actually used in the final phrase table.

Possible extensions of the models in our fashion are not only tied to POS information. One could for example incorporate more structured information such as dependency relations. This information would be assigned to a word just like the POS tag has been. More specifically, we suggest to consider the following two approaches: (1) Tokens get assigned the number of their dependants, e.g. Peter`/0` likes`/2` Mary`/0`. (2) Dependent tokens get assigned a tuple specifying their dependency type and their head word, e.g Peter`/(subj,likes)` likes`/(root,nil)` Mary`/(obj,likes)`. As this approach might run into data sparsity problems, as a variant, the dependency type could be omitted. Once one of the above syntax taggings is generated, the mapping and scores for the phrase table can then be obtained just as before with the POS-Mapping/Scoring approach.

6 Conclusion

We have described a language-independent approach to incorporate linguistic information such as POS tags into phrase-based SMT. We achieved this by enriching the phrase pairs in the standard phrase table with additional POS scores which reflect the correspondence between the underlying POS sequences of the phrases of each pair. Two kinds of POS scores have been proposed: *POS Phrase Translation* scores from a learned phrase table based on POS sequences and *POS Phrase Frequency* scores which are raw counts of POS sequence pairs. To assign the scores to the standard phrase pairs, they have been mapped to their underlying POS sequences (via a word/POS phrase table). In order to extract the same phrases across all phrase tables, the word alignment of the standard phrase table has been reused. In experiments for German-English, automatic evaluation showed minor differences in performance between the extended systems and the baseline. Additional manual inspection of the results revealed promising local improvements. Compared to the factored models, our extension uses linguistic information implicitly, does not provide additional translation options and therefore does not introduce further complexity for decoding.

Acknowledgments

This work was part of a project seminar at Saarland University. We would like to thank our supervisor Andreas Eisele from DFKI for the ideas that got us started and his support. Part of this research was funded through the European Community's Seventh Framework Programme under grant agreement no. 231720, EuroMatrix Plus.

References

Chris Callison-Burch, Miles Osborne, and Philipp Koehn. 2006. Re-evaluating the Role of BLEU in Machine Translation Research. In *Proceedings of EACL*, pages 249–256.

Marine Carpuat. 2009. Toward Using Morphology in French-English Phrase-Based SMT. In *Proceedings of the Fourth Workshop on Statistical Machine Translation*, pages 150–154, Athens, Greece. ACL.

Michael Collins, Philipp Koehn, and Ivona Kucerova. 2005. Clause Restructuring for Statistical Machine Translation. In *Proceedings of the 43rd Annual Meeting of the ACL*, Ann Arbor, Michigan. ACL.

Maria Holmqvist, Sara Stymne, and Lars Ahrenberg. 2007. Getting to Know Moses: Initial Experiments on German-English Factored Translation. In *Proceedings of the Second Workshop on Statistical Machine Translation*, Prague, Czech Republic. ACL.

Philipp Koehn and Hieu Hoang. 2007. Factored Translation Models. In *Proceedings of the 2007 Joint Conference on EMNLP and CoNLL*, pages 868–876.

Philipp Koehn and Kevin Knight. 2003. Feature-Rich Statistical Translation of Noun Phrases. In *Proceedings of the 41st Annual Meeting of the ACL*, pages 311–318, Sapporo, Japan.

Philipp Koehn, Franz Josef Och, and Daniel Marcu. 2003. Statistical Phrase-Based Translation. In *Proceedings of HLT-NAACL 2003*, pages 48–45.

Philipp Koehn, Hieu Hoang, Alexandra Birch, Chris Callison-Burch, Marcello Federico, Nicola Bertoldi, Brooke Cowan, Wade Shen, Christine Moran, Richard Zens, Chris Dyer, Ondrej Bojar, Alexandra Constantin, and Evan Herbst. 2007. Moses: Open Source Toolkit for Statistical Machine Translation. In *Annual Meeting of the ACL*.

Philipp Koehn. 2005. Europarl: A Parallel Corpus for Statistical Machine Translation. In *Proceedings of MT Summit*.

Philipp Koehn, 2010. *Moses. Statistical Machine Translation System*. User Manual and Code Guide.

Franz Josef Och and Hermann Ney. 2002. Discriminative Training and Maximum Entropy Models for Statistical Machine Translation. In *Proceedings of the 40th Annual Meeting of ACL*, pages 295–302.

Franz Josef Och and Hermann Ney. 2003. A Systematic Comparison of Various Statistical Alignment Models. *Computational Linguistics*, 29:19–51, March.

Franz Josef Och. 2003. Minimum Error Rate Training in Statistical Machine Translation. In *Proceedings of the 41st Annual Meeting of ACL*, pages 160–167.

Maja Popović and Hermann Ney. 2006. POS-based Word Reorderings for Statistical Machine Translation. In *Proceedings of the International Conference on Language Resources and Evaluation*, pages 1278–1283, Genoa, Italy.

Kay Rottmann and Stephan Vogel. 2007. Word Reordering in Statistical Machine Translation with a POS-Based Distortion Model. In *Proceedings of the 11th International Conference on Theoretical and Methodological Issues in Machine Translation (TMI)*, Skövde, Sweden.

Thoudam Doren Singh and Sivaji Bandyopadhyay. 2010. Manipuri-English Bidirectional Statistical Machine Translation Systems using Morphology and Dependency Relations. In *Proceedings of the 4th Workshop on Syntax and Structure in Statistical Translation*, pages 83–91, Beijing, China. Coling 2010 Organizing Committee.

Omar F. Zaidan and Chris Callison-Burch. 2009. Feasibility of Human-in-the-loop Minimum Error Rate Training. In *Proceedings of the 2009 Conference on EMNLP*, pages 52–61, Singapore. ACL.

German	sechsundsechzig prozent der gesamtbeschäftigung der gemeinschaft entfallen auf kleine und mittlere unternehmen [...]
Baseline	the community sechsundsechzig per cent of total employment in small and medium-sized enterprises [...]
4 PPT	sechsundsechzig % of total employment of the community is generated by small and medium-sized enterprises [...]
Reference	smes account for 66 % of total employment in the community [...]

(a) Handling genitive constructions and translating the main verb correctly

German	es gibt kein volk in europa , das im philosophischen sinne neutral ist .
Baseline	there are no people in europe , in the philosophical sense is neutral .
4 PPT	there is no people in europe , which is neutral in philosophical sense .
Reference	there is no nation in europe that is philosophically neutral .

(b) Handling a relative clause correctly

German	wie ist nun der konkrete stand der verhandlungen ?
Baseline	as is now the real state of negotiations ?
4 PPT	so what exactly is the real state of negotiations ?
Reference	what stage has actually been reached in these negotiations ?

(c) Translating interrogative pronoun properly

German	sie haben natürlich recht , immer wieder auf diese frage zu verweisen .
Baseline	you are right , of course , to this question again and again .
4 PPT	you are right , of course , always to refer to this question .
Reference	you are , of course , quite right to keep reverting to this question .

(d) Missing verb in baseline translated properly in our model

German	abschließend möchte ich noch sagen , dass die postdienstleistungen in schweden nicht schlechter und in gewisser weise sogar besser geworden sind .
Baseline	finally , i would like to say that the postal services in sweden and in some way not worse even improved .
4 PPT	finally , i would like to say that the postal services not worse in sweden and in some way have become even better .
Reference	in conclusion , i would like to say that the postal service in sweden has not deteriorated , in some respects it has even improved .

(e) Tricky coordinate construction with omitted verb

German	auf diese weise [...] könnten machtzentren geschaffen werden , die untereinander in konflikt geraten könnten .
Baseline	in this way [...] machtzentren could be created , in conflict with each other .
4 PPT	in this way [...] machtzentren could be created , which could come into conflict with each other .
Reference	[...] there is a real danger that this will result in conflicting centres of power .

(f) Conveying correct semantics

German	schließlich beruht jedes demokratische system auf dem vertrauen und dem zutrauen der menschen .
Baseline	finally , any democratic system is based on the confidence and the trust of the people .
4 PPT	finally , any democratic system based on the confidence and the trust of the people .
Reference	after all , any democratic system is built upon the trust and confidence of the people .

(g) Wrong translation due to missing verb

German	der rat möchte daran erinnern , dass seine politik stets darauf abzielt , ein möglichst hohes niveau des verbraucherschutzes zu gewährleisten .
Baseline	the council would like to remind you that its policy has always been at the highest possible level of consumer protection .
4 PPT	the council would like to remind you that his policy always aims , as a high level of consumer protection .
Reference	the council wishes to point out that its policy is always to afford consumers the highest possible level of protection .

(h) Wrong pronoun chosen for translation

Figure 2: Example sentences for comparing our PPT extended model with the baseline. (2a) – (2f) reveal improvements, (2g) – (2h) show weaknesses.

Inter-domain Opinion Phrase Extraction Based on Feature Augmentation

Gábor Berend[1], **István Nagy T.**[1], **György Móra**[1] and **Veronika Vincze**[1,2]
[1]Department of Informatics, University of Szeged
{berendg,nistvan,gymora}@inf.u-szeged.hu
[2]Hungarian Academy of Sciences, Research Group on Artificial Intelligence
vinczev@inf.u-szeged.hu

Abstract

In this paper, a system for the extraction of key argument phrases – which make the opinion holder feel negative or positive towards a particular product – from product reviews is introduced. Since the necessary amount of training examples from any arbitrary product type (target domain) is not always available, the possible usage of domain adaptation in the task of opinion phrase extraction is also examined. Experimental results show that models relying on training examples mainly from a different domain can still yield results that are comparable to that of the intra-domain settings.

1 Introduction

There has been a growing interest in the NLP treatment of subjectivity and sentiment analysis (see e.g. Balahur et al. (2011)) and that of keyphrase extraction, e.g. Kim et al. (2010). Product reviews serve as perfect objects for the combination of the above mentioned research areas as the opinion bearing phrases of a product review can be interpreted analogously to regular keyphrases of scientific documents, i.e. in both cases proper phrases have decisive role within the document where they were present. The fact that some review portals have the possibility to leave a set of pro and con phrases underlines this resemblance between opinion phrases and scientific keyphrases.

However, despite the somewhat common nature of opinion phrases and keyphrases, methods that work on the well studied field of scientific keyphrase extraction are not necessarily successful in the extraction of opinion phrases from product reviews. On the one hand, although proper phrases have their decisive role in both types of genres, opinion phrases are the ones that form the sentiments of the opinion holder, whereas in the case of scientific keyphrases they should be such phrases that summarize well the content of a document. Note the difference between opinion-forming phrases and those which summarize well the content of a document, i.e. one can frequently use such phrases in a review that does not have much importance in the opinion-forming aspect, whereas in the case of scientific documents frequently used phrases tend to be proper keyphrases as well.

Most of the standard keyphrase extraction algorithms employ supervised learning, which makes the accessibility of training instances generated from reviews and the sets of opinion phrases assigned to them prerequisite. In the case of training an opinion phrase extractor on one domain, this criterion is not easily fulfilled in every case, due to the fact that it is not necessary that one can find abundant training examples for any kind of product types. For this reason, exploiting domain adaptation techniques during the task of opinion phrase mining among different domains might be useful. This paper examines the possible utility of domain adaptation in the inter-domain opinion phrase mining task.

2 Related Work

There have been many studies on opinion mining (Turney, 2002; Pang et al., 2002; Titov and McDonald, 2008; Liu and Seneff, 2009). Our approach relates to previous work on the extraction of reasons for opinions. Most of these papers treat the task of mining reasons from product reviews as one of identifying sentences that express the author's negative or positive feelings (Hu and Liu, 2004a; Popescu and Etzioni, 2005). This paper is clearly distinguishable from previous opinion mining systems as our goal is to find the reasons for opinions expressed and we aim the task of phrase extraction instead of sentence recognition.

This work differs in important aspects even from the frequent pattern mining-based approach of Hu and Liu (2004b), since they regarded the main task of mining opinion features with respect to a group of products, not individually at review-level as we did. Even if an opinion feature phrase is feasible for a given product-type, it is not necessary that all of its occurrences are accompanied with sentiments expressed towards it (e.g. *The phone comes in red and black colors*, where *color* could be an appropriate product feature).

The approach presented here differs from these studies in the sense that it looks for the reason phrases themselves review by review, instead of multi-labeling some aspects. These approaches are intended for applications used by companies who would like to obtain a general overview about a product or would like to monitor the polarity relating to their products in a particular community. In contrast, we introduce here a keyphrase extraction-based approach which works at the document level as it extracts keyphrases from reviews which are handled independently of each other. This approach is more appropriate for the consumers, who would like to be informed before purchasing some product.

The work of Kim and Hovy (2006) lies probably the closest to ours. They addressed the task of extracting con and pro sentences, i.e. the sentences on why the reviewers liked or disliked the product. They also note that such pro and con expressions can differ from positive and negative opinion expressions as factual sentences can also be reason sentences (e.g. *Video drains battery.*). Here the difference is that they extracted sentences, but we targeted phrase extraction.

Most of the keyphrase extraction approaches (Witten et al., 1999; Turney, 2003; Medelyan et al., 2009; Kim et al., 2010) extract phrases from one document that are the most characteristic of its content. In these supervised approaches keyphrase extraction is regarded as a classification task, in which certain n-grams of a specific document function as keyphrase candidates, and the task is to classify them as proper or improper keyphrases. Here, our task formalization of keyphrase extraction is adapted from this line of research for opinion mining and we focus on the extraction of argument phrases from product reviews that induce sentiments in its author. As community generated pros and cons can provide training samples and our goal is to extract the users' own words, here we also follow this supervised keyphrase extraction procedure.

As stated earlier, abundant training examples are not necessarily available from a single domain (product type) in the case of opinion phrase extraction, so domain adaptation techniques might be useful in the detection of opinion phrases. Formally, in the case of domain adaptation we are given two sets of instances, $S \subseteq D_S \in \mathbb{R}^n$ and $T \subseteq D_T \in \mathbb{R}^m$, D_S and D_T being the feature spaces of the source and target domain and S and T the set of source and target instances, respectively. Typically $|S| \gg |T|$ also holds for the sizes of the two distinct domains.

As a possible solution for domain adaptation Daumé and Marcu (2006) proposes an approach which learns three separate models, one for the source specific, target specific and general information as well. They also report that the usage of EM for the training of the models can be computationally costly.

Although the feature augmentation technique of Daumé (2007) uses a similar intuition (i.e. the existence of source-, target specific and general information), it is much simpler as it learns one model including both source and target domain instances in an extended feature space, instead of learning three models at a time. Here the original feature space is mapped to a higher-dimension space, so that source and target domain and general information are incorporated. To achieve this, the mapping Φ_S or Φ_T is employed to every instance x from the original feature space, depending on the fact whether the original vector x is representing a source or a target domain instance, respectively. The two mappings are of the forms $\Phi_S(x) =< x, x, \mathbf{0} >$ and $\Phi_T(x) =< x, \mathbf{0}, x >$, where **0** is the null vector.

3 Opinion Phrase Extraction

Experiments were inspired by the standard – mainly scientific – keyphrase extraction systems. In these systems, such in KEA (Witten et al., 1999) or Turney (2003), the extraction of such phrases (i.e. keyphrases) that circumscribe the main content of individual documents is regarded as a supervised learning task, where the author or reader-assigned keyphrases are used as positive training examples.

Here we adapted these standard scientific keyphrase extraction approaches to the task of opinion phrase extraction, however, in our case training examples were such phrases that make the author feel negative or positive towards a given object. Our setting was also similar to standard keyphrase extraction as the task of opinion phrase extraction was regarded as a supervised learning task, where training instances are generated from consecutive n-grams of product reviews. Although the opinion phrase extraction setting shows resemblance to scientific keyphrase extraction, the different nature of scientific keyphrases compared to opinion phrases makes different approaches reasonable.

3.1 Feature Space

In our supervised learning approach, opinion phrase candidates were described by a set of features that were used in a MALLET (McCallum, 2002) implementation of the Maximum Entropy classifier. Opinionated phrases were finally determined by regarding those candidate phrases that were among the (top-5, 10 and 15) highest rated phrases based on the probability,

$$P(Class = +|X) = \frac{exp(\sum_{i}^{n} \lambda_i f_i(+,X))}{\sum_{c \in C} exp(\sum_{i}^{n} \lambda_i f_i(c,X))}$$

, where X is the feature vector describing a candidate phrase, n is the dimension of the feature space, the set $C = \{+, -\}$ refers to the set of possible outcome classes of an instance (i.e. proper and improper opinion phrases), λ_i is the weight determined by the model for the ith feature and $f_i(c, X)$ is the feature function with respect to a class label c and the input vector X.

3.1.1 General Features

Since we assumed that the underlying principles of extracting opinionated phrases are similar to some extent to the extraction of standard (mostly scientific) keyphrases, features of the standard setting were applied in this task as well. The most common ones, introduced by KEA (Witten et al., 1999) are the **Tf-idf** value and the **relative position** of the first occurrence of a candidate phrase within a document. We should note that KEA is primarily designed for keyphrase extraction from scientific publications and whereas the position of the first occurrence might be indicative in research papers, product reviews usually do not contain a summarizing "abstract" at the beginning. For these reasons we chose these features as the ones which form our baseline system. **Phrase length** is also a common feature, which was defined here as the number of the non-stopword tokens of an opinion candidate phrase.

3.1.2 Task Specific Features

Due to the differences pointed out so far, different features can attribute to opinion phrase extraction compared to scientific keyphrase extraction. This subsection is dedicated to present some of the novel features that were introduced to favor the unique characteristics of opinion phrase extraction.

Opinionated phrases often bear special orthographic characteristics, e.g. in the case of *so slooow* or *CHEAP*. Features that represent this phenomenon were also incorporated in the feature space: the first feature is responsible for **character runs** (i.e. more than 2 of the same consecutive characters), and another is responsible for **strange capitalization** (i.e. the presence of uppercase characters besides the initial one).

One feature used external information on the individual tokens of a candidate phrase. It relied on the **sentiment scores** of SentiWordNet (Baccianella et al., 2010), a publicly available database that contains a subset of the synsets of the Princeton Wordnet with positivity, negativity and neutrality scores assigned to each one, depending on the use of its sentiment orientation (which can be regarded as the probability of a phrase belonging to a synset being mentioned in a positive, negative or neutral context). These scores were utilized for the calculation of the sentiment orientations of each token of a candidate phrase. Surface-based SentiWordNet-calculated feature values for a candidate phrase included the *maximal positivity and negativity and subjectivity* scores of the individual tokens and the *total sum* over all the tokens of one phrase.

Sentence-based features were also defined based on SentiWordNet. Previous studies have shown that upon extracting keyphrases from scientific documents, the use of external knowledge such as checking Wikipedia to see whether there exists an article that has the same title as a candidate phrase can be beneficial. One possible use of SentiWordNet seems somewhat analogous to these findings since it was also used to gather **indicator terms** from sentences. Those elements of SentiWordNet synsets were gathered as potential indicator words for which the sum of the average positivity and negativity sentiments scores among all its synsets were above 0.5 (i.e. whose word forms are more likely to have some kind of polarity). Then for a given candidate phrase of a

	Mobiles	Movies
Number of reviews	2,009	1,962
Sentences/review	31.9	29.8
Tokens/sentence	16.1	17.0
Keyphrases/review	4.7	3.2
Candidate phrases/review	130.38	135.89

Table 1: Various statistics on the size of the corpora

given document, a true value was assigned to the SentiWordNet-derived indicator features that had at least one co-occurrence within the same sentence within the review of the candidate phrase.

SentiWordnet was also used to investigate the entire sentences that contained a phrase candidate. This kind of feature calculated the sum of every sentiment score in each sentence where a given candidate phrase was present. Then the **mean** and the deviation of the sum of the sentiment scores were calculated for each token of the phrase-containing sentences and assigned to the candidate phrase. The mean of the sentiment scores of the individual sentences yielded a general score on the **sentiment orientation** of the sentences containing a candidate phrase, while higher values for the **deviation** was intended to capture cases when a reviewer writes both factual (i.e. uses few opinionated words) and non-factual (i.e. uses more emotional phrases and opinions) sentences about a product.

A more detailed description on the framework and evaluation results dealing with the intra-domain setting (including human evaluation as well) can be found in Berend (2011). In addition to that system, here the feature augmentation technique of) was applyed to improve inter-domain results.

4 Evaluation

Evaluation was carried out on two fairly different domains, i.e. on reviews dealing with mobile phones and movies from the site `epinions.com`. Section 4.1 presents the dataset of product reviews and the way the set of proper opinion phrases (which served as positive training examples) were determined for its elements, and Section 4.2 describes experimental results achieved on that dataset. The evaluation procedure was strict in the sense that only perfect matches (after some normalization step) were accepted, i.e. the normalized version of an opinion phrase returned from a document must be identical to at least one of the normalized versions from the set of refined author keyphrases (pros and cons) of the very document.

4.1 Dataset

In our experiments, we crawled two quite different domains of product reviews, i.e. mobile phone and movie reviews from the review portal `epinions.com`. For both domains, 2000 reviews were crawled from `epinions.com` and an additional of 50 and 75 reviews, respectively. [1] This corpus is quite noisy (similarly to other user-generated contents); run-on sentences and improper punctuation were very common, as well as grammatically incorrect sentences since reviews were often written by non-native English speakers.

The list of pros and cons was inconsistent too in the sense that some reviewers used full sentences to express their opinions, while usually a few token-long phrases were given by others. The segmentation of their elements was marked in various ways among reviews (e.g. comma, semicolon, ampersand or the *and* token) and even differed sometimes within the very same review. There were many general or uninformative pros and cons (like *none* or *everything* as a pro phrase) as well.

In order to have a consistent gold-standard annotation for training and evaluation, we refined the pros and cons of the reviews in the corpora. In the first step, the **segmentation** of pros and cons was manually checked by human annotators. Our automatic segmentation method split the lines containing pros and cons along the most frequent separators. This segmentation was corrected by the annotators in 7.5% of the reviews. Then the human annotators also marked the general pros and cons (11.1% of the pro and con phrases) and the reviews without any identified keyphrases were discarded.

Linguistic analysis included the POS tagging (Toutanova and Manning, 2000) and syntactic parsing (Klein and Manning, 2003) of the reviews using Stanford CoreNLP.

4.2 Experimental Results

Several experiments were conducted in order to see the effect of domain adaptation in the opinion phrase extracting task. Where not stated differently experiments were carried out in 10-fold

[1] All the data used in our experiments are available at `http://rgai.inf.u-szeged.hu/proCon`

	Mobiles			Movies		
	P	R	F	P	R	F
Baseline	1.72	1.84	1.77	1.21	1.93	1.49
Target	14.8	15.7	15.27	10.0	15.8	12.22
Source	3.5	3.7	3.58	3.2	5.0	3.92
Mixed	11.1	11.8	11.46	6.5	10.3	8.0
$Mixed_{DA}$	12.7	13.4	13.04	7.2	11.3	8.84

Table 2: Results obtained on the mobile and movie dataset relying on the top-5 ranked phrases.

	Mobiles			Movies		
	P	R	F	P	R	F
Baseline	1.42	3.04	1.94	0.98	3.13	1.5
Target	10.4	22.0	14.11	7.0	21.9	10.63
Source	3.6	7.7	4.93	2.7	8.5	4.1
Mixed	8.0	16.9	10.82	4.6	14.6	7.05
$Mixed_{DA}$	8.6	18.3	11.72	5.0	15.8	7.65

Table 3: Results obtained on the mobile and movie dataset relying on the top-10 ranked phrases.

cross validation, the results of which are present in Tables 2, 3 and 4. Results are reported in the form of Precision, Recall and F-score (indicated with P, R and F, respectively) at the levels of top-5,10 and 15-ranked keyphrases for both mobile phones and movies. In the tables the row *Baseline* corresponds to that intra-domain setting when only the two standard features (i.e. tf-idf and position of first occurrence) were used. As for the rows *Target*, *Source* and *Mixed* the extended feature space was utilized and they indicate that the training and testing domains were the same, differed and originated from both source and target domains, respectively. The row $Mixed_{DA}$ refers to the result when source and target domain documents were incorporated among the training instances (similarly to *Mixed*) and feature augmentation-based domain adaptation was applied as well.

First of all, before conducting experiments involving domain adaptation, the intra-domain performance of the opinion phrase extraction system was measured on the datasets. Intra-domain evaluation refers to the fact that during these runs all the instances of the training set were derived from the very same domain as the test instances. Obviously, these results can serve as an upper bound on the final results which used domain adaptation, i.e. on a more noisy training set. These results are found in the row *Target*.

Secondly, that case was investigated when the weights of the Maximum Entropy model that fitted the training instances the best were based on the different domain compared to the domain of the evaluation, meaning that no instances originating from the target domain were present during the creation of a particular model. Evaluating elements of the target domain based on the model that was learnt on a different source domain is present in the rows *Source* of Tables 2, 3 and 4. In this case it was not necessary to apply 10-fold cross validation, since the evaluation and the training of models took place on entirely different domains.

	Mobiles			Movies		
	P	R	F	P	R	F
Baseline	1.39	4.48	2.12	0.89	4.26	1.48
Target	8.0	25.4	12.17	5.3	24.6	8.67
Source	3.6	11.4	5.44	2.4	11.2	3.92
Mixed	11.1	11.8	11.46	3.7	17.4	6.13
$Mixed_{DA}$	6.7	21.2	10.17	4.0	18.6	6.53

Table 4: Results obtained on the mobile and movie dataset relying on the top-15 ranked phrases.

The row *Mixed* contains result achieved when models were created in such a manner that during 10 runs 10% of the target domain instances (choosing different elements every time) were added to the set of all the source domain instances. In these cases the evaluation took place on the remaining 90% of the target domain that were not selected to be added to the instances for the training originating from the source domain.

In the case of the results in the row *Mixed+DA* the selection of training and test instances was carried out exactly the same way as described in the case of the row *Mixed*, but this time the feature space was augmented as described in Daumé (2007) that is briefly outlined at the end of Section 2.

5 Discussion

Intra-domain results can be interpreted as an upper bound for a system that is based on domain adaptation, due to the fact that in the intra-domain setting data points that make up the set of training instances are drawn from the same distribution as the test instances. Similarly, when instances originating from a different source domain are added, it can easily bias the model on which predictions are based.

Best results in the intra-domain setting around an F-score of 15 might not seem so solid for the first time, but for the proper judgement of these results, it is worth to know that at the shared task of SemEval-2010 (Kim et al., 2010) that dealt with the extraction of keyphrases from scientific publications, the best performing system achieved an F-score of 19.3 when evaluating it against the top-15 author keywords. Naturally, product reviews are far more noisy and heterogeneous in language than scientific publications, and the determination of keyphrase-behaving opinion reasons is far more ambiguous and difficult. It is also true that the language of product reviews is more 'creative', i.e. there are more possibilities to express proper and similarly functioning keyphrases compared to the scientific genre, which makes exact match-based evaluation more prone to underestimate the results in the case of opinionated texts.

The fact that the highest F-scores for keyphrases are achieved when the number of extracted phrases is around the average number of pro and con phrases per reviews (i.e. between 4.7 and 3.2 for mobiles and movies, respectively) also suggests that our ordering of keyphrase candidates is quite effective (since once we find the number of keyphrases a document has, performance cannot really grow anymore).

It is also unequivocal from the results of the rows *Source* of Tables 2, 3 and 4 that training a model solely on one source domain (without any target domain instances) and evaluating it on a different target domain causes severe drop in performance. Despite the serious decline in the result in the latter settings, giving a small set of target domain documents (having a size equalling only to 10% of the size of the source domain documents) yields much better results.

However, since $|S| \gg |T|$, it is still true that the effect of adding elements from T to the training set is easily oppressed by the much higher mass of the element of S. It is shown that the simple, yet efficient method of feature augmentation can still help, yielding final domain-adaptation results that are comparable to those results when the training and the testing took place within the same domain.

Besides all, it can also be seen that the domain of mobiles phones seems to be an easier task (which was confirmed by human annotator agreement rates as well).

6 Conclusions and Future Work

In this paper an extension of the standard scientific keyphrase extraction was introduced, and a possible way to overcome the absence of abundant tagged training examples was shown, using the simple method of feature augmentation. Using the simple feature augmentation domain adaptation technique, results achieved on the target domain were comparable to those settings when the parameters of our model were estimated on a large set of instances from the very same domain as the test instances. However, this highly idealistic assumption that one has access to a fair amount of training material from the domain of the target documents is not always met. In these cases domain adaptation approaches seem to be useful.

The basic idea of treating opinion phrases similarly to scientific keyphrases raises the question whether domain adaptation methods would work in the aspect of scientific articles and product reviews as well. Although these two genres definitely seem to be more distant from each other than two sets of reviews dealing with different product families, we find it as one possible way to extend this work to thoroughly examine this particular question.

Acknowledgments

This work was supported by the Project "TÁMOP-4.2.1/B-09/1/KONV-2010-0005 – Creating the Center of Excellence at the University of Szeged", supported by the European Union and co-financed by the European Regional Development Fund and by the project BELAMI financed by the National Innovation Office of the Hungarian government.

References

Stefano Baccianella, Andrea Esuli, and Fabrizio Sebastiani. 2010. Sentiwordnet 3.0: An enhanced lexical resource for sentiment analysis and opinion mining. In *Proceedings of the Seventh conference on International Language Resources and Evaluation (LREC'10)*, Valletta, Malta, May. European Language Resources Association (ELRA).

Alexandra Balahur, Ester Boldrini, Andres Montoyo, and Patricio Martinez-Barco, editors. 2011. *Proceedings of the 2nd Workshop on Computational Approaches to Subjectivity and Sentiment Analysis (WASSA 2.011)*. Association for Computational Linguistics, Portland, Oregon, June.

Gábor Berend. 2011. Opinion expression mining by exploiting keyphrase extraction. In *Proceedings of the 5th International Joint Conference on Natural Language Processing*, IJCNLP '11, Chiang Mai, Thailand, November.

Hal Daumé, III and Daniel Marcu. 2006. Domain adaptation for statistical classifiers. *J. Artif. Int. Res.*, 26:101–126, May.

Hal Daumé, III. 2007. Frustratingly Easy Domain Adaptation. In *Proceedings of the 45th Annual Meeting of the Association of Computational Linguistics*, pages 256–263, Prague, Czech Republic, June. Association for Computational Linguistics.

Minqing Hu and Bing Liu. 2004a. Mining and summarizing customer reviews. In *Proceedings of the tenth ACM SIGKDD international conference on Knowledge discovery and data mining*, KDD '04, pages 168–177, New York, NY, USA. ACM.

Minqing Hu and Bing Liu. 2004b. Mining opinion features in customer reviews. In *Proceedings of the 19th national conference on Artifical intelligence*, AAAI'04, pages 755–760. AAAI Press.

Soo-Min Kim and Eduard Hovy. 2006. Automatic identification of pro and con reasons in online reviews. In *Proceedings of the COLING/ACL 2006 Main Conference Poster Sessions*, pages 483–490, Sydney, Australia, July. Association for Computational Linguistics.

Su Nam Kim, Olena Medelyan, Min-Yen Kan, and Timothy Baldwin. 2010. Semeval-2010 task 5: Automatic keyphrase extraction from scientific articles. In *Proceedings of the 5th International Workshop on Semantic Evaluation*, SemEval '10, pages 21–26, Morristown, NJ, USA. Association for Computational Linguistics.

Dan Klein and Christopher D. Manning. 2003. Accurate unlexicalized parsing. In *Proceedings of the 41st ACL*, pages 423–430.

Jingjing Liu and Stephanie Seneff. 2009. Review sentiment scoring via a parse-and-paraphrase paradigm. In *Proceedings of the 2009 Conference on Empirical Methods in Natural Language Processing*, pages 161–169, Singapore, August. Association for Computational Linguistics.

Andrew Kachites McCallum. 2002. Mallet: A machine learning for language toolkit. http://mallet.cs.umass.edu.

Olena Medelyan, Eibe Frank, and Ian H. Witten. 2009. Human-competitive tagging using automatic keyphrase extraction. In *Proceedings of the 2009 Conference on Empirical Methods in Natural Language Processing*, pages 1318–1327, Singapore, August. Association for Computational Linguistics.

Bo Pang, Lillian Lee, and Shivakumar Vaithyanathan. 2002. Thumbs up?: sentiment classification using machine learning techniques. In *EMNLP '02: Proceedings of the ACL-02 conference on Empirical methods in natural language processing*, pages 79–86, Morristown, NJ, USA. Association for Computational Linguistics.

Ana-Maria Popescu and Oren Etzioni. 2005. Extracting product features and opinions from reviews. In *Proceedings of Human Language Technology Conference and Conference on Empirical Methods in Natural Language Processing*, pages 339–346, Vancouver, British Columbia, Canada, October. Association for Computational Linguistics.

Ivan Titov and Ryan McDonald. 2008. A joint model of text and aspect ratings for sentiment summarization. In *Proceedings of ACL-08: HLT*, pages 308–316, Columbus, Ohio, June. Association for Computational Linguistics.

Kristina Toutanova and Christopher D. Manning. 2000. Enriching the knowledge sources used in a maximum entropy part-of-speech tagger. In *Proceedings of the 2000 Joint SIGDAT conference on Empirical methods in natural language processing and very large corpora*, EMNLP '00, pages 63–70, Stroudsburg, PA, USA. ACL.

Peter Turney. 2002. Thumbs up or thumbs down? semantic orientation applied to unsupervised classification of reviews. In *Proceedings of the 40th Annual Meeting of the Association for Computational Linguistics (ACL)*, pages 417–424.

Peter Turney. 2003. Coherent keyphrase extraction via web mining. In *Proceedings of IJCAI*, pages 434–439.

Ian H. Witten, Gordon W. Paynter, Eibe Frank, Carl Gutwin, and Craig. 1999. Kea: Practical automatic keyphrase extraction. In *ACM DL*, pages 254–255.

ArbTE: Arabic Textual Entailment

Maytham Alabbas
School of Computer Science
University of Manchester
Manchester, M13 9PL, UK
alabbasm@cs.man.ac.uk

Abstract

The aim of the current work is to see how well existing techniques for textual entailment work when applied to Arabic, and to propose extensions which deal with the specific problems posed by the language. Arabic has a number of characteristics, described below, which make it particularly challenging to determine the relations between sentences. In particular, the lack of diacritics means that determining which sense of a word is intended in a given context is extremely difficult, since many related senses have the same surface form; and the syntactic flexibility of the language, notably the combination of free word-order, pro-drop subjects, verbless sentences, and compound NPs of various kinds, means that it is also extremely difficult to determine the relationships between words.

1 Introduction

The aim of the work described here is to investigate how well existing techniques for 'Recognising Textual Entailment' (RTE: the task of determining, for two sentences *text (T)* and *hypothesis (H)*, whether '...typically, a human reading *T* would infer that *H* is most likely true' (Dagan et al., 2005)). The RTE tasks contrasts with the standard definition of entailment, which states the *T* entails *H* if *H* is true whenever *T* is. The RTE task is in some ways easier than the classical entailment task, and has led to a number of approaches that diverge from the tradition of translating from natural language into 'logical forms' and using standard theorem proving techniques to determine the relationships between these logical forms (Blackburn et al., 2001).

The current system, Arabic Textual Entailment (ArbTE), will investigate the effectiveness of existing TE approaches when they are applied to Modern Standard Arabic (MSA, or Arabic). These approaches have been developed very recently and have largely been applied to English texts. There is very little work on applying textual entailment techniques to Arabic (we have, in fact, so far found no such work), and little evidence that the existing approaches will work for it. The key problem for Arabic is that it is massively more ambiguous than English, for reasons described below, so that many of the existing approaches to textual entailment are likely to be inapplicable.

Lexical ambiguity:

- the Arabic writing system omits characters corresponding to short vowels and other features that distinguish words. This means that written Arabic resembles textese, but the situation is in fact far worse than this analogy suggests, because Arabic has highly productive derivational morphology, which means that a single root form can give rise to numerous derived forms, *most of which are confusable when the short vowels and other markers are omitted.* For instance, the following table shows the Arabic word (علم), which has 7 different reading with diacritics marks.

Arabic	Meaning
عِلْمٌ	knowledge
عَلَمٌ	flag
عَلِمَ	knew
عُلِمَ	is known
عَلَّمَ	taught
عَلِّمْ	teach!
عُلِّمَ	is taught

Table 1: ambiguity caused by the lack of diacritics.

- Arabic also contains numerous clitic items

(prepositions, pronouns and conjunctions), so that it is often difficult to determine just what items are present in the first place. For example the word والى can be analyzed as والي *'ruler'*, و+الى+ي *'and to me'*, و+ألي *'and I follow'*, و+آل+ي *'and my clan'* or و+آلي *'and automatic'* (Habash et al., 2009). Each of these cases has a different diacritization.

Syntactic ambiguity (Daimi, 2001):

- Arabic has a comparatively free word order, with VSO, VOS, SVO and OVS all being possible orders for the arguments of a transitive verb under appropriate conditions.

- It is a pro-drop language. According to the pro-drop theory (Baptista, 1995), *"a null class (pro) is permitted in a finite clause subject place if the agreement features on the verb are rich enough to enable its content to be recovered"*. The potential absence of a subject is not unique to Arabic, but it causes more problems here than in a number of other languages because Arabic verbs can typically occur either intransitively or transitively. In such cases, it is hard to tell whether a sequence consisting of a verb and a following NP is actually an intransitive use of the verb, with the NP as subject, or a transitive use with a zero subject (or indeed a passive). For example, the Arabic sentence (سأل الطالب سؤالا) has two different meaning, which are *'(He) asked the student a question.'* or *'The student asked a question.'*

- Nouns can be used as adjectives, or as possessive determiners (in so-called 'construct phrases'), with typically little inflectional morphology to mark such uses. Nouns that are being used as possessive determiners, for instance, should be marked as being genitive, but the case markers are almost always omitted in written MSA and hence this clue is unavailable. For instance,the Arabic construct phrase (مفاتيح السيارة) has many comparables in English: *'the keys of the car'* or *'the car's keys'* or *'the car keys'* (Habash, 2010). In this example, the word (السيارة) specifies, defines, limits or explains the particular identity of the word (مفاتيح).

- The copula is omitted in simple positive equational sentences, so that a sequence of a noun and a predicative item (i.e. another noun, an adjective or a PP) may make a sentence. For instance, the Arabic equational sentence has a PP predicate(المعلم في المدرسة) (the-teacher in the-school)*'The teacher (is) in the school.'*

Taken together, these make assigning a structural analysis to a sequence of Arabic forms an extremely difficult task. We have carried out a number of experiments using state-of-the-art taggers (AMIRA 2.0 (Diab, 2009), MADA 3.1 (Habash et al., 2009; Habash, 2010) and a home-grown tagger, MXL, with comparable accuracy) and parsers (notably MALTParser (Nivre et al., 2007) and (McDonald and Pereira, 2006))), using the Penn Arabic Treebank (PATB) (Maamouri and Bies, 2004) as training data. The PATB contains over 5000 phrase-structure trees whereas we want dependency trees. Therefore, we adapted the algorithm described by (Xia and Palmer, 2001), which uses the idea of a *head percolation table* as explained in (Collins, 1997). In the current work, the head percolation table is semi-automatically generated from the PATB by grouping the related tags in one tag and then finding the possible heads for each one, which order manually according to its priority (e.g. in our work *'CONJ'* has high priority for each entry). The outcome of these experiments is that we can achieve around 80% accuracy when assigning unlabelled dependency trees to input texts, and around 70% when we try to attach labels to these trees. These scores are considerably lower than the scores that have been achieved using these parsers on other languages using similar sized training corpora. This reflects the observations above about Arabic, and especially written Arabic: the numerous sources of uncertainty listed above just make parsing difficult.

Given that most TE algorithms operate over parse trees, we have to consider ways of making these algorithms more robust. It is unlikely that we will find ways of parsing Arabic much more accurately–the taggers and parsers we are using are as good as it gets, and the training sets we are using are comparable in size to training sets that have been used for other languages (and experimentation suggests that the data-set/accuracy curve has indeed levelled off by the time we have exhausted the training set). We will be using a

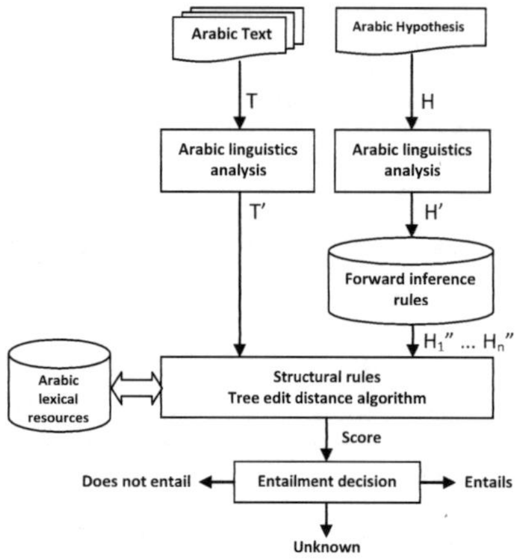

Figure 1: General diagram of ArbTE system.

fairly orthodox TE architecture, as shown in Fig 1. At each stage we will attempt to exploit variations on the standard machinery to help us overcome the extra problems raised by written Arabic.

2 ArbTE

Arabic linguistic analysis: as noted above, we have carried out a number of experiments with state-of-the-art taggers and parsers. These experiments show in particular two main results:

- Combining the output of multiple data-driven dependency parsers can produce more accurate results, even for imperfectly tagged text, than each parser produces by itself for texts with the gold-standard tags. We have recently published preliminary results from these experiments (Alabbas and Ramsay, 2011) and have submitted a more detailed paper to somewhere. Table 2 shows labelled accuracy (LA) of combining MST, MALT1 (*Nivre arc-eager*) and MALT2 (*Stackeager*) compared with retagged (by MADA) and gold-standard corpuses. The first technique (TECHNIQUE1) combines the outputs of the parsers where at least two parsers agree, otherwise the head is taken from MST, whereas the dependency relation is taken from MALT1. The second technique (TECHNIQUE2) combines the outputs of the parsers where MALT1 and MALT2 agree, otherwise the output of MST is taken.

  It is notable that the LA for combining multiple parsers are higher than the LA of the individual parsers for both retagged and gold-standard corpuses.

Best LA for individual parser		TECHNIQUE1	TECHNIQUE2
Retagged	Gold-St.		
0.784	0.793	0.803	0.804

Table 2: LA for combining multiple parsers techniques for MST, MALT1 and MALT2 parsers with voting.

- Combining the output of three different taggers can also produce more accurate results than either parser produces by itself. We describe this result in detail elsewhere. Table 3 shows the results of three taggers when tested on PATB with a coarse-grained tagset.

Taggers accuracy			Combine taggers		
AMIRA	MXL	MADA	P	R	F-score
89.59	95.17	94.05	0.9947	0.83	0.9049

Table 3: Precision (P), recall (R) and F-score for agreement output for three taggers and gold standard.

  It is notable that the precision on the cases where the taggers agree are considerably higher than the accuracy of the individual taggers.

These experiments suggest that obtaining dependency trees from Arabic text is an inherently difficult task. We therefore plan to look more closely at the specific mistakes that the parsers make, in order to identify fragments which are consistently analysed correctly. If we apply our inference rules only to those subtrees which can be trusted then we will improve the accuracy of the inferences that are carried out.

We will also investigate the relative benefits of using labelled and unlabelled dependency trees at this point. Unlabelled trees are, clearly, less reliable as a basis for extracting and applying inference rules. Labelled trees, however, are significantly more difficult for the parsers to get right. We therefore intend to investigate whether it is better to use labelled trees (semantically informative but only found with 70% accuracy) or unlabelled ones (less informative but found with 80% accuracy).

Forward inference rules: we intend to extract transfer-like rules (Hutchins and Somers, 1992) for transforming the parse tree that we extract from the text to other entailed trees, to be used as a set of forward inference rules. The work mentioned above for determining which subtrees can be reliably identified will be exploited here to ensure that we only extract rules from elements of the parse tree that we trust. We will leave reasoning about open class lexical items to the backward chaining stage that is embodied in the tree matching part of the architecture. As shown in Fig. 1, the forward inference rules are applied before the dependency trees are matched.

Tree edit distance: to match text:hypothesis dependency tree pairs effectively, we will use an extended version of Zhang and Shasha (1989)'s tree edit distance (TED) algorithm, as explained below.

One of the main drawbacks of the TED (Kouylekov, 2006) is that transformation operations (insert, delete and exchange) are applied solely on single nodes and not on subtrees. Heilman and Smith (2010) extended the available operations in standard TED to `INSERT-CHILD`, `INSERT-PARENT`, `DELETE-LEAF`, `DELETE-&- MERGE`, `RELABEL-NODE` and `RELABEL-EDGE`. The authors also identify three new operations, `MOVE-SUBTREE`, which means move a node *X* in a tree *T* to be the last child on the left/right side of a node *Y* in *T* (s.t. *Y* is not a descendant of *X*), `NEW-ROOT` and `MOVE-SIBLING`, to enable succinct edit sequences for complex transformation. This extended set of edit operations allows certain combinations of the basic operations to be treated as single steps, and hence provides shorter (and therefore cheaper) derivations. The fine-grained distinctions between, for instance, different kinds of insertions also make it possible to assign different weights to different variations on the same operation. Nonetheless, these operations continue to operate on individual nodes rather than on subtrees (despite its name, even `MOVE-SUBTREE` appears to be defined as an operation on nodes rather than on subtrees). Therefore, we have extended the basic version of the TED algorithm so that operations that insert/delete/exchange subtrees cost less than the sum of the costs of inserting/deleting/exchanging their parts (e.g. deleting a modifier subtree should be less expensive than the sum of deleting its components individually). This will enable us to find the minimum edit operations to transform one tree to another. Also, this will allow us to be sensitive to the fact that the links in a dependency tree carry linguistic information about relations between complex units, and hence to ensure that when we compare two trees we are paying attention to these relations. For instance, this enables us to be sensitive to the fact that operations involving modifiers, in particular, should be applied to the subtree as a whole rather than to its individual elements. Thus, we transform tree (a) to tree (b) in Fig 2 by deleting *'in the park'* in a single operation, removing the modifier as a whole, rather than three operations removing *'in'*, *'the'* and *'park'* one by one. We have applied the current technique to transform different trees to another trees and obtained encouraging results. So, we just need in this part of the system to find a suitable values of edit operation costs to make matching between two dependency trees more accurate.

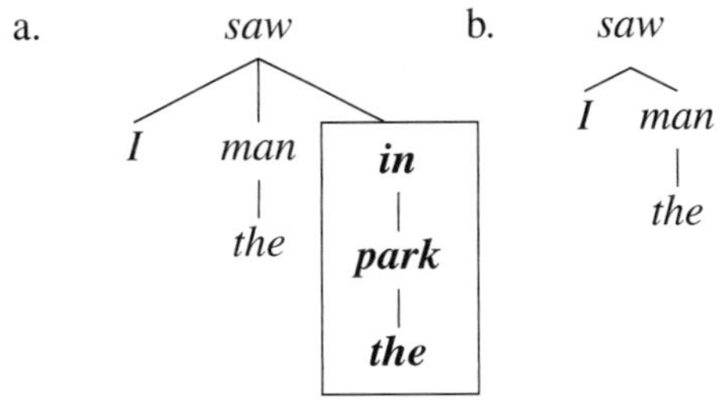

Figure 2: Two dependency trees.

In this part of the system, we also intend to exploit the subset/superset relations encoded by Arabic WordNet (Black et al. (2006)) when exchanging items in a tree. Roughly speaking, if comparing one tree to another requires us to swap two lexical items, we will be happier doing so if the item in the source tree is a hyponym of the one in the target tree. Doing this will allow us to delay making decisions about potentially ambiguous lexical items: it is reasonably safe to assume that if W_1 has a sense which is a hyponym of some sense of W_2 then a sentence involving W_1 will entail a similar sentence involving W_2. This will definitely be quicker, and may be more reliable, than trying to disambiguate the two from first principles and then looking for entailment relationships.

This reflects the widely accepted view that contextual information is the key to lexical disambiguation. Within the RTE task, the text provides the context for disambiguation of the hypothesis, and the hypothesis provides the context for disambiguation of the text. Almost any human reader would, for instance, accept that *T1* entails *H1*, despite the potential ambiguity of the word *'bank'*.

***T1:** My money is all tied up at the bank.*
***H1:** I cannot easily spend my money.*

We therefore intend to deal with lexical ambiguity by allowing T to entail H if there is *any* reading of T which entails *any* reading of H (this is similar to Hobbs' approach to disambiguation via *'abduction'* (Hobbs et al. (1993); Hobbs (2005))).

Finally, we investigated another Arabic resource to provide us more information about relations between words, *i.e.* Openoffice Arabic dictionary, which contains POS and synonyms for many Arabic words. Currently, we intend to investigate the Microsoft Word Arabic dictionary, which contains a huge amount of Arabic information.

Arabic dataset: in order to train and test our work, we need an appropriate data set. This adds a further level of complexity to our task: there are, to our knowledge, no such data sets available for Arabic, so we have to develop one. We do not want to produce a set of text:hypothesis pairs by hand–partly because doing so is a lengthy and tedious process, but more importantly because hand-coded data sets are liable to embody biases introduced by the developer. If the data set is used for training the system, then the rules that are extracted will be little more than an unfolding of information explicitly supplied by the developers. If it is used for testing then it will only test the examples that the developers have chosen, which are likely to be biased, albeit unwittingly, towards the way they think about the problem.

We therefore need to find some way of extracting such pairs at least semi-automatically. The most promising idea is by posing queries to a search engine and filtering the responses for sentences that do (and don't) entail the query. We are currently building a corpus of text:hypothesis pairs by using headlines from Arabic newspapers and channels TV websites as queries to be input to Google via the standard Google-API, and then selecting the first sentence, which usually represents the most related sentence in the article with the headline, of each of the first N returned pages. This technique produces a large number of potential pairs without any bias in either the texts or the hypotheses. To increase the quality of the sentence's pair that resulted from the query, we add some conditions to filter the results. For instance, the number of common words between both sentences must be less than a specific threshold to avoid having very similar sentences and the length of a headline must be at least more than N words to avoid very small headlines. This technique has different advantages, especially the presence of the same headline in several newspapers but it express in different words for the same day. For instance, one of the CNN headline is *'Berlusconi says he won't seek another term.'* and the related sentence as shown in Table 4. We make the same query but for another website, such as BBC and Reuters and the results as shown in Table 4. Therefore, we can swap between a headline of one newspaper with related sentences from another to increase the quality of the sentences's pair. We have tested this technique on different languages, such as Arabic, English, Spanish, German, Turkish, Bulgarian and French. We carried out a series of informal experiment with native speakers. The results were encouraging, but the nature of the experiments mean that they are not robust.

The Arabic articles that are returned by this process typically contain very long sentences (upwards of 100 words), where only a small part has a direct relationship to the query. This is typical of Arabic text, which is often written with very little punctuation, with elements of the text linked by conjunctions rather than being broken into implicit segments by punctuation marks such as full stops and question marks. We have carried out some initial experiments aimed at segmenting the large parse trees that we obtain for such sentences into smaller linked elements. This is more reliable than simply segmenting the surface strings at conjunctions, since many conjunctions link non-sentential structures, and are therefore not sensible places to break the text.

These pairs still have to be marked-up by human annotators, but at least the process of collecting them is as nearly bias-free as possible. Therefore, to annotated our dataset, we are currently developing an online annotation system, which will be soon available for the annotators. The system normally presents the annotator with sentences that they have not yet seen, but there is also an option to revisit previously annotated examples. Finally, each pair of sentences must be annotated by three different users before we get the result of annotation which represents the agreement of at least two users. The system will be flexible with the number of annotators for each pair of sentences and maybe increase it to five when we need that.

3 Conclusions and Future Work

We have outlined a number of approaches to the task of adapting existing TE algorithms for work-

Website	Headline (Hypothesis)	Related sentence (Text)	Results
CNN	Berlusconi says he won't seek another term.	Italian Prime Minister Silvio Berlusconi said Friday he will not run again when his term expires in 2013.	Entails
BBC	Silvio Berlusconi vows not to run for new term in 2013.	Italian Prime Minister Silvio Berlusconi has confirmed that he will not run for office again when his current term expires in 2013.	Entails
Reuters	Berlusconi says he will not seek new term.	Italian Prime Minister Silvio Berlusconi declared on Friday he would not run again when his term expires in 2013.	Entails

Table 4: Some English text:hypothesis pairs.

ing with a language where we are faced with an exceptional level of lexical and structural ambiguity. As we previously mentioned, there are different options for each stage, so we will try to test different combinations between the system components to find the best structure of ArbTE system.

Also we speculate that further work by marking the 'polarity' of subtrees in the dependency trees obtained by the parser(s) and making rules sensitive to the polarity of the items they are being applied to would further improve ArbTE results. This will make the use of TED as a way of determining consequence relations more reliable for all languages, not just Arabic: the fact that *T2* entails *H2*, whereas *T3* does not entail *H3*, arises from the fact that *'doubt'* reverses the polarity of its sentential complement. Systems that pay no attention to polarity will inevitably make mistakes, and we intend to adapt the TED algorithm so that it pays attention to this issue.

T2: *I believe that a woman did it.*
H2: *I believe that a human being did it.*

T3: *I doubt that a woman being did it.*
H3: *I doubt that a human did it.*

References

Alabbas, M. and Ramsay, A. (2011). Evaluation of dependency parsers for long arabic sentences. In *Proceeding of International Conference on Semantic Technology and Information Retrieval (STAIR'11)*, pages 243–248. IEEE.

Baptista, M. (1995). On the nature of pro-drop in Capeverdean Creole. Technical report, Harvard Working Papers in Linguistics, 5: 3-17.

Black, W., Elkateb, S., Rodriguez, H., and Alkhalifa, M. (2006). Introducing the Arabic WordNet project. In *Proceedings of the Third International WordNet Conference (GWC-06)*.

Blackburn, P., Bos, J., Kohlhase, M., and De Nivelle, H. (2001). Inference and computational semantics. *Studies in linguistics and philosophy*, pages 11–28.

Collins, M. (1997). Three generative, lexicalised models for statistical parsing. In *Proceedings of the 34th Annual Meeting of the Association for Computational Linguistics*, pages 16–23, Madrid.

Dagan, I., Magnini, B., and Glickman, O. (2005). The PASCAL recognising textual entailment challenge. In *Proceedings of Pascal Challenge Workshop on Recognizing Textual Entailment*.

Daimi, K. (2001). Identifying Syntactic Ambiguities in Single-Parse Arabic Sentence. *Computers and the Humanities*, 35(3):333–349.

Diab, M. (2009). Second generation tools (amira 2.0): Fast and robust tokenization, pos tagging, and base phrase chunking. In *Proceedings of the Second International Conference on Arabic Language Resources and Tools*, pages 285–288.

Habash, N. (2010). *Introduction to Arabic Natural Language Processing*. Synthesis Lectures on Human Language Technologies. Morgan & Claypool Publishers.

Habash, N., Rambow, O., and R., R. (2009). Mada+tokan: A toolkit for arabic tokenization, diacritization, morphological disambiguation, pos tagging, stemming and lemmatization. In Choukri, K. and Maegaard, B., editors, *Proceedings of the Second International Conference on Arabic Language Resources and Tools*, Cairo, Egypt. The MEDAR Consortium.

Heilman, M. and Smith, N. (2010). Tree edit models for recognizing textual entailments, paraphrases, and answers to questions. In *Human Language Technologies: The 2010 Annual Conference of the North American Chapter of the Association for Computational Linguistics*, pages 1011–1019. Association for Computational Linguistics.

Hobbs, J. R. (2005). *The handbook of pragmatics*, chapter Abduction in Natural Language Understading, pages 724–740. Blackwell Publishing.

Hobbs, J. R., Stickel, M. E., Appelt, D. E., and Martin, P. (1993). Interpretation as abduction. *Artificial Intelligence*, 63:69–142.

Hutchins, W. J. and Somers, H. L. (1992). *An introduction to machine translation*. Academic Press.

Kouylekov, M. (2006). *Recognizing textual entailment with tree edit distance: Application to question answering and information extraction*. PhD thesis.

Maamouri, M. and Bies, A. (2004). Developing an Arabic treebank: Methods, guidelines, procedures, and tools. In *Proceedings of COLING*, pages 2–9.

McDonald, R. and Pereira, F. (2006). Online learning of approximate dependency parsing algorithms. In *Proceedings of EACL*, volume 6, pages 81–88.

Nivre, J., Hall, J., Nilsson, J., Chanev, A., Eryigit, G., Kübler, S., Marinov, S., and Marsi, E. (2007). MaltParser: A language-independent system for data-driven dependency parsing. *Natural Language Engineering*, 13(02):95–135.

Xia, F. and Palmer, M. (2001). Converting dependency structures to phrase structures. In *1st Human Language Technology Conference (HLT-2001)*, pages 1–5, San Diego.

Zhang, K. and Shasha, D. (1989). Simple fast algorithms for the editing distance between trees and related problems. *SIAM J. Comput.*, 18(6):1245–1262.

RDFa Editor for Ontological Annotation

Melania Duma
Faculty of Mathematics and Computer Science
University of Bucharest
Academiei Street number 14, Bucharest
melaniaduma@gmail.com

Abstract

One of the purposes of semantic web is to provide machine understandable content and this can be achieved by annotating information. At the moment, annotations can be created manually and also automatically, both of the approaches having advantages and disadvantages. The goal of this article is to present a new semi-automatic annotation tool, which given a text will annotate words with concepts from an ontology.

1 Introduction

In the present days, World Wide Web has proven to be one of the easiest and most useful ways of gaining access to information. One of the main characteristics of this information is that it requires human intervention in order to be managed and presented. The main goal of Semantic Web is to provide a way of transforming this information, so that it is also machine comprehensible, idea that is captured in the definition provided by World Wide Web Consortium: "The Semantic Web is about two things. It is about common formats for integration and combination of data drawn from diverse sources, where on the original Web mainly concentrated on the interchange of documents. It is also about language for recording how the data relates to real world objects" (Ivan, 2011). In order to achieve the ideas presented in this definition, a need for annotation systems arises.

Document annotation can be defined as the process of providing data about the content of the documents. In some ways, the process of annotating is very similar to that of tagging, and the similarity comes from the fact that they both enrich the information by providing metadata and they both improve the search capabilities of a system. However, annotations go one step further than tags - they help create more organized metadata which can be further exploited by specialized systems.

The process of annotating documents can be done both manually, as well as automatically, both of these approaches having advantages and disadvantages.

One of the biggest advantages of manual annotation is that it has a high accuracy rate, but it has proven to be both cost and time inefficient. It also often requires for an exact procedure to be followed. At first, the human annotator must familiarize himself with the text, then proceed with the annotations. Any difficult decision regarding an annotation is then saved in a file, and a curator later reviews the specific annotations and makes any necessary changes. This whole procedure proves to be very expensive because it requires the constant training of personnel, as the level of accuracy of annotation depends drastically of the level of domain specific knowledge of the human annotator.

On the other hand, automatic annotation can offer a method of annotating in a time efficient way, while having the disadvantage that it is highly error prone, mainly because of the fact that it lacks human intervention.

In order to overcome these shortcomings, a series of semi-automatic annotation systems have been developed. Many present themselves under the form of an editor that annotates specific parts of a document (word, paragraph, section or an entire document).

Different approaches on how to perform semi-automatic annotation where implemented in a series of platforms and a survey of these platforms is presented in (Reeve and Han, 2005). AeroDAML is a pattern based system, in which nouns and relationships are connected with concepts and properties that are part of the DARPA Agent Markup Language (DAML) ontologies (Reeve and Han, 2005). Regarding the architecture, AeroDAML is made up of a series of components: a text extraction component based on AeroText, a mapping component and an annotation editor.

Armadillo is also a pattern based system, that given a set of initial words called seeds, will annotate them and extract the context surrounding these words. Based on these contexts, a set of rules is constructed, which is then used in order to discover other words surrounded by similar contexts. The process takes place again with the new words acting as seeds.

Another system that can be used for annotating documents is the KIM Platform which contains an ontology, a knowledge base, an annotation system, and an indexing and retrieval system based on the Lucene engine. During the annotation process, the token is not only mapped to a concept in the ontology but also to a reference in the knowledge base, so that word disambiguation can be provided.

MnM is a machine learning based system, based on the Lazy-NLP algorithm. The result of this algorithm is a set of rules, which are then used to tag information in the document or correct existing tags.

MUSE is another semantic annotation platform based, like KIM platform, on the GATE framework. The component that deals with semantic annotation is based on Java Annotation Pattern Engine (JAPE), which provides a grammar that helps in constructing rules. These rules are then used in order to create annotations.

Ont-O-Mat is based on S-CREAM (Semi-automatic CREAtion of Metadata), a semantic annotation framework. Information extraction in Ont-O-Mat is done with the help of Amilcare, and tagging and correction rules are created using the LP algorithm. Furthermore, the process of annotation in Ont-O-Mat is based on the PANKOW (Pattern-based Annotation through Knowledge On the Web) algorithm, which returns a set of hypothesis phrases, that are used to create annotations.

All of the systems mentioned above have been evaluated in terms of precision and recall, and the MnM and MUSE platforms have proven to have the highest performance among them, with a precision of 95%, respectively 93.5% (Reeve and Han, 2005).

In this paper, a new RDFa editor, that aims to semi-automatically annotate data, will be introduced. This new system differentiates from the others in that it helps create valid RDFa annotations, which integrated in the content of the Web pages, will make them not only human readable, but also machine understandable. Furthermore, the full potential of these annotations can be attained later on, by creating a reasoning module which can be integrated in the platform.

The paper is structured as follows. In section 2, the main functionalities of the system are presented, together with a description of the main components that form the new editor. An evaluation of the new software is provided in section 3, while section 4 contains the conclusion and ideas for future work.

2 System Design and Challenges

2.1 System Functionalities

The aim of this article is to describe the design and implementation of an ongoing project, that aims to provide a RDFa editor for semantic annotation of documents. The aim of RDFa, which is "a way to express RDF data within XHTML, by reusing the existing human-readable data" (Birbeck and Adida, 2008), is to provide a series of attributes. These attributes can be used in order to enrich the information contained in the web pages with the help of new metadata.

Regarding the domain, the editor accepts any kind of document and ontology, as it was constructed with the purpose of being an open-domain tool.

A list of the most important functionalities that have been implemented in the new annotating platform is presented below:

- The application creates annotations based on text chunks, from a given document and a selected concept from an ontology. At the moment the system works with Nounphrases (NP)
- The ontology used for annotation can be selected by the user of the application, together with the document to be annotated
- All the annotations made to a documents are saved in a new file and respect the RDFa format
- After annotations have been made, a version of the annotated document can be viewed and saved
- After a document is opened, it is possible to also open an annotation file and merge them

- The details regarding an annotation can be viewed for every annotated NP
- Any specific annotation can be deleted at any point in time

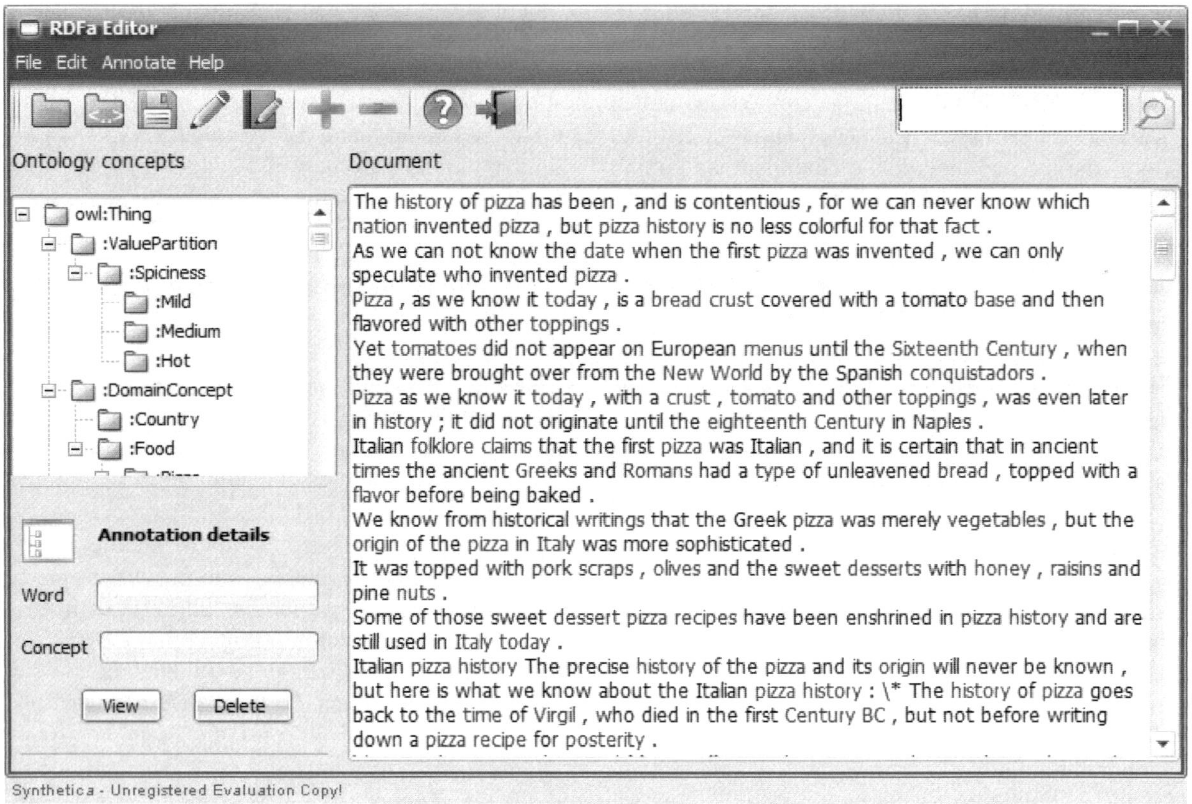

Fig. 1: The interface of the system

2.2 System Components

Regarding its architecture, the system is made up of a series of different components, that combined achieve the goal of semi-automatically annotating a document (Figure 2).

The Ontology Manager component, used for importing and presenting the ontology, was created with help of Jena, a Java framework used for writing Semantic Web applications and Pellet, an open-source Java based OWL DL reasoner. The Pellet API provides a class, that given an ontology, it presents the class hierarchy under the form of a tree component that can be easily integrated in the application.

The Document component deals with the management of the document that will be annotated. Thus, a document is opened and then the text is retrieved and passed to the Document Parser component.

The Document Parser component is concerned with the parsing of the document, which results in the creation of a list of tokens. In order to determine which of the tokens are Nounphrases, a part of speech tagger was needed. Therefore, the tagger selected was Stanford Log-linear Part-Of-Speech Tagger developed by the Stanford Natural Language Processing Group. This particular tagger has been chosen because it was developed in Java and it was easy to be integrated into the rest of the application, but also because of its high performance rate.

The tagger provides two models for the English language: bidirectional-distsim-wsj-0-18.tagger and left3words-wsj-0-18.tagger.

In the development of the new system the first of the options above was chosen mainly because, even though it is slower than the other model, it has an increased accuracy (97.32% over 96.97%).

The Annotation component of the application deals with the automatic annotation when a noun has been selected from the text and a concept has also been selected from the ontology. In order to achieve this, a lemmatizer was needed, which has the goal "to reduce inflectional forms and sometimes derivationally related forms of a word to a common base form" (Manning et al., 2008).

The use of a lemmatizer was preferred to that of a stemmer, mainly because while the stemmer uses only heuristics in order to determine a base form of a word, a lemmatizer uses vocabularies and morphological analysis in order to determine the dictionary form of an word. Thus, due to the way in which it is constructed, a lemmatizer could help increase the accuracy of annotations.

WordNet is constructed as a lexical database for the English language. It provides software tools that support automatic text analysis and one of these tools is the lemmatizer. The lemmatizer was used to automatically annotate all the nouns that share the same lemma with the selected noun.

All the annotations made are saved in a file in XML format. Every annotation is characterized by a noun, represented by the interval indicating the position it occupies in the text, and by the concept used in the annotation, specified by the RDFa attribute @about.

Resource Description Framework (RDF) is a language whose goal is to create statements regarding Web sources. In order to create the statements, RDFa, a recommendation of W3C, uses a set of attributes composed of a few XHTML attributes together with some newly created ones (Birbeck and Adida, 2008).

Among the latter ones, the @about attribute is used in order to define the subject of the data. Because of the fact that the system annotates only nouns, it was assumed that all the nouns represent the subject of the data, and therefore they have all been annotated using the @about attribute.

The file, in which the annotations are saved, can be later opened again and used in order to organize the existing annotations. More precisely, once the text document is displayed, and an annotation file is opened, the annotations from this file are retrieved and then processed.

The processing of an annotation requires the extraction of the concept it references and the interval which characterizes the position of a noun. Once this interval is retrieved, the position is searched in the current document and the corresponding noun is highlighted.

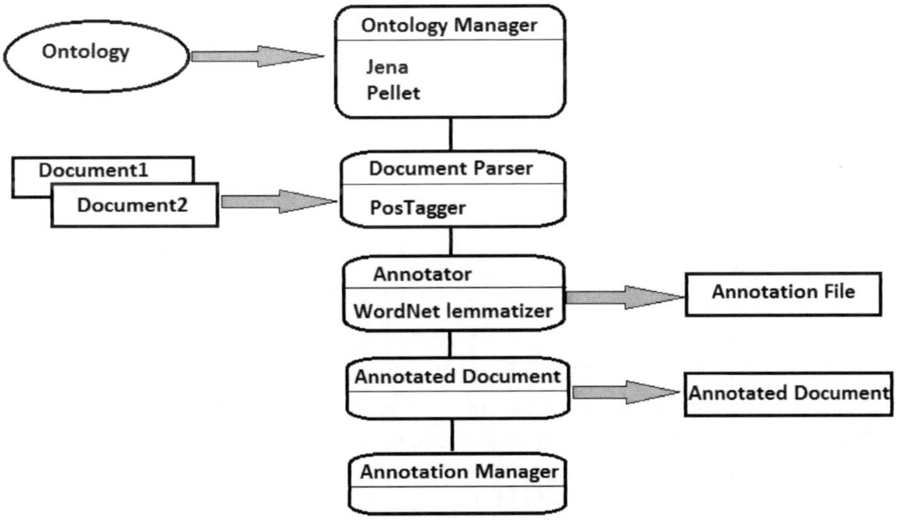

Fig. 2: Components of the system

The Annotated Document component provides the possibility to view the annotated file. In order to achieve this, the list of annotations specific to the current document is merged with the text and they form a new document which can be viewed and saved.

In more details, the interval, which describes the position of the noun in the text, is determined for every annotation. The ends of the interval are then searched in the text and the RDFa attribute is inserted in the corresponding position. These insertions are done in a new document so that the original one remains unaffected by these changes.

The Annotation Manager component deals with the management of annotations. It provides a way to view and analyze the concept which was used during the annotation of a noun and also to delete the specified annotation if proven inaccurate.

3 Evaluation

In this section an evaluation of the new system is presented. In order to achieve this, the metrics used for evaluation will be defined. Recall is defined as the number of accurate annotation divided by the number of all the annotations made by a human annotator, while precision is defined by the number of accurate annotations divided by the number of accurate plus the number of inaccurate annotations generated by the annotation platform.

The new system was tested using a document base created with the help of 35 Web pages. The Web pages were parsed and the content was extracted and saved in text files. The ontology used in the evaluation was the pizza.owl ontology and it was chosen because it is constructed in a way that allows correct extraction of the tree component using Jena and Pellet.

In order to evaluate the new tool, a number of factors were taken into consideration like the time required by the annotation process and the accuracy of the annotations decided by a human annotator.

The time is in direct correlation with the length of the document being processed and annotated, and it ranges from 0.8 seconds for a 500 words document to 4.6 seconds for a 3000 words document. This has been measured on a 3 GB RAM, 2.4. GHz machine.

In the evaluation stage, the application was tested on a number of 35 documents written in English, having a length on average of 1700 words. After the automatic annotation of the documents, 1427 annotation were generated.

In order to determine the accuracy of the annotations, one human annotator verified every annotation. Next, the accurate and inaccurate annotations were counted in order to compute the measures of precision and recall. So, the precision for this set of documents was determined to be 78.3% and the recall to be 69.1%.

These results could be explained by the part-of-speech tagger used, which has an accuracy of 97.32% and also by the accuracy of the WordNet lemmatizer, but also by the fact that at the moment the system, does not use word disambiguation techniques.

4 Conclusion and Future Work

The goal of the new editor is to provide a way of annotating documents using concepts from an ontology. In the same time, the annotations made, are valid under the RDFa recommendation. In this way, the main goal of Semantic Web, that of presenting information so that computers can understand and utilize it, is achieved.

One of the current limitations of the application is that it only annotates Nounphrases. The annotation process makes use of only a taxonomy extracted from the ontology. In the future, the annotation process could be extended so that adjectives are also annotated.

Another limitation is that the current version of the software supports only documents written in English and having the .txt extension. In the future, the system will be improved, so that a spidering component is added. It will extract content directly from the web pages, which will be afterwards annotated.

At the moment, when a noun is annotated, all the nouns that share the same lemma with the selected token, are also annotated with the same concept. This process could be further extended in the near future so that synonyms of the selected noun, obtained with the help of synsets from WordNet, could be also, automatically, annotated with the same concept.

Another question that arises is if it would be possible to store the annotation files on a server so that other persons would have access to them, which will surely broaden the perspective of the application. The application would then become a client-server application. This would raise some issues, that would have to be taken in consideration, like concurrent changes of an annotation file.

Another improvement that could be made is to increase the speed of the document parsing. This can be achieved by altering the implementation of the parsing algorithm, so that it becomes more time efficient.

As a conclusion, the new system presented has achieved its goal - it provides a new way of semi-automatically annotating documents. The annotations constructed are based on the RDFa recommendation, and in this way they can be further used by specialized systems. This proves to be one of the main advantages of the new platform. Nonetheless, improvements can and will be made to the system, that will help make it more efficient and flexible.

Acknowledgments

I would like to express my gratitude to Prof. dr. Monica Tataram, University of Bucharest and to Prof. dr. Walther von Hahn and Prof. dr. Cristina Vertan, University of Hamburg, for their supervision, help and guidance.

References

Ben Adida, Mark Birbeck, Shane McCarron and Steven Pemberton. 2008. *RDFa in XHTML - Syntax and Processing.* June 2011 <http://www.w3.org/TR/rdfa-syntax/>.

Mark Birbeck and Ben Adida. 2008. *RDFa Primer.* June 2011 <http://www.w3.org/TR/xhtml-rdfa-primer/>.

Sam Chapman, Alexiei Dingli and Fabio Ciravegna. 2004. *Armadillo: Harvesting Information for the Semantic Web.* 27th Annual International ACM SIGIR Conference on Research and Development in Information Retrieval, 25-27 July 2004, Sheffield, UK.

Stephen Dill, Nadav Eiron, David Gibson, Daniel Gruhl, R. Guha, Anant Jhingran, Tapas Kanungo, Kevin S. Mccurley, Sridhar Rajagopalan and Andrew Tomkins. 2003. *A Case for Automated Large Scale Semantic Annotation.* Web Semantics: Science, Services and Agents on the World Wide Web, Vol. 1, No. 1: 115-132.

Siegfried Handschuh, Steffen Staab and Fabio Ciravegna. 2002. *S-CREAM Semi-automatic CREAtion of Metadata.* Proceedings of the 13th International Conference on Knowledge Engineering and Knowledge Management. Ontologies and the Semantic Web.

Herman Ivan. 2011. *W3C Semantic Web Activity.* July 2011. <http://www.w3.org/2001/sw/>.

Herman Ivan. 2009. *W3C Semantic Web Frequently Asked Questions.* July 2011. <http://www.w3.org/RDF/FAQ>.

Atanas Kiryakov, Borislav Popov, Dimitar Manov, Damyan Ognyanoff, Rosen Marinov and Ivan Terziev. 2004. *Automatic Semantic Annotation with KIM.* 3rd International Semantic Web Conference (ISWC2004).

Nadzeya Kiyavitskaya, Nicola Zeni, James R. Cordy, Luisa Mich and John Mylopoulos. 2005. *Semi-Automatic Semantic Annotations for Web Documents.* Proceedings of SWAP 2005, 2nd Italian Semantic Web Workshop.

Paul Kogut and William Holmes. 2001. *AeroDAML Applying Information Extraction to generate DAML annotations from Web Pages.* Proceedings of K-CAP 2001.

Jacob Köhler, Stephan Philippi, Michael Specht, and Alexander Rüegg. 2006. *Ontology based text indexing and querying for the semantic web.* Journal Knowledge-Based Systems archive Vol. 19 No. 8

Lothar Lemnitzer and Paola Monachesi. 2007. *Keyword extraction for metadata annotation of Learning Objects.* Workshop on Natural Language Processing and Knowledge Representation for eLearning environments

Lothar Lemnitzer, Cristina Vertan, Alex Killing, Kiril Simov, Diane Evans, Dan Cristea and Paola Monachesi. 2007. *Improving the search for learning objects with keywords and ontologies.* EC-TEL 2007 - Second European Conference on Technology Enhanced Learning.

Christopher D. Manning, Prabhakar Raghavan and Hinrich Schütze. 2008. *Introduction to Information Retrieval.* Cambridge University Press, Cambridge, UK.

Frank Manola and Eric Miller. 2004. *RDF Primer.* June 2011 <http://www.w3.org/TR/rdf-primer/>.

Matthew Petrillo and Jessica Baycroft. 2010. *Introduction to manual annotation.* July 2011. <http://gate.ac.uk/wiki/IntroToManualAnnotation_April2010.pdf>.

Borislav Popov, Atanas Kiryakov, Angel Kirilov, Dimitar Manov, Damyan Ognyanoff and Miroslav Goranov. 2003. *KIM - Semantic Annotation Platform.* Proceedings of the International Semantic Web Conference.

Borislav Popov, Atanas Kiryakov, Damyan Ognyanoff, Dimitar Manov and Angel Kirilov. 2004. *KIM – a semantic platform for information extraction and retrieval.* Natural Language Engineering, Vol. 10, No. 3-4: 375-392.

Lawrence Reeve and Hyoil Han. 2005. *Survey of Semantic annotation platforms.* Proceedings of the 20th Annual ACM Symposium on Applied Computing, Web Technologies and Applications track.

Antonio Sanfilippo, Stephen Tratz, Michelle Gregory, Alan Chappell, Paul Whitney, Christian Posse, Patrick Paulson, Bob Baddeley, Ryan Hohimer and Amanda White. 2006. *Automating Ontological Annotation with WordNet.* Proceedings of SemAnnot 2005

David Vallet, Miriam Fernandez and Pablo Castells. 2005. *An Ontology-Based Information Retrieval Model.* Proceedings of Extended Semantic Web Conference.

Semantic Annotation. June 2011. <http://www.ontotext.com/kim/semantic-annotation>.

Extracting Protein-Protein Interactions with Language Modelling

Ali Reza Ebadat
INRIA-INSA
ali_reza.ebadat@inria.fr

Abstract

In this paper, we model the corpus-based relation extraction task, namely protein-protein interaction, as a classification problem. In that framework, we first show that standard machine learning systems exploiting representations simply based on shallow linguistic information can rival state-of-the-art systems that rely on deep linguistic analysis. We also show that it is possible to obtain even more effective systems, still using these easy and reliable pieces of information, if the specifics of the extraction task and the data are taken into account. Our original method combining lazy learning and language modelling out-performs the existing systems when evaluated on the LLL2005 protein-protein interaction extraction task data[1].

1 Introduction

Since the nineties, a lot of research work has been dedicated to the problem of corpus-based knowledge acquisition, whether the aimed knowledge is terminology, special cases of vocabulary (e.g. named entities), lexical relations between words or more functional ones. This paper focuses on this last kind of acquisition, i.e., relation extraction, and more specifically on Protein-Protein Interaction (PPI) extraction from bio-medical texts. The goal of PPI is to find pairs of proteins within sentences such that one protein is described as regulating, inhibiting, or binding the other. In functional genomics, these interactions, which are not available in structured database but scatterd in scientific papers, are central to determine the function of the genes.

In order to extract PPIs, the texts which contain the interactions have to be analyzed. Two kinds of linguistic analysis can be performed for this purpose: deep and shallow. Automatic deep analysis, which provides a syntactic or semantic parsing of each sentence, can be a useful source of information. However, tools for automatic deep analysis are available only for a limited number of natural languages, and produce imperfect results. Manual deep analysis, on the other hand, is time consuming and expensive. Another way to analyze texts is to rely only on a shallow linguistic analysis, taking into account the sole words, lemmas or parts of speech (POS) tags. Automatic tools for shallow analysis are available for many languages, and are (sufficiently) reliable.

In this paper, we advocate the use of shallow linguistic features for relation extraction tasks. First, we show that these easy and reliable pieces of information can be efficiently used as features in a machine learning (ML) framework, resulting in good PPI extraction systems, as effective as many systems relying on deep linguistic analysis. Furthering this idea, we propose a new simple yet original system, called LM-kNN and based on language modeling, that out-performs the state-of-the-art systems.

The paper is organized as follows. Section 2 reviews related work on PPI extraction from biomedical texts. Section 3 specifies the problem and our methodology. Results when using classical machine learning algorithms are given in Section 4, together with a comparison with existing systems. The last section presents a conclusion and some future work.

2 Related Work

In this literature review, focus is set on researches dedicated to relation extraction from bio-medical texts, especially those evaluated in a PPI framework. The systems proposed for this task can be organized into different groups, depending on the source of knowledge (deep vs. shallow linguistic information) and on the approach used (manual vs. ML).

[1]This work was achieved as part of the Quaero Programme, funded by OSEO, French State agency for innovation.

For instance , RelEx (Fundel et al., 2007) exploits manually built extraction rules handling deep and shallow linguistic information. This system yields good results, yet using such an hand-elaborated knowledge is a bottleneck requiring expertise for any new domain. Thus, many ML-based approaches were proposed to overcome this limitation. The ML techniques range from SVM with complex kernels (Airola et al., 2008; Kim et al., 2010) or CRF (?), to expressive techniques like inductive logic programming (Phuong et al., 2003). Lexical or linguistic features of words surrounding a pair of proteins can be considered as shallow linguistic features to train the systems (Bunescu and Mooney, 2006; ?; Sun et al., 2007). Yet, most of the techniques rely on deep linguistic analysis like syntactic parsing. Indeed, grammatical relations are assumed to be important for PPI extraction, especially when few training data compared to test data are available (Fayruzov et al., 2009). Yet, the performance of extraction systems being sensitive to the accuracy of automatic parsers (Fayruzov et al., 2008), shallow linguistic information still remains an option (Xiao et al., 2005), though up-to-now less effective than deep one.

In this work, we defend the hypothesis that shallow linguistic information combined with standard ML approaches is sufficient to reach good results. Furthermore, we propose a system demonstrating that when this simple information is cleverly used, it even out-performs these state-of-the-art systems.

3 Approach

This section is dedicated to the different machine learning approaches, based on shallow linguistic features, that we experimented. The two first subsections respectively present how to model the PPI task as a machine learning problem —and in particular how relations are described— and the classification tools commonly used for similar tasks. In the last subsection, we propose a new relation extraction technique, based on language modelling, which is expected to be more efficient than the existing ones.

3.1 Modelling the Relation Extraction Task as a Machine Learning Problem

The goal of relation extraction is to predict, at the occurrence level, if two entities share a defined relation. Expert systems, with manually defined extraction patterns, are usually very costly to build, cannot be adapted to new domains and require an expert knowledge both for the pattern design and the domain which is rarely available. Thus, it is usual to try to build relation extraction systems by machine learning. Such approaches require examples of the spotted relations, but the necessary expert knowledge is cheaper in this case than for pattern design. Moreover, bootstrapping and iterative approaches (Hearst, 1992) or active learning can be used to lower this cost.

In PPI extraction, the goal is to predict if there is any interaction between two proteins. In such a case, the relation is directed, that is, one of the entity is an agent and the other is the target. For example, in the sentence reported in Figure 1 in which entities (proteins) are in bold, there is a relation between *GerE* and *cotD* for which *GerE* is the agent and *cotD* is the target.

> ***GerE*** *stimulates* ***cotD*** *transcription and inhibits* ***cotA*** *transcription in vitro by* ***sigma K*** *RNA polymersase, as expected from in vivo studies, and, unexpectedly, profoundly inhibits in vitro transcription of the gene (****sigK****) that encode* ***sigma K****.*

Figure 1: Sample sentence for protein-protein interaction

To handle this directed relation problem, we model it as a 3-class machine learning task. For each training sentence, each pair of entities is either tagged as *None* if the entity pair does not have any interaction, *LTR* if the interaction is from the left to the right (agent to target in the sentence word order), and *RTL* if the interaction is from the right to the left.

The representation, that is, the set of features describing our examples for the machine learning algorithms is voluntarily chosen as very simple. Indeed, a relation is simply represented by the bag of lemmas occurring between the two entities. Grammatical words are kept since they may be important clues to detect the direction of the interaction (like the word *by*). For instance, Table 1 reports the examples found in the sentence: *Most cot genes, and the gerE, are transcribed by sigma K RNA polymerase*. More formally, each example is described by a vector; each dimension of this vector corresponds to a lemma and its value is 1 if the word occurs between the entities and 0 otherwise. The sparse vector obtained is expected to be a representation both performant and robust since it does not rely on any complex pre-processing.

Example pair	Bag of lemmas	Class
cot,gerE	gene,and,the	None
cot,sigmaK	gene,and,the,gerE, gene,be,transcribe,by	RTL
gerE,sigmaK	gene,be,transcribe,by	RTL

Table 1: Examples of bag of lemmas to be used as feature vector

3.2 Machine Learning for the Bag of Lemmas Representation

In the experiments reported below, this bag-of-lemmas representation is exploited with machine learning techniques popularly used for similar tasks: Support Vector Machine (SVM), Random Tree and Random Forest (as implemented in the Weka toolkit (Hall et al., 2009)).

SVM aims at constructing a set of hyperplanes in the representation space dividing the examples according to their class. When used with complex kernels, the hyperplanes are searched in a higher space, resulting in a complex separation in the original representation space. Random Tree and Random Forest (Breiman, 2001) are two classification algorithms based on the well-known decision trees offering a better robustness especially when tackling problems with small or noisy training data. Random Tree constructs a classical decision tree but considers only a subset of attributes (features) that are randomly selected at each node. Random Forest extends this technique: it builds a large set of decision trees by randomly sampling the training data and the features. It is important to note that all these techniques learn explicitly or implicitly to divide the representation space—in our case the lemma vector space—into different parts corresponding to our 3 classes.

3.3 Nearest Neighbors with Language Modelling

Besides these somewhat classical machine learning approaches, we propose a new technique to extract relations. As the previous ones, it still uses shallow linguistic information, which is easy to obtain and ensures the necessary robustness. One of the main differences with the previous approaches concerns the representation of the examples: it takes into account the sequential aspect of the task with the help of n-gram language models. Thus, a relation is represented by the sequence of lemmas occurring between the agent and the target, if the agent occurs before the target, or between the target and the agent otherwise. A language model is built for each example Ex, that is, the probabilities based on the occurrences of n-grams in Ex are computed; this language model is written $\mathcal{M}_{Ex}$. The class (LTR, RTL or none) of each example is also memorized.

Given a relation candidate (that is, two proteins or genes in a sentence), it is possible to evaluate its proximity with any example, or more precisely the probability that this example has generated the candidate. Let us note $C =< w_1, w_2, ..., w_m >$ the sequence of lemmas between the proteins. For n-grams of n lemmas, this probability is classically computed as:

$$P(C|\mathcal{M}_{Ex})) = \prod_{i=1}^{m} P(w_i|w_{i-n}..w_{i-1}, \mathcal{M}_{Ex})$$

As for any language model in practice, probabilities are smoothed in order to prevent unseen n-grams to yield 0 for the whole sequence. In the experiments reported below, we consider bigrams of lemmas and simply use interpolation with lower order n-grams (unigram in this case) combined with an absolute discounting (Ney et al., 1994).

In order to prevent examples with long sequences to be favored, the probability of generating the example from the candidate ($P(Ex|\mathcal{M}_C)$) is also taken into account. Finally, the similarity between an example and a candidate is

$$sim(Ex, C) = \min\left(P(Ex|\mathcal{M}_C), P(C|\mathcal{M}_{Ex})\right).$$

The class is finally attributed to the candidate by a k-nearest neighbor algorithm: the 10 most similar examples (highest sim) are calculated and a majority vote is performed. This lazy-learning technique is expected to be more suited to this kind of tasks than the model-based ones proposed in the previous sub-section since it better takes into account the variety of ways to express a relation (see Section 4.3 for a discussion on this issue).

4 Experiments

In this section, the experiments with the different relation extraction systems described above are presented. The data used and the evaluation metrics and methodologies are first detailed. Then the results obtained through cross-validation and on held-out test data are given and compared with existing systems. Finally, some insights raised by these results are given.

4.1 LLL Data

To evaluate the different relation extraction systems, we use the data developed for the Learning Language in Logic 2005 (LLL05) shared task (Nédellec, 2005). The goal of LLL05 was to extract protein/gene interactions in abstracts from the Medline bibliography database.

The provided training set is composed of sentences in which a total of 161 interactions between genes/proteins are identified. Since only positive examples (RTL or LTR in our case) are provided in the training data, we need to consider negative examples for training. As explained before, all interactions are directed; thus, each pair of proteins within a sentence having no interaction between its constituents is considered as a negative example. The test set is composed of another set of sentences for which the groundtruth is kept unknown; the results are computed by submitting the predictions to a web service. The original LLL challenge offered the possibility to train and test the systems only on interactions expressed without the help of co-references (mostly with pronouns designating a previously montionned entity). Also, the training and test data were also provided with or without manual syntactic annotations of the sentences (dependency analysis). Of course, in order to evaluate our systems in a realistic way, we used the data containing interactions expressed with or without co-references, and we did not considered the manual syntactic annotation.

4.2 Evaluation

The evaluation metrics chosen in our experiments are those classically used in this domain: precision, recall and f-measure. It is important to note that in this evaluation, partially correct answers, like an interaction between two entities correctly detected but with the wrong interaction direction, are considered as wrong answers.

We evaluate our LM approach and compare it with the more traditional machine learning techniques and the state-of-the-art systems in two ways. First, we classically use cross-validation. Yet, with so few examples, it is important to choose a number of folds important enough to provide reliable figures; in the results presented below, 30-fold cross-validation is considered. The second way is by using an unseen test dataset. This dataset was developed for the evaluation of the LLL challenge. The groundtruth is kept unknown; and the results are computed by submitting the predictions to a web service.

The differences between these two evaluation procedures shed light on inherent difficulties and biases in some studies that we discuss after presenting our results.

4.2.1 Cross Validation Evaluation

Table 2 reports the recall (R), precision (P) and f-measure (F) computed by 30-fold cross-validation on the different machine learning techniques presented in the previous section. More precisely, the SVM used is the popular libSVM implementation (Chang and Lin, 2001), which was tested with usual kernels (linear and RBF); Random Forest was used with 700 trees, and Naive Bayes and Random tree were used with their default parameters in Weka if any.

Algorithm	**P**	**R**	**F**
libSVM linear kernel	77.1	77.4	77.2
libSVM RBF kernel ($\gamma = 0.1$)	40.7	63.8	49.7
libSVM RBF kernel ($\gamma = 0.5$)	81.4	74.9	78
Random Forest	80.4	80.6	80.4
Random Tree	77.6	77.4	77.5
Naive Bayes	75.1	68.1	69.3
Naive Bayes Multinomial	70.4	70.3	70.3
LM-kNN	**82.2**	**80.3**	**81.2**

Table 2: Performance of shallow linguistic based techniques with 30-fold cross validation

It is interesting to note that all the techniques perform very well, achieving very high scores, except for the SVM with a RBF kernel and $\gamma = 0.1$. This negative result can be explained by the fact that the SVM with such settings and so few training data has a tendency to over-fit, especially because of the training data amount. Apart from this problem, the closeness of the other results tends to show that, for the same bag-of-lemmas representation, the choice of the classifier does not strongly impact on the performance. Yet, overall, Random Forest, SVM with adequate settings and our LM-kNN technique show the highest f-measures.

4.2.2 Held Out Data Evaluation

The held out test data provided for the LLL challenge allows us to evaluate the previous techniques in another evaluation framework. Table 3 reports the performance obtained by these techniques on the complete test set (interaction expressed with or without co-references). For comparison purposes, the results on this dataset reported by other studies are also included. Since many teams have only considered the evaluation without coreferences, which is supposed to correspond to an easier task, we also report the results of our LM-kNN approach and other state-of-the-art systems in this context in Table 4. The first part of each table concerns systems using raw data (no manual annotation), which corresponds to a realistic evaluation of the systems, and the second part contains results of other systems using the provided manual syntactic analysis.

System	P	R	F
systems on raw data			
Goadrich et al. (2005)	25.0	81.4	38.2
Random Forest	57.9	48.1	52.6
libSVM linear kernel	58.0	56.6	57.3
LM-kNN	**70.9**	**79.5**	**75**
systems on manually annotated data			
Katrenko et al. (2005)	**51.8**	**16.8**	**25.4**
Goadrich et al. (2005)	14.0	93.1	24.4

Table 3: Results for held-out test set of LLL, with or whitout co-references

System	P	R	F
systems on raw data			
Hakenberg et al. (2005)	50.0	53.8	51.8
Greenwood et al. (2005)	10.6	98.1	19.1
Kim et al. (2010)	68.5	68.5	68.5
Fundel et al. (2007)	68	78	72
LM-kNN	**67.1**	**87**	**75.8**
systems on manually annotated data			
Popelínský and Blaťák (2005)	37.9	55.5	45.1
Riedel and Klein (2005)	60.9	46.2	52.6
Kim et al. (2010)	**79.3**	**85.1**	**82.1**

Table 4: Results for held-out test set of LLL, without co-references

The first thing one can note from Table 3 is that the results are lower than those obtained by cross-validation. This loss is particularly important for the classical approaches based on a bag-of-lemmas representation. This point is not specific to our approaches and was already noticed by previous studies using the LLL dataset. It is due in part to a difference between the way the training and the test sets were built: the distributions of positive examples and negative ones are very different in these two sets since the test data contains much more sentences without any valid interaction. With respect to this, our LM-kNN approach over-performs the other ones and still produces high results for this task.

Besides our LM-kNN technique which ranks first (+6.5% over the best known results for fully automatic systems), it is interesting to note that our other machine learning approaches also perform well compared with state-of-the-art techniques, even though the latter could be considered as more complex than our methods. Indeed, Hakenberg et al. (2005) used finite state automata to generate extraction patterns. In addition to LLL corpora, these authors took advantage of 256 additional positive examples manually annotated. The method of Greenwood et al. (2005) generates candidate patterns from examples with the help of MiniPar for a syntactic analysis and WordNet and PASBio for a semantic analysis and tagging. Goadrich et al. (2005) applied Inductive Logic Programming and Markov Logic methods. The approach used by Kim et al. (2010), as we explained in Section 2, relies on the shortest path in the syntactic parse tree and a specially developed kernel for SVM.

Results of systems tested with manual syntactic information are also worth noting. Katrenko et al. (2005) used the manual syntactic annotations and a ad'hoc ontology to induce extraction patterns. Popelínský and Blaťák (2005) also applied Inductive Logic Programming on the manual syntactic annotation and enriched the data by using WordNet. It is interesting to note that, even with this manual syntactic analysis and the fact that some systems carried tests only on the easiest part of the test set, most of these systems (the case of Kim et al. (2010) is discussed below) perform worse than our simple machine learning approaches.

4.3 Discussion

With the development and the availability of powerful machine learning systems, many NLP problems are now modelled as classification tasks. As

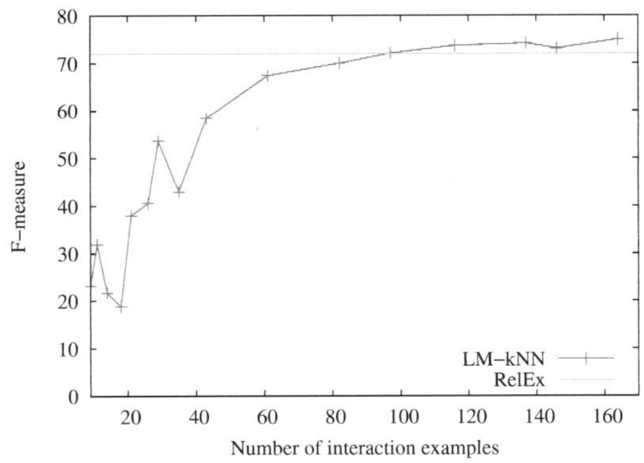

Figure 2: F-measure according to the number of interaction examples

with our Random Forest or SVM experiments, such approaches usually yield good results. Yet, when taking into account the specifics of the task and the data, a huge improvement can be expected.

As the performance of our LM-kNN approach suggests it, lazy learning approaches combined with simple tools like language modelling can offer an interesting alternative to complex tools, especially when dealing with small dataset and a complex classification task.

Another advantage of using a lazy-learning approach such as LM-kNN is that it may offer more robustness than model-based learning approaches when dealing with few examples. And if one wants to reduce the cost of the development of a relation extraction system, it is interesting to see how few examples are necessary to yield good enough results. Figure 2 shows the evolution of f-measure of our LM-kNN system on the LLL test set according to the number of interaction given as examples. For comparison, we also report the result of the rule-based system RelEx (Fundel et al., 2007), which was up to now the best performing system for this task (on raw data, but only tested on interaction without co-references). The evolution of the LM-kNN performance describes an expected curve: important variations are noticed when dealing with very few examples, the improvement is more important when adding examples to a small set of examples, and then the improvement is getting smaller; yet it is interesting to note that the curve suggests that more examples could still improve the f-measure of the system. The performance of RelEx is reached by our technique with less than 100 examples. Therefore, it suggests that instead of hand-crafting complex extraction rules that cannot be adapted to another extraction task, annotating only 100 examples is enough, which corresponds to about 50 sentences.

Systems using syntax for relation extraction obtain promising results; yet, as we pointed it out before, they are highly dependent on the availability and the quality of the syntactic analysis (see (Fayruzov et al., 2008)). For instance, the f-measure of Kim et al. (2010) declines by 15% when moving from a manual, perfect syntactic annotation to an automatic one.

5 Conclusion

In this paper we have presented and experimented several systems, that can be easily implemented, to extract directed Protein-Protein Interactions in bio-medical texts. We have shown that modeling the PPI extraction task as a classification problem and simply using shallow linguistic information is sufficient to reach good results. Moreover, we have proposed a simple yet very efficient relation extraction system, LM-kNN, based on language modeling which better takes the specifics of the task and data into account. The results, evaluated on a publicly available dataset, underlined the interest of using shallow linguistic information and our new LM-kNN method yielded the best known results.

This good result is very promising, and many perspectives are foreseen. From a technical point of view, it is possible to integrate these machine learning frameworks into an iterative process: newly retrieved relations are used as additional examples to re-train a system. Such approaches, like the one of (Hearst, 1992), as well as active learning techniques are of course straightforward for our lazy-learning approach. From an applicative point of view, our LM-kNN has to be tested over other relation extraction tasks. In particular, we foresee its use for the detection of relations in speech transcripts of sporting events. As it was previously said, shallow linguistic approaches is a necessity in such a context in which the oral characteristics and the speech-to-text process prevent the use of any deep linguistic analysis tools.

References

Antti Airola, Sampo Pyysalo, Jari Björne, Tapio Pahikkala, Filip Ginter, and Tapio Salakoski. 2008. A graph kernel for protein-protein interaction extraction. In *Proc. of the Workshop on Current Trends in Biomedical Natural Language Processing*, pages 1–9, Columbus, Ohio, USA.

Christian Blaschke and Alfonso Valencia. 2002. The frame-based module of the SUISEKI information extraction system. *IEEE Intelligent Systems*, 17(2):14–20. doi:10.1109/5254.999215.

Leo Breiman. 2001. Random forests. *Machine Learning*, 45(1):5–32. doi:10.1023/A:1010933404324.

Razvan Bunescu and Raymond Mooney. 2006. Subsequence kernels for relation extraction. *Advances in Neural Information Processing Systems*, 18:171–178.

Chih-Chung Chang and Chih-Jen Lin, 2001. *LIBSVM: a library for support vector machines.* Software available at `http://www.csie.ntu.edu.tw/~cjlin/libsvm`.

Timur Fayruzov, Martine De Cock, Chris Cornelis, and Veronique Hoste. 2008. The role of syntactic features in protein interaction extraction. In *Proc. of the 17th Conference on Information and Knowledge Management (CIKM'08)*, pages 61–68, Napa Valley, CA, USA. doi:10.1145/1458449.1458463.

Timur Fayruzov, Martine De Cock, Chris Cornelis, and Veronique Hoste. 2009. Linguistic feature analysis for protein interaction extraction. *BMC Bioinformatics*, 10. doi:10.1186/1471-2105-10-374.

Katrin Fundel, Robert Kuffner, and Ralf Zimmer. 2007. RelEx–relation extraction using dependency parse trees. *Bioinformatics*, 23(3):365–371. doi: 10.1093/bioinformatics/btl616.

Mark Goadrich, Louis Oliphant, and Jude Shavlik. 2005. Learning to extract genic interactions using gleaner. In Nédellec (Nédellec, 2005), pages 62–68.

Mark A. Greenwood, Mark Stevenson, Yikun Guo, Henk Harkema, and Angus Roberts. 2005. Automatically acquiring a linguistically motivated genic interaction extraction system. In Nédellec (Nédellec, 2005), pages 46–52.

Jorg Hakenberg, Conrad Plake, Ulf Leser, Harald Kirsch, and Dietrich Rebholz-Schuhmann. 2005. Identification of language patterns based on alignement and finite state automata. In Nédellec (Nédellec, 2005), pages 38–45.

Mark Hall, Eibe Frank, Geoffrey Holmes, Bernhard Pfahringer, Peter Reutemann, and Ian H. Witten. 2009. The WEKA data mining software: An update. *SIGKDD Explorations*, 11(1):10–18.

Min He, Yi Wang, and Wei Li. 2009. PPI finder: A mining tool for human protein-protein interactions. *PLoS ONE*, 4(2). doi:10.1371/journal.pone.0004554.

Marti A. Hearst. 1992. Automatic acquisition of hyponyms from large text corpora. In *Proc. of the 14th International Conference on Computational Linguistics (COLING'92)*, pages 539–545, Nantes, France.

Sophia Katrenko, M. Scott Marshall, Marco Roos, and Pieter Adriaans. 2005. Learning biological interactions from medline abstracts. In Nédellec (Nédellec, 2005), pages 53–58.

Seonho Kim, Juntae Yoon, Jihoon Yang, and Seog Park. 2010. Walk-weighted subsequence kernels for protein-protein interaction extraction. *BMC Bioinformatics*, 11. doi:10.1186/1471-2105-11-107.

H. Ney, U. Essen, and R. Kneser. 1994. On structuring probabilistic dependencies in stochastic language modelling. *Computer Speech and Language*, 8:1–38.

Claire Nédellec, editor. 2005. *Learning language in logic – Genic interaction extraction challenge*, in Proc. of the 4th Learning Language in Logic Workshop (LLL'05), Bonn, Germany.

Tu Minh Phuong, Doheon Lee, and Kwang Hyung Lee, 2003. *Learning rules to extract protein interactions from biomedical text*, volume 2637, pages 148–158. Springer Verlag. doi:10.1007/3-540-36175-8_15.

Luboš Popelínský and Jan Blaťák. 2005. Learning genic interactions without expert domain knowledge: Comparison of different ILP algorithms. In Nédellec (Nédellec, 2005), pages 59–61.

Sampo Pyysalo, Antti Airola, Juho Heimonen, Jari Björne, Filip Ginter, and Tapio Salakoski. 2008. Comparative analysis of five protein-protein interaction corpora. *BMC Bioinformatics*, 9(Suppl 3). doi:10.1186/1471-2105-9-S3-S6.

Sebastian Riedel and Ewan Klein. 2005. Genic interaction extraction with semantic and syntactic chains. In Nédellec (Nédellec, 2005), pages 69–74.

Chengjie Sun, Lei Lin, Xiaolong Wang, and Yi Guan, 2007. *Using maximum entropy model to extract protein-protein interaction information from biomedical literature*, volume 4681, pages 730–737. Springer Verlag. doi:10.1007/978-3-540-74171-8_72.

Juan Xiao, Jian Su, GuoDong Zhou, and ChewLim Tan. 2005. Protein-protein interaction extraction: A supervised learning approach. In *Proc. of the 1st International Symposium on Semantic Mining in Biomedicine (SMBM 2005)*, pages 51–59, Hinxton, Cambridgeshire, UK.

Experiments with Small-sized Corpora in CBMT

Monica Gavrila
Hamburg University
gavrila@informatik.
uni-hamburg.de

Natalia Elita
Hamburg University
elita@informatik.
uni-hamburg.de

Abstract

There is no doubt that in the last couple of years corpus-based machine translation (CBMT) approaches have been in focus. Each of the approaches has its advantages and disadvantages. Therefore, hybrid approaches have been developed. This paper presents a comparative study of CBMT approaches, using three types of systems: a statistical MT (SMT) system, an example-based MT (EBMT) system and a hybrid (EBMT-SMT) system. We considered for our experiments three languages, from different language families: Romanian, German and English. Two different types of corpora have been used: while the first is manually created, the latter is automatically built.

1 Introduction

There is no doubt that in the last couple of years corpus-based machine translation (CBMT) approaches have been in focus. Among them, the statistical MT (SMT) approach has been by far more dominant, but the example-based machine translation (EBMT) Workshop at the end of 2009[1] and the new open-source systems (e.g. OpenMaTrEx – see section 2.3) showed a revived interest in the EBMT and hybrid approaches.

The unclear definitions and the mixture of ideas make the difference between the two CBMT approaches difficult to distinguish. In order to show the advantages of one or another method, comparisons between SMT and EBMT (or hybrid) systems have been presented in the literature. To get advantage of positive sides of both CBMT approaches, hybrid systems have been developed. The results, depending on the data type and the systems considered, seem to be positive for various approaches. The marker-based EBMT system described in (Way and Gough, 2005) outperformed the SMT system presented in the same paper. In (Smith and Clark, 2009) the hybrid EBMT-SMT system is outperformed by a Moses-based SMT system. In both papers the language pair under consideration is English - French.

In this paper we compare several CBMT approaches, using three MT systems: an SMT system (**Mb_SMT**), an EBMT system ($Lin - EBMT^{REC+}$) and a hybrid (EBMT-SMT) system (OpenMaTrEx). MT experiments are run for two language pairs, in both directions of translation: Romanian (ro)-English (en), Romanian (ro)-German (ge). In contrast to other authors, for example (Smith and Clark, 2009), we use small-sized domain-restricted corpora for training. It is usually believed that small-size copora better fit into the EBMT environment. The use of small-sized copora for SMT has been tried before: (Popovic and Ney, 2006) present results for Serbian-English and a training data size of approx. 2.6K sentences. However, to our knowledge, no comparisons among CBMT systems using small-sized data have been published.

Even more, for the language pairs employed in this paper no other comparative studies have been published. Nevertheless, separate results for EBMT and SMT have been presented: EBMT results in (Irimia, 2009)[2] and SMT in (Cristea, 2009) and (Ignat, 2009). All these experiments use for training and testing the JRC-Acquis corpus.

Our paper is organized as follows: the following section presents the MT systems employed. In Section 3 the data used is described and the translation results are interpreted. The paper ends with conclusions and further work.

2 System Description

In this section we present the three CBMT systems we used: an SMT system (**Mb_SMT**), an

[1] computing.dcu.ie/~mforcada/ebmt3/ - last accessed on June 21st, 2011.

[2] Only English and Romanian have been under consideration.

EBMT system ($Lin - EBMT^{REC+}$) and a hybrid (EBMT-SMT) system (OpenMaTrEx).

2.1 The SMT System: Mb_SMT

The pure SMT system (**Mb_SMT**) follows the description of the baseline architecture given for the Sixth Workshop on SMT[3] at the EMNLP 2011 Conference. **Mb_SMT** uses Moses[4], an SMT system that allows the user to automatically train translation models for the language pair needed, considering that the user has the necessary parallel aligned corpus. More details about Moses can be found in (Koehn et al., 2007).

While running Moses, we used SRILM – (Stolcke, 2002)– for building the language model (LM) and GIZA++ – (Och and Ney, 2003) – for obtaining word alignment information. We made two changes to the specifications given at the Workshop on SMT: we left out the tuning step and we changed the order of the language model (LM) from 5 to 3. Leaving out the tuning step has been motivated by results we obtained in experiments which are not the topic of this paper, when comparing different settings for the SMT system. Not all tests for the system configuration which included tuning showed an improvement. Changing the LM order has been motivated by results reported in the SMART project[5].

2.2 The EBMT System: $Lin - EBMT^{REC+}$

$Lin - EBMT^{REC+}$ is an EBMT system which combines the linear EBMT approach with the template-based one – see (McTait, 2001) for the classification of EBMT approaches and the definition of a template. Before starting the translation, training and test data are pre-processed (such as tokenization and lowercasing) as in the Moses-based SMT system. We use a token[6]-index in order to reduce the search space in the matching process. In case the test sentence is found in the training corpus during the matching procedure, its translation represents the output. Otherwise, the alignment and recombination steps are performed. The matching procedure is an approach based on surface-forms, focusing in recursively finding the longest common substrings. The alignment information is extracted from the GIZA++ output of the **Mb_SMT** system. The longest target language (TL) aligned subsequences are used in the recombination step, which is based on 2-gram information and word-order constraints. In $Lin - EBMT^{REC+}$ ideas from the template-based EBMT approach are incorporated in the recombination step, by extracting and imposing three types of word-order constraints: First word constraints; Constraints extracted from the target language side of a template; Constraints extracted from both sides of a template. More information about the system, templates and how combinations of constraints influence the evaluation results has been presented in (Gavrila, 2011).

2.3 The Hybrid System: OpenMaTrEx

OpenMaTrEx is a free (open-source) EBMT system based on the marker hypothesis (Dandapat et al., 2010).

The marker hypothesis (Green, 1979) is a universal psycholinguistic constraint which states that natural languages are '*marked*' for complex syntactic structures at surface form by a closed set of specific lexemes and morphemes. That is, a basic phrase-level segmentation of an input sentence can be achieved by exploiting a closed list of known marker words to signalize the start and end of each segment.

OpenMaTrEx consists of a marker-driven chunker, several chunk aligners and two engines: one is based on the simple proof-of-concept monotone recombinator (called Marclator[7]) and the other uses a Moses-based decoder (called MaTrEx[8]).

The system uses GIZA++ for word alignments and IRSTLM[9] to obtain the LM. The complete architecture of OpenMaTrEx is described in (Dandapat et al., 2010) and (Stroppa et al., 2006). OpenMaTrEx can be run in two modes: Marclator and MaTrEx. In the MaTrEx mode it wraps around the Moses statistical decoder, using a hybrid translation table containing marker-based chunks as well as statistically extracted phrase pairs. For our experiments we followed the training and translation steps as described in (Dandapat et al., 2010). Only

[3] `www.statmt.org/wmt11/baseline.html` - last accessed on July 14th, 2011.

[4] `www.statmt.org/moses/` - last accessed on July 14th, 2011.

[5] `www.smart-project.eu` - last accessed on July 14th, 2011.

[6] A token is represented by a word form, a number or a punctuation sign.

[7] `www.openmatrex.org/marclator/` - last accessed on July 1st, 2011.

[8] `www.sf.net/projects/mosesdecoder/` - last accessed on July 1st, 2011.

[9] `http://hlt.fbk.eu/en/irstlm` - last accessed on July 21sth, 2011.

the results of the run in MaTrEx mode (the hybrid MT architecture) are shown in the current article, as this is the usual way to use OpenMaTrEx, according to its developers.

2.3.1 Marker Words Files

In this subsection we present the marker words files for Romanian developed during this research. The markers for English and German have been already contained in the system: The English markers were derived from the Apertium English-Catalan dictionaries[10]; The German markers were extracted from the "Ding" dictionary by Sarah Ebling[11].

We extracted the markers for Romanian during the experiments presented in this paper by considering the morpho-syntactic specifications from MULTEXT-East[12] and Wikipedia[13].

The set of markers for Romanian consists of the chunking and non-chunking punctuation that has been acquired from the English marker words file. The other word categories included in the file are: determiners, pronouns (personal, demonstrative, possessive, interrogative, relative), prepositions, conjunctions (coordinative and subordinative), (cardinal) numerals, adverbs and auxiliary verbs.

Definite articles and weak forms of the personal pronouns are two examples of clitic forms in Romanian. We have not considered the definite articles as markers, as they appear within the word as endings (e.g. ro: *dosareLE* – en: *THE files*). Personal pronouns separated by a hyphen have not been included in the set of markers (e.g. ro: *LE-am citit* – en: *I read THEM*).

Some of the determiners are ambiguous, as they can also be pronouns or numerals (e.g. ro. *O fată*) – en: *A girl*; ro: *ia-O* – en: *take IT*; ro: *O pară şi două mere* – en: *A pear and two apples*). Only given the context it can be determined whether the word is a determiner, a numeral or a pronoun. In order to avoid ambiguity, indefinite articles were introduced as determiners in the set of markers and the category *determiner pronoun* was included only once under the category of pronouns.

[10]www.apertium.org/?id=whatisapertium\&lang=en - last accessed on June 21st, 2011.

[11]www-user.tu-chemnitz.de/~fri/ding/ - last accessed on June 21st, 2011.

[12]nl.ijs.si/ME/V4/msd/html/msd-ro.html - last accessed on July 1st, 2011.

[13]ro.wikipedia.org/wiki/Parte_de_vorbire - last accessed on July 1st, 2011.

There are currently 366 Romanian, 307 English and 656 German markers. Both German and Romanian have diacritics: in case of German - both versions (with and without diacritics) of the same marker word are included in the file. In case of Romanian, we created two separate sets of markers: one with and one without diacritics.

3 Evaluation

In this section, before the evaluation results are presented, we describe the training and test data used in the experiments.

3.1 Data Description

We used for the evaluation two different types of corpora, both having the same size: RoGER, a manual of an electronic device, and JRC-Acquis$_{SMALL}$, a sub-part of JRC-Acquis which contains regulations of the European Union (EU).

RoGER is a domain-restricted parallel corpus, including four languages (**Ro**manian, **E**nglish, **G**erman and **R**ussian). It is manually aligned at sentence level. Moreover, the text is manually preprocessed, by replacing concepts such as numbers and web pages, with '*meta-notions*' – for example numbers with *NUM*. It contains no diacritics. More information about the RoGER corpus can be found in (Gavrila and Elita, 2006).

Its small size (2333 sentences) is compensated by the correctness of the translations and sentence alignments. We randomly extracted 133 sentences, which we used as test data for all three MT systems. The rest of 2200 sentences represent the training data. Statistical information about RoGER is shown in Table 1.

Data SL	**No. of tokens**	**Voc.**	**Average sent. length**
English-Romanian			
Training	27889	2367	12.68
Test	1613	522	12.13
Romanian-English, Romanian-German			
Training	28946	3349	13.16
Test	1649	659	12.40
German-Romanian			
Training	28361	3230	12.89
Test	1657	604	12.46

Table 1: RoGER statistics (SL= source language, voc.=vocabulary, sent.=sentence or sentences).

The second corpus considered, JRC-

Acquis$_{SMALL}$, is a sub-corpus of the JRC-Acquis (Steinberger et al., 2006). To analyze how the systems behave in case of another type of small-sized corpus, 2333 sentences have been randomly extracted from the center of the whole JRC-Acquis data. These sentences form the JRC-Acquis$_{SMALL}$ corpus. From this data, 133 sentences have been randomly selected as test data. The rest of 2200 remain as training data. JRC-Acquis$_{SMALL}$ has not been manually verified or modified. More information about the corpus can be found in Table 2.

Data SL	No. of tokens	Voc.	Average sent. length
English-Romanian			
Training	75405	3578	34.27
Test	4434	992	33.33
Romanian-English			
Training	72170	5581	32.80
Test	4325	1260	32.51
German-Romanian			
Training	69735	5929	31.69
Test	3947	1178	29.67
Romanian-German			
Training	75156	6390	34.16
Test	4366	1320	32.82

Table 2: JRC-Acquis$_{SMALL}$ statistics.

The three languages used in this paper present different morphological and syntactical characteristics. As English has been used quite often in MT experiments, for a better understanding of the translation challenges, we will briefly describe Romanian and German in the following paragraphs .

Romanian is a lesser resourced language with a highly infected morphology and high demand for translation after joining the European Union in 2007. It is a Romance language, with influence from Slavic languages especially on vocabulary and phonetics. Features, such as its inflectional system, or the three genders, make difficult the adaptation of language technology systems for other family-related languages.

German is a Germanic language, which is also inflected and presents a 3-gender system and well defined inflection classes. Two special features are represented by the verbs with particles (the separation of the particle from the verb inside the sentence and the challenge that the particle can be ambiguous) and the compounds. Compounds in German are normally written as single words, without spaces or other word boundaries.[14]

Analyzing Tables 1 and 2 ifferences in the text style can be also noticed in the average length of the sentences: between 12 and 13 tokens for RoGER and between 29 and 34 for JRC-Acquis$_{SMALL}$. The total number of tokens and the vocabulary size reinforce the differences between the languages: the vocabulary size for the inflected languages is higher as the one for English; the total numbers of tokens for German is lower, as German uses more compounds.

3.2 Automatic Evaluation Results

We evaluated the obtained translations automatically by using the BLEU (**bil**ingual **e**valuation **u**nderstudy) score. BLEU measures the number of n-grams, of different lengths, of the system output that appear in a set of references. More information on BLEU can be found in (Papineni et al., 2002). We considered the twelfth version of the BLEU implementation from the National Institute of Standards and Technology (NIST)[15]: *mteval_v12*.

Although BLEU is criticized in the research environment, the choice of the metrics is motivated by our resources (software, linguistic resources, etc.) and, for comparison reasons, by results reported in the literature. Due to lack of data and further translation possibilities, the comparison with only one reference translation is considered.

The obtained results are presented in Tables 3 (for RoGER)and 4 (for JRC-Acquis$_{SMALL}$). In the following subsection we will analyze these results.

3.3 Interpretation of the Results

In order to be able to analyze better the results, we examined the test data set from two points of view: the number of out-of-vocabulary words (OOV-words) and the number of test sentences already found in the training data. Both aspects have a direct influence on the translation quality and

[14]The longest German word verified to be actually in (albeit very limited) use is Rindfleischetikettierungsüberwachungsaufgabenübertragungsgesetz, which, literally translated, is "beef labelling supervision duty assignment law" [from Rind (cattle), Fleisch (meat), Etikettierung(s) (labelling), Überwachung(s) (supervision), Aufgaben (duties), Übertragung(s) (assignment), Gesetz (law)].

[15]`www.itl.nist.gov/iad/mig//tests/mt/2008/scoring.html` - last accessed on June 14th, 2011.

Mb_SMT	$Lin - EBMT^{REC+}$	Open-MaTrEx
English – Romanian		
0.4386	0.3085	0.4320
Romanian – English		
0.4765	0.3668	0.4663
German – Romanian		
0.3240	0.2646	0.2564
Romanian – German		
0.3405	0.2894	0.3058

Table 3: BLEU results (RoGER).

Mb_SMT	$Lin - EBMT^{REC+}$	Open-MaTrEx
English – Romanian		
0.4801	0.3550	0.4446
Romanian – English		
0.4904	0.3910	0.4771
German – Romanian		
0.2811	0.2167	0.2468
Romanian – German		
0.2926	0.2458	0.2433

Table 4: BLEU results (JRC-Acquis$_{SMALL}$).

evaluation results. These results for RoGER and JRC-Acquis$_{SMALL}$ are presented in Tables 5 and 6.

No. OOV-words (% from voc. size)	Sent. in the training corpus
English-Romanian	
60 (11.49%)	37 (27.8%)
Romanian-English	
84 (12.75%)	34 (25.5%)
German-Romanian	
101 (16.72%)	31 (23.3%)
Romanian-German	
84 (12.75%)	34 (25.5%)

Table 5: Analysis of the test data set (RoGER).

It could be noticed that all systems work better for English-Romanian (both directions of translations) than for German-Romanian (both directions of translations). The lower results for the translation direction German-Romanian can be also explained by the number of OOV-words and sentences found in the training data. We notice a similar behavior for both corpora for Romanian-English, in both directions of translation. For

No. OOV-words (% from voc. size)	Sent. in the training corpus
English-Romanian	
72 (7.25%)	38 (28.5%)
Romanian-English	
129 (10.23%)	33 (24.8%)
German-Romanian	
171 (14.51%)	41 (30.82%)
Romanian-German	
160 (12.12%)	40 (30.0%)

Table 6: Analysis of the test data set (JRC-Acquis$_{SMALL}$).

all three MT systems the results for Romanian-English are better than for English-Romanian. Generally, also the results for Romanian-German are better than the ones for German-Romanian. This behavior could mean that building the output for Romanian is more difficult than for the other two languages. Moreover, the German compound nouns could cause data-sparsity.

Compared with the other systems **Mb_SMT** works the best. OpenMaTrEx has the results quite close to the ones of **Mb_SMT**. It is better than the EBMT system with only two exceptions: for German-Romanian and the RoGER data or for Romanian-German and the JRC-Acquis$_{SMALL}$ data, $Lin - EBMT^{REC+}$ gives slightly better results than OpenMaTrEx. While comparing the **Mb_SMT** and OpenMaTrEx, we obtained results similar to the ones in (Smith and Clark, 2009)[16]. The difference is only the corpus size: (Smith and Clark, 2009) used a large-sized corpus (the Europarl corpus) in their experiments.

4 Conclusions and Further Work

In this paper three corpus-based MT systems have been compared using the same test and training data. MT experiments were made for two language pairs (Romanian-English, Romanian-German), in both directions of translation. Two small-sized domain-restricted corpora of different types were used in the experiments – a framework which is thought to better fit the EBMT approach.

In order to establish which system is really the best, as the BLEU score has been criticized in the last couple of years, a manual analysis of the results is currently being made. Splitting Ger-

[16] A one-to-one comparison is not possible, as the training and test data are different.

man compounds to avoid data sparsity is our next action point. We also need to test the systems with larger copora to analyze how the quality of translation changes when the size of the corpus is progressively incremented. Other interesting aspects we consider is running OpenMaTrEx under the Marclator mode and testing how changing (increasing) the list of markers influences the results.

References

Dan Cristea. 2009. Romanian language technology and resources go to europe. Presentated at the FP7 Language Technology Informative Days, January, 20-11. To be found at: ftp://ftp.cordis.europe.eu/pub/fp7/ict/docs/language-technologies/cristea_en.pdf - last accessed on 10.04.2009.

Sandipan Dandapat, Mikel L. Forcada, Declan Groves, Sergio Penkale, John Tinsley, and Andy Way. 2010. Openmatrex: A free/open-source marker-driven example-based machine translation system. In *IceTAL'10*, pages 121–126.

Monica Gavrila and Natalia Elita. 2006. Roger - un corpus paralel aliniat. In *Resurse Lingvistice şi Instrumente pentru Prelucrarea Limbii Române Workshop Proceedings*, pages 63–67, 63-67, December. Workshop held in November 2006, Publisher: Ed. Univ. Alexandru Ioan Cuza, ISBN: 978-973-703-208-9.

Monica Gavrila. 2011. Constrained recombination in an example-based machine translation system. In Vincent Vondeghinste, Mikel L. Forcada, and Heidi Depraetere, editors, *Proceedings of the EAMT-2011: the 15th Annual Conference of the European Association for Machine Translation*, pages 193–200, Leuven, Belgium, May. ISBN 9789081486118.

Thomas R.G. Green. 1979. The necessity of syntax markers: Two experiments with artificial languages. *Journal of Verbal Learning and Verbal Behavior*, 18(4):481 – 496.

Camelia Ignat. 2009. *Improving Statistical Alignment and Translation Using Highly Multilingual Corpora*. Ph.D. thesis, INSA - LGeco- LICIA, Strasbourg, France, June, 16th. It can be found on: http://sites.google.com/site/cameliaignat/home/phd-thesis - last accessed on 3.08.09.

Elena Irimia. 2009. Ebmt experiments for the english-romanian language pair. In *Proceedings of the Recent Advances in Intelligent Information Systems*, pages 91–102. ISBN 978-83-60434-59-8.

Philipp Koehn, Hieu Hoang, Alexandra Birch, Chris Callison-Burch, Marcello Federico, Nicola Bertoldi, Brooke Cowan, Wade Shen, Christine Moran, Richard Zens, Chris Dyer, Ondrej Bojar, Alexandra Constantin, and Evan Herbst. 2007. Moses: Open source toolkit for statistical machine translation. In *Annual Meeting of the Association for Computational Linguistics (ACL), demonstration session*, Prague, Czech Republic, June.

Kevin McTait. 2001. *Translation Pattern Extraction and Recombination for Example-Based Machine Translation*. Ph.D. thesis, Centre for Computational Linguistics, Department of Language Engineering, PhD Thesis, UMIST.

Franz Josef Och and Hermann Ney. 2003. A systematic comparison of various statistical alignment models. *Computational Linguistics*, 29(1):19–51.

Kishore Papineni, Salim Roukos, Todd Ward, and Wei-Jing Zhu. 2002. Bleu: a method for automatic evaluation of machine translation. In *Proceedings of the 40th Annual Meeting on Association for Computational Linguistics, Session: Machine translation and evaluation*, pages 311 – 318, Philadelphia, Pennsylvania. Publisher: Association for Computational Linguistics Morristown, NJ, USA.

Maja Popovic and Hermann Ney. 2006. Statistical machine translation with a small amount of bilingual training data. In *LREC-2006: Fifth International Conference on Language Resources and Evaluation. 5th SALTMIL Workshop on Minority Languages: Strategies for developing machine translation for minority languages*, pages 25–29, Genoa, Italy, May.

James Smith and Stephan Clark. 2009. Ebmt for smt: A new ebmt-smt hybrid. In Mikel L. Forcada and Andy Way, editors, *Proceedings of the 3rd Intyernational Workshop on Example-Based Machine Translation*, pages 3–10, Dublin, Ireland, November, 12-13.

Ralf Steinberger, Bruno Pouliquen, Anna Widiger, Camelia Ignat, Tomaz Erjavec, Dan Tufis, and Daniel Varga. 2006. The jrc-acquis: A multilingual aligned parallel corpus with 20+ languages. In *Proceedings of the 5th International Conference on Language Resources and Evaluation (LREC'2006)*, Genoa, Italy, May, 24-16.

Andreas Stolcke. 2002. Srilm - an extensible language modeling toolkit. In *Proc. Intl. Conf. Spoken Language Processing*, pages 901–904, Denver, Colorado, September.

Nicolas Stroppa, Declan Groves, Andy Way, and Kepa Sarasola. 2006. Example-based machine translation of the basque language. In *Proceedings of AMTA 2006 – 7th Conference of the Association for Machine Translation in the Americas*, pages 232–241, Cambridge, MA, USA., August.

Andy Way and Nano Gough. 2005. Comparing example-based and statistical machine translation. *Natural Language Engineering*, 11:295–309, September.

Question Parsing for QA in Spanish

Iria Gayo
University of Santiago de Compostela
iria.delrio@usc.es

Abstract

Question processing is a key step in Question Answering systems. For this task, it has been shown that a good syntactic analysis of questions helps to improve the results. However, general parsers seem to present some disadvantages in question analysis. We present a specific tool under development for Spanish question analysis in a QA context: SpQA. SpQA is a parser designed to deal with the special syntactic features of Spanish questions and to cover some needs of question analysis in QA systems such as target identification. The system has been evaluated together with three Spanish general parsers. In this comparative evaluation, SpQA shows the best results in Spanish question analysis.

1 Introduction

In Question Answering (QA) systems, question processing is a crucial step to obtain a right answer (Carvalho et al., 2010). For this reason, QA systems usually have a specific module that addresses question analysis (Vicedo, 2004). Question treatment can have different levels of complexity, but, in most cases, it entails a syntactic analysis. Furthermore, in this analysis, the correct processing of the interrogative constituent has a special relevance, taking into account that this element can play an important role in the definition of the question target. Correct syntactic analysis of questions constitutes, therefore, a key stage in QA systems process (Moldovan et al., 2002; Hermjakob, 2001): if we want a good processing of the question, a good syntactic analysis is a helpful starting point.

Consequently, in order to get a good syntactic analysis of questions, we need a tool for processing them correctly. For Spanish there are free general parsers that could carry out this task. However, this option presents some disadvantages as we will see in detail in section 2. In this paper we present a tool under development for Spanish question analysis in a QA context, SpQA (Spanish Parser for QA). SpQA is a parser focused on question analysis, designed to be used in the question processing module of a QA system. As a result, it is thought to deal with the special syntactic features of Spanish questions and to cover some needs of QA systems such as question target identification. The parser has been evaluated comparing its results with those presented for general Spanish parsers in Gayo (2011). As we will see in section 5, this comparative evaluation shows that, currently, SpQA gets the best results in syntactic analysis of questions.

The paper is structured as follows: in section 2 we show some data related to the performance of general parsers in question analysis. In section 3 we briefly present SpQA. Section 4 accounts for the evaluation method and section 5 shows the results of this evaluation. Finally, in section 6 we present some conclusions and future work.

2 Parsing Questions

To confront the task of question analysis, we could think to make use of available general parsers. However, this option carries some drawbacks.

It has been shown, at least for English, that parsing accuracies of general parsers drop significantly on out-of-domain data (Gildea, 2001; Mcclosky et al., 2006; Foster, 2010). This fact has also been shown, in particular, for question analysis in English (Petrov et al., 2010).

Unfortunately, for Spanish there are not such studies that compare general accuracies of available parsers with those obtained parsing questions. Therefore, in order to obtain this kind of data, we can use available studies that measure question parsing performance and comparing them with others that measure general performance.

Related with question parsing in Spanish, we have only the data of Gayo (2011). Gayo (2011) shows the accuracy in question analysis of three general Spanish parsers: DepPattern (Gamallo and Sánchez, 2009), Txala (Atserias et al., 2005) and Hispal (Bick, 2006). As we will see, this evaluation uses PARSEVAL metrics for two variables: constituent recognition and constituent labeling. These variables are applied to all consituents in the question and to the interrogative constituent in particular.

We can see the results of Gayo (2011) summarized in Table 1.

	Hispal	Txala	DepPatt.
All-Recognition	87.8	91.6	86.1
Int-Recognition	97.0	100.0	90.0
All-Labeling	68.2	71.3	51.1
Int-Labeling	52.5	62.0	25.0

Table 1: Evaluation of three Spanish parsers in question analysis Gayo (2011).

On the other hand, there are general evaluations only for two of the three parsers measured in Gayo (2011): Hispal (Bick, 2006) and Txala (Lloberes et al., 2010). Comparing these general results with those for questions showed in Table 1, we obtain the following data:[1]

	Txala	Hispal
G-Recognition	81.1/80.9	
Q-Recognition	91.6	87.8
Qint-Recognition	100.0	97.0
G-Labeling	73.9/74.3	95.3
Q-Labeling	71.3	68.2
Qint-Labeling	62.0	52.5

Table 2: Comparison of results in general (G) and question analysis (Q for all constituents; Qint for the interrogative contituent) of two Spanish parsers.

Because we do not have data for Hispal about general constituent recognition (see note 2), it is only possible to make an exhaustive comparison of both parsers concerning labeling. As we can see in Table 2, compared with general labeling (G-Labeling), accuracies of both parsers drop in tasks of question labelling (Q-Recognition and Qint-Recognition). This decrease is especially marked labeling the interrogative constituent (Qint-Labeling). However, the distance between accuracies in general and question analysis is considerably bigger in Hispal than in Txala. In fact, Txala only shows a remarkable drop labeling the interrogative constituent. We can conclude that Hispal seems to suffer considerably the change of domain, whereas Txala only shows some problems when it is confronted with one specific aspect of questions syntax: the role of the interrogative constituent.

3 SpQA

SpQA is a parser (under development) designed for Spanish question analysis in a QA context. Therefore, it is thought to be part of the question analysis module of QA systems. SpQA is a rule-based parser/transducer, wich is generated by means of the AGFL parser generator from an attribute grammar written in the AGFL formalism[2]. This grammar (with its lexicons and fact tables) is an extension of a general Spanish grammar for IR applications that is also under development, ASPIRA. The generated parser is a Top-Down Chart parser, using the Best-Only heuristic (Koster et al., 2007). It can perform constituent and dependency analysis (the latter by transduction).

The aim of the parser is to obtain as much linguistic information as possible from questions to facilitate the extraction of the right answer in a QA system. For this reason, we are interested in syntactic as well as semantic information, although, for the time being, the parser gets mostly syntactic information. Concerning the type of questions to analyze, we want to cover all types of Spanish direct interrogative structures (wh- and yes/no questions). At the current stage of development, the parser analyzes only wh- questions like:

¿Qué dibujó Leonardo Da Vinci en 1492?

(What did Leonardo Da Vinci draw in 1492?)

Given a question like this, SpQA

- recognizes and labels all the syntactic constituents in the sentence, showing the dependency relations between constituents
- identifies the syntactic and semantic target of the question (qt)

[1]In Lloberes et al. (2010), Txala was evaluated with two different corpora, so there are two different results. Unfortunately, Bick (2006) does not show general results for constituent identification (G-Recognition).

[2]http://www.agfl.cs.ru.nl/

- recognizes specific structures as dates, quantities and personal NP's

  [[PN[3]: Leonardo Da Vinci] <SUBJ [V:dibujar <**qtOBJ [ENTITY]** <DATEen 1492]]

  ([[PN: Leonardo Da Vinci] <SUBJ [V:draw <**qtOBJ [ENTITY]** <DATEin 1492]])

Currently, SpQA identifies six different semantic targets: PERSON, ENTITY, QUANT, TIME, PLACE, MANNER. To identify them, the parser uses the linguistic information encoded in the wh-words.

- PERSON: when the target is human.

  ¿Quién era el presidente de Francia durante las pruebas de armas nucleares en el Pacífico Sur?

  (Who was the president of France during the tests of nuclear weapons in the South Pacific?)

- ENTITY: when the target is no human.

  ¿Qué fue levantado el 13 de agosto de 1961?

  (What was built the 13th of August 1961?)

- QUANT: when the target is a quantity.

  ¿Cuántos goles se marcaron en total en el Mundial de Fútbol de 1982?

  (How many goals were scored in total in the World Cup of 1982?)

- TIME: when the target is related with time (a date, time, etc).

  ¿Cuándo se firmó el Tratado de Maastricht?

  (When was the Maastricht Treaty signed?)

- PLACE: when the target is a location.

  ¿Dónde se celebraron los JJ.OO. de 1992?

  (Where were celebrated the Olympic Games of 1992?)

- MANNER: when the target is a process, a description or an explanation.

  ¿Cómo actúa la hormona del crecimiento?

  (How does growth hormone work?)

When the question has a more complex interrogative constituent like

> ¿**Cuántos kilos de anchoas** *capturó la flota del Cantábrico durante 1994?*
>
> (How many kilos of anchovies did the fleet of the Cantabric fish in 1994?)

SpQA identifies the semantic target with the nucleus of the interrogative constituent:

> [[[[N: flota] <PREPde [PN: Cantábrico]] <DET la] <SUBJ [V:capturar <**qtOBJquant [[N: kilos] <PREPde [N: anchoas]]** <DATEdurante 1994]]
>
> ([[[[N: fleet] <PREPof [PN: Cantabric]] <DET the] <SUBJ [V:fish <**qtOBJquant [[N: kilos] <PREPof [N: anchovies]**] <DATEin 1994]])

4 Question Parsing Evaluation

We are interested in a comparative evaluation of SpQA against other Spanish general parsers. However, building the methodology and the necessary data for parsing evaluation is a very complex and hard task (especially if the parsers have different frameworks, like in our case). For this reason, for our evaluation we have used the same data and evaluation methodology of Gayo (2011), applying them to SpQA and comparing our results with those of Gayo (2011) for DepPattern, Txala and Hispal.

In this section, we present first the three Spanish parsers used for the comparative evaluation of SpQA: Txala, Hispal and DepPattern. Then, we explain in detail the comparative evaluation method taken from Gayo (2011).

4.1 Spanish Parsers for the Comparative Evaluation

TXALA is the Spanish parser in the suite *Freeling*[4] (Padró et al., 2010). It can be downloaded for free (as a part of *Freeling*) and it is also available on-line. It offers dependency parsing with functional labeling.

HISPAL is the Spanish parser of the VISL[5] project. It is only available for use on-line, but it allows the uploading of files for analysis with a maximum of 2 Mb. It performs constituent parsing with functional labeling in the Constraint Grammar framework.

DEPPATTERN is the Spanish parser in the suite *DepPattern Toolkit*[6] (Gamallo and Sánchez, 2009). It can be downloaded for free and it is also available on-line. It offers dependency parsing with functional labeling.

[3]PN = Proper Noun

[4]http://nlp.lsi.upc.edu/freeling/

[5]http://beta.visl.sdu.dk/

[6]http://gramatica.usc.es/pln/tools/deppattern.html

4.2 Evaluation Methodology

For the comparative evaluation of SpQA, we have used the parser evaluation methodology presented in Gayo (2011). We applied the metrics of PARSEVAL scheme (Black et al., 1991) to measure two variables in question analysis: constituent recognition and constituent labeling. For each variable, we measure

- **Precision**: number of correct constituents (constituents in the gold standard) in parser output divided by number of constituents in the parser output.
- **Recall**: number of correct constituents (constituents in the gold standard) in parser output divided by the number of constituents in the gold standard.
- **F1 score**.

We applied these two variables to constituents in general (all the constituents in the sentence) and to the interrogative constituent in particular (for the importance of this element in QA systems). To make possible the comparison of SpQA with the results showed in Gayo (2011), we also used the same testing corpus of questions and the same gold standard.

4.2.1 The Testing Corpus

The corpus is made up of 100 questions extracted from monolingual Spanish sets of CLEF[7] 2004, 2006 and 2007. All the examples in the testing corpus are wh- questions. Questions were selected from CLEF sets according to their syntactic structure. The idea was to choose questions that presented a variety of syntactic structures, like different interrogative constituents, subordinated clauses, dates or named entities.

4.2.2 The Gold Standard

The gold standard is made up of the 100 questions of the testing corpus analyzed manually by one person. The analysis consists of the identification of the main syntactic structure (constituents in the sentence): verb and arguments/adjuncts, labeled with their syntactic function.

¿Qué robaba el oso Yogui?
What did Yogi Bear steal?
3 constituents:
Verb: *robaba* (did...steal)
Interrogative Direct Object: *Qué* (what)
Subject: *el oso Yogui* (Yogi Bear)

To minimize possible differences between parsers caused by their different frameworks, some linguistic decisions were taken in the annotation. These decisions tried to simplify as much as possible the syntactic analysis. For example, we only consider six syntactic labels: subject (S), direct object (O), indirect object (IO), predicative (PR), adjunct (CC; bounded or unbounded) and modifier (MOD); we analyze the verbal phrase always as one constituent (even if it was a complex unit: *ha sido premiado*, has been awarded); we do not compute as constituents functional clitics as *lo* (direct object clitic) or *se* (impersonal clitic); etc.

4.3 Parsers Output Analysis

For Txala, Hispal and DepPattern we use directly the data of Gayo (2011). For SpQA, we analyzed the testing corpus with the parser and we extracted:

- Number of constituents recognized: total number of constituents in the parser output.
- Identification of constituents: number of correct and incorrect constituents (compared with the gold standard) in the parser output.
- Labeling: number of correct and incorrect labeled constituents (compared with the gold standard) in the parser output.

5 Results

We show first the results concerning question constituents in general. Then, the results related to the interrogative constituents in particular (identification and labeling for both).

5.1 Question Constituents

We can see the results of general constituent recognition in Table 4.

	Hispal	Txala	DepPatt.	SpQA
precision	86.9	89.9	88.8	91.2
recall	88.7	93.3	83.6	93.6
F-score	87.8	91.6	86.1	92.4

Table 3: Constituent recognition.

The four parsers have good results: around or over 90. SpQA has the best results, although they are very close to those of Txala.

[7] http://www.clef-campaign.org/

In general constituent labeling, we have the next results:

	Hispal	Txala	DepPatt.	SpQA
precision	72.5	73.9	56.1	94.5
recall	64.3	69.0	46.9	88.5
F-score	68.2	71.3	51.1	91.4

Table 4: Constituent labeling.

Again SpQA has the best results. However, for this variable there is a clear distance between SpQA and the other three parsers. Whereas the accuracies of Txala, Hispal and DepPattern drop significantly in this task (comparing their results with Table 4), SpQA maintains its performance (only the recall is a bit lower).

So, as we can see, SpQA shows very close results in general constituent recognition and labeling.

5.2 Interrogative Constituent

Table 5 shows the results for interrogative constituent recognition:

	Hispal	Txala	DepPatt.	SpQA
precision	96.1	100.0	90.0	99.0
recall	98.0	100.0	90.0	99.0
F-score	97.0	100.0	90.0	99.0

Table 5: Interrogative constituent recognition.

Again, the four parsers have good results, all over 90. Txala has the best accuracy, followed very closely by SpQA.

The reason that SpQA does not achieve an accuracy of 100 is simple: the parser fails in the recognition of one of the sentences as a question, due to structural syntactic reasons (the question has a syntactic order that is not in the grammar). As a consequence, with the current architecture of the system, this causes it to fail in the recognition of the interrogative constituent. However, the important thing to note is that the problem is not in the recognition of the interrogative and it can be easily solved.

Concerning labeling, these are the results:

We can see again a substantial difference in parser accuracies between recognition and labeling. Hispal, Txala and DepPattern especially, have worse results again, whereas SpQA keeps its accuracy.

	Hispal	Txala	DepPatt.	SpQA
precision	52.0	62.0	25.0	94.9
recall	53.0	62.0	25.0	94.0
F-score	52.5	62.0	25.0	94.5

Table 6: Interrogative constituent labeling.

The accuracy in interrogative constituent labeling is even lower than in general constituent labeling (Table 5) for Hispal, Txala and DepPattern. From accuracies around 70, Hispal and Txala drop to numbers around 50 and 60, respectively; DepPattern falls from 51 to 25.

On the other hand, SpQA still maintains its performance, and, contrary to the other two parsers, it has even better results labeling the interrogative constituent (94%) than in general labeling (91%).

6 Conclusions and Future Work

Question processing is a crucial step in QA systems. In this processing, syntactic analysis of questions plays an important role.

For this task, we have presented SpQA, a parser focused on question analysis in Spanish. Currently, the system recognizes and labels all the constituents in the question. In addition, it identifies the syntactic and semantic target of the questions, as well as dates, proper nouns and quantities.

Compared to three freely available Spanish parsers, Hispal, Txala and DepPattern, SpQA shows the best results in four tasks: recognition and labeling of general constituents and recognition and labeling of the interrogative constituent. Besides this, whereas Hispal, Txala and DepPattern show a considerable difference between their accuracies in constituent recognition and labeling (general and for the interrogative constituent), SpQA keeps its accuracy, which is always over 90.

Future work concerns syntax and semantics aspects of SpQA. First, we have to make the grammar more complete to cover all possible syntactic structures of Spanish questions. Then, it will be necessary to concentrate on semantic aspects of questions, especially on the aspects related to target identification.

References

Jordi Atserias, Elisabet Comelles, and Aingeru Mayor. 2005. Txala un analizador libre de dependencias para el castellano. *Procesamiento del Lenguaje Natural*, (35):455–456, September.

Eckhard Bick. 2006. A Constraint Grammar-based Parser for Spanish. In *Proceedings of TIL 2006 - 4th Workshop on Information and Human Language Technology*.

Ezra Black, Steven P. Abney, D. Flickenger, Claudia Gdaniec, Ralph Grishman, P. Harrison, Donald Hindle, Robert Ingria, Frederick Jelinek, Judith L. Klavans, Mark Liberman, Mitchell P. Marcus, Salim Roukos, Beatrice Santorini, and Tomek Strzalkowski. 1991. A Procedure for Quantitatively Comparing the Syntactic Coverage of English Grammars. In *North American Chapter of the Association for Computational Linguistics*.

Gracinda Carvalho, David Martins de Matos, and Vitor Rocio. 2010. Improving IdSay: A Characterization of Strengths and Weaknesses in Question Answering Systems for Portuguese. In Thiago Alexandre Salgueiro Pardo, António Branco, Aldebaro Klautau, Renata Vieira, and Vera Lúcia Strube de Lima, editors, *PROPOR*, volume 6001 of *Lecture Notes in Computer Science*, pages 1–10. Springer.

Jennifer Foster. 2010. "cba to check the spelling" Investigating Parser Performance on Discussion Forum Posts. In *Human Language Technologies: The 2010 Annual Conference of the North American Chapter of the Association for Computational Linguistics*, HLT '10, pages 381–384, Stroudsburg, PA, USA. Association for Computational Linguistics.

Pablo Gamallo and Isaac González. 2009. Una gramática de dependencias basada en patrones de etiquetas. *Procesamiento del Lenguaje Natural*, (43):315–323.

Iria Gayo. 2011. Análisis de preguntas para Búsqueda de Respuestas: evaluación de tres parsers del español (Question Analysis for QA: Evaluation of three Spanish Parsers). In *Proceedings of SEPLN'11 (to appear)*.

Daniel Gildea. 2001. Corpus Variation and Parser Performance. In Lillian Lee and Donna Harman, editors, *Proceedings of the 2001 Conference on Empirical Methods in Natural Language Processing*, pages 167–202.

Ulf Hermjakob. 2001. Parsing and Question Classification for Question Answering. In *Proceedings of the workshop on Open-domain question answering - Volume 12*, ODQA '01, pages 1–6, Stroudsburg, PA, USA. Association for Computational Linguistics.

Cornelis H. A. Koster, Marc Seutter, and Olaf Seibert. 2007. Parsing the Medline Corpus. In *Proceedings RANLP 2007*, pages 325–329.

Marina Lloberes, Irene Castellón, and Lluís Padró. 2010. Spanish FreeLing Dependency Grammar. In Nicoletta Calzolari (Conference Chair), Khalid Choukri, Bente Maegaard, Joseph Mariani, Jan Odijk, Stelios Piperidis, Mike Rosner, and Daniel Tapias, editors, *Proceedings of the Seventh conference on International Language Resources and Evaluation (LREC'10)*, Valletta, Malta, may. European Language Resources Association (ELRA).

David Mcclosky, Eugene Charniak, and Mark Johnson. 2006. Reranking and Self-training for Parser Adaptation. *ACL-COLING*.

D. Moldovan, S. Harabagiu, R. Girju, P. Morarescu, F. Lacatusu, A. Novischi, A. Badulescu, and O. Bolohan. 2002. Lcc Tools for Question Answering. In Voorhees and Buckland, editors, *Proceedings of the 11th Text REtrieval Conference (TREC-2002)*, NIST, Gaithersburg.

Lluís Padró, Miquel Collado, Samuel Reese, Marina Lloberes, and Irene Castellón. 2010. Freeling 2.1: Five Years of Open-source Language Processing Tools. In Nicoletta Calzolari (Conference Chair), Khalid Choukri, Bente Maegaard, Joseph Mariani, Jan Odijk, Stelios Piperidis, Mike Rosner, and Daniel Tapias, editors, *Proceedings of the Seventh conference on International Language Resources and Evaluation (LREC'10)*, Valletta, Malta, may. European Language Resources Association (ELRA).

Slav Petrov, Pi-Chuan Chang, Michael Ringgaard, and Hiyan Alshawi. 2010. Uptraining for Accurate Deterministic Question Parsing. In *Proceedings of the 2010 Conference on Empirical Methods in Natural Language Processing*, pages 705–713, Cambridge, MA, October. Association for Computational Linguistics.

José Luis Vicedo. 2004. La búsqueda de respuestas: Estado actual y perspectivas de futuro. *Inteligencia Artificial, Revista Iberoamericana de Inteligencia Artificial*, 8(22):37–56.

Incremental Semantics Driven Natural Language Generation With Self-Repairing Capability

Julian Hough
Interaction, Media and Communication Research Group,
School of Electronic Engineering and Computer Science,
Queen Mary University of London
julian.hough@eecs.qmul.ac.uk

Abstract

This paper presents the on-going development of a model of incremental semantics driven natural language generation (NLG) for incremental dialogue systems. The approach is novel in its tight integration of incremental goal-driven semantics and syntactic construction, utilizing Type Theory with Records (TTR) record types for goal concepts as its input and the grammar formalism Dynamic Syntax (DS) for a word-by-word tactical generation procedure. The characterization of generation in terms of semantic input and word output graphs allows an integration into the incremental dialogue system Jindigo and facilitates the generation of human-like self-repairs in a semantically and syntactically motivated way.

1 Introduction

Recently, the arrival of incremental frameworks such as that described by Schlangen and Skantze (2011) has reignited the challenges for dialogue systems. Their implementation has recently shown success in micro-domains (Skantze and Schlangen, 2009) and has included some incremental natural language generation (NLG) capabilities which have been shown to be favored by users over non-incremental counterparts (Skantze and Hjalmarsson, 2010). However, this new brand of system has not taken account of incremental semantic processing on a word-by-word level in generation, which is the nature of the model for NLG described here.

The consequences of taking a fine-grained incremental semantics approach for NLG include the possibility of closer integration with parsing, and the incorporation of *self-repair* in a natural and context-sensitive way. Integrating self-repair into generation in the way described here should be beneficial for incremental dialogue systems with fragmentary and changing inputs to generation, and could also give some insights for modeling speech production.

1.1 Related Work

Traditionally, incremental generation has been motivated by developing autonomous processing models of human speech production. In particular, Kempen and Hoenkamp (1987) and Levelt (1989)'s functional decomposition of distinct *conceptualization*, *formulation* and *articulation* phases provided a psycholinguistic model which continues to have an influence on NLG. Motivated by modeling memory limitation, the principle of incrementality was generally taken that the syntactic formulator was able to begin its processing without complete input from the conceptualizer- in grammatical terms, tree formation could be both lexically and conceptually guided- see e.g. De Smedt (1990).

Guhe (2007) modeled an incremental conceptualizer which generated pre-verbal messages in a piece-meal fashion. While formulation was not the focus, the benefit of incremental semantic construction was clear: the conceptualizer's incremental modification of pre-verbal messages could influence downstream tactical generation decisions, particularly with 'correction' increments causing self-repairs.

Albeit less psychologically motivated, Skantze and Hjalmarsson (2010) provide a similar approach to Guhe in implementing incremental speech generation in a dialogue system. Generation input is defined as canned-text *speech plans* sent from the dialogue manager divided up into word-length *speech units*. Incremental generation is invoked to allow speech plans to change dynamically during interaction with a user: a simple string-based comparison of the incoming plan with the current one being vocalized allows both *covert* and *overt* self-repairs to be generated depending on the number of units in the plan realized at the point of difference detection.

This paper describes a new model for incremental generation that incorporates word-by-word semantic construction and self-repairing capability, going beyond string-based plan corrections and strict delineation of conceptualization and surface realization. The model is also portable into incremental dialogue systems.

2 Background

2.1 Dynamic Syntax (DS)

Dynamic Syntax (DS, Kempson et al., 2001) is an action-based and semantically oriented incremental grammar that defines grammaticality as parsability. The DS lexicon consists of *lexical actions* keyed to words, and also a set of globally applicable *computational actions*, both of which constitute packages of monotonic update operations on semantic trees and take the form of IF-THEN action-like structures such as (1).

(1)
john:
IF $?Ty(e)$
THEN $\mathtt{put}(Ty(e))$
$\mathtt{put}(fo(john'))$
ELSE $\mathtt{abort}$

(2)
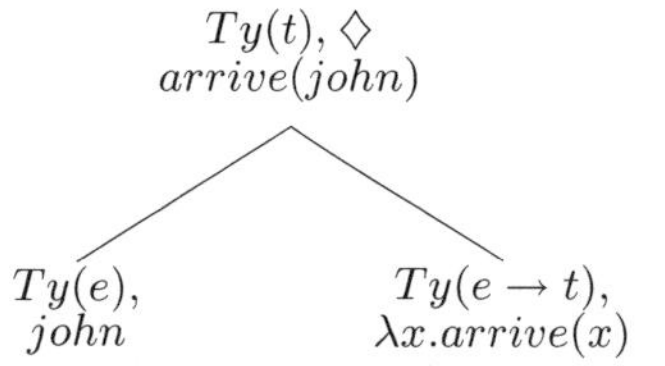

In DS parsing, if the pointer object ($\diamond$) currently satisfies the precondition of an action, (e.g. is at a node of type $?Ty(e)$), then simple monotonic tree update operations of the tree logic LOFT (Blackburn and Meyer-Viol, 1994) are licensed. The trees represent terms in the typed lambda calculus, with mother-daughter node relations corresponding to semantic predicate-argument structure with no independent layer of syntax- see (2). Parsing begins with an axiom tree with a single node of requirement type $?Ty(t)$, and intersperses testing and application of lexical actions triggered by input words and execution of permissible (Kleene* iterated) sequences of computational actions.

Successful parses are sequences of applications of actions that lead to a tree which is complete (i.e. has no type requirements $?Ty(..)$ on any node, and has type $Ty(t)$ at its root node as in (2)) with a compiled formula. Incomplete *partial* structures are also maintained in the parse state as words are scanned in the input.

2.2 DS Generation as Parsing

As Purver and Kempson (2004) demonstrate, a tactical model of DS generation can be neatly defined in terms of the DS parsing process and a *subsumption check* against a *goal tree*. Goal trees are complete and fully specified DS trees such as (2), and generation consists of attempting to parse each word in the lexicon given the trees under construction, followed by a check to remove trees which do not subsume the goal tree from the parse state. Due to the stage-by-stage iteration through the lexicon, the DS generation process effectively combines lexical selection and linearization into a single action. Also, while no formal model of self-repair has hitherto been proposed in DS, self-monitoring is inherently part of the generation process, as each word generated is parsed.

2.3 Jindigo and the DyLan Interpreter

Jindigo (Skantze and Hjalmarsson, 2010) is a Java-implemented dialogue system following the abstract framework described by Schlangen and Skantze (2011). Its system is a network of modules, each consisting of a *left buffer* for input increments, a *processor* and a *right buffer* for the output increments. It is the *adding*, *commitment* and *revoking* of *incremental units* (IUs) in a module's right buffer and the effect of doing so on another module's left buffer that determines system behaviour, and the IUs can have *groundedIn* relations between one another if it is desirable that they should be in some way inter-dependent. The buffers are defined graphically, with vertices and edges representing IUs, allowing for multiple hypotheses in speech recognition and, as mentioned, revision of canned-text speech plans in generation (Skantze and Hjalmarsson, 2010).

There is an implementation of a DS parser in Jindigo in the `DyLan` interpreter module (Purver et al., 2011), where a parse state is characterized as a Directed Acyclic Graph (DAG), following Sato (2011), with DS *actions* for edges and *trees* for nodes. The characterization allows an exploitation of Jindigo's graph-based buffers, particularly the interface with word graphs sent from a voice recognition (ASR) module: `DyLan` incrementally attempts to parse word hypothesis edges as they become available, and parse paths in the DAG are *groundedIn* the corresponding word edges of the ASR graph- see figure 1.

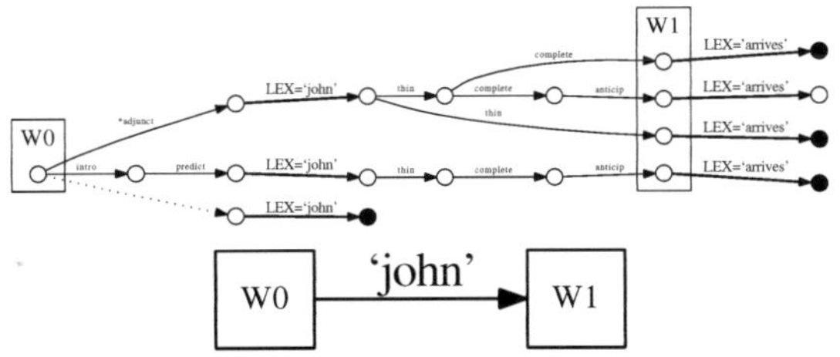

Figure 1: DS parsing process as a DAG, *groundedIn* corresponding word graph hypothesis edge 'john' spanning vertices W0 and W1

The application of a computational or lexical action can be seen as a labeled left-right transition edge between the trees under construction, which are represented by circular white nodes in the graph. Parts of the parse DAG are *groundedIn* the edge labelled with the word whose parse process they represent.

The other addition to DS in `DyLan` is the incorporation of Type Theory with Records (TTR) (Cooper, 2005), which can seen in (3). TTR *record types* decorate the nodes of the tree as opposed to simple atomic formulae, with each *field* in the record type containing a variable name, a value (after the =), which can be null for *unmanifest* fields, and a type (after the colon) which represents the node type of the DS tree at which its potential formula value is situated- basic types e and t are used here for clarity.

(3) *"John arrived"* $\longmapsto$

$$\Diamond, Ty(t), \left[\begin{array}{ll} x =_{john} & : e \\ p =_{arrive(x)} & : t \end{array}\right]$$

$$Ty(e), \quad [\ x =_{john} \ : e\ ]$$

$$Ty(e \rightarrow t), \quad \lambda r : [\ x1 \ : e\ ] \left[\begin{array}{ll} x =_{r.x1} & : e \\ p =_{arrive(x)} & : t \end{array}\right]$$

The TTR adaptation is made to provide representations that can interface with domain conceptual structures in the rest of the dialogue system. `DyLan` automatically compiles a record type at the root node of a complete tree and checks this against system domain concepts.

3 Incremental Semantics Driven NLG

3.1 Goal Concepts and Incremental TTR Construction

To achieve thorough-going incrementality in terms of semantic content, the model proposed here modifies the DS generation procedure described in (Purver and Kempson, 2004) in two principal ways. Firstly, a TTR record type is compiled after each word candidate is parsed, giving maximal TTR representations for *partial trees* in addition to complete ones. Implementationally, this is achieved by a simple two-stage algorithm of firstly decorating nodes lacking formulae with record types containing the appropriate types- e.g. $[p =_{U(x)}: t]$ for a $Ty(e \rightarrow t)$ node, $[p =_{U(x,y)}: t]$ for a $Ty(e \rightarrow (e \rightarrow t))$ node etc.[1] Secondly, the functional application from the record types of the functor nodes to the record types of their sister argument nodes is carried out, compiling a β-reduced record type at their mother node. The ordering of the applications is achieved through an iterative search for functor nodes with uncompiled mother nodes, halting upon compilation of a formula at the root node.

The second principal modification is the replacement of a goal tree with a *goal concept* represented by a TTR record type. Consequently, tree subsumption checking is replaced by a *semantic pruning* stage, whereby parse paths that do not compile a valid *supertype* of the goal TTR record type are abandoned. The supertype check involves a recursive mapping of the fields of the candidate record type under inspection to the goal subtype, with testing for type consistency, arity of predicates, and position of arguments[2].

An example of a successful generation path is shown in figure 2, where the incremental generation of "john arrives" succeeds as successful lexical action applications are interspersed with applicable computational action sequences (e.g. transitions $\boxed{0} \mapsto \boxed{1}$ and $\boxed{2} \mapsto \boxed{3}$), at each stage passing the supertype relation check against the goal, until arriving at a tree that *type matches* in $\boxed{4}$.

[1]Technically, these functor node record types should be functions from record type to record type, as can be seen on the $Ty(e \rightarrow t)$ node in figure 3, for simplicity they are not fully represented in the discussion from here on but as simple record types with metavariable arguments.

[2]The fields with the underspecified value U are mapped successfully if they pass this type-checking stage, as they have underspecified semantics.

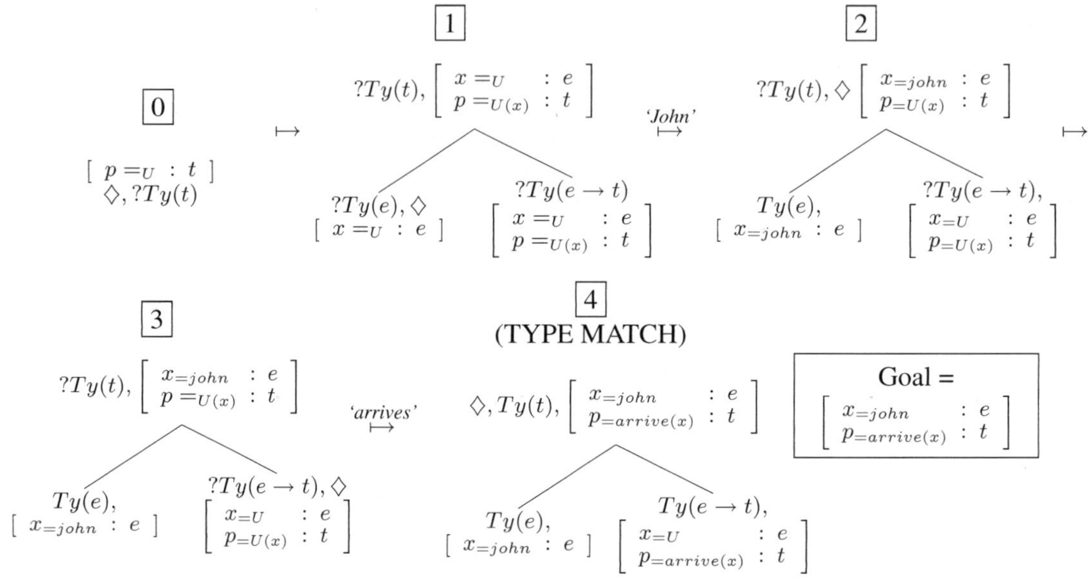

Figure 2: Successful generation path in DS-TTR

3.2 Implementation In Jindigo

The proposed DS-TTR generator has been implemented in Jindigo as a prototype module, not only facilitating tight integration with the DS parsing module `DyLan`, but also allowing dynamically changing inputs to generation and revisions of word selection.

In our module, incremental units (IUs) in the left buffer are defined as goal concept TTR record types (as in the Goal in figure 2), encoded in a simple XML attribute-value structure and posted by the dialogue manager. Our module's other input IUs are DS *parse state edges* from the `DyLan` parsing module which are used to update the module's current parse state during generation. Output IUs in the right buffer are *word edges* in a word graph made available to the speech synthesizer module, and *parse state edges* available to `DyLan's` left buffer[3]. Word edges in the word graph are *groundedIn* their corresponding parse state edge IUs, the same way as shown for parsing in figure 1.

Schematically, the procedure for word-by-word generation is as follows: At a state vertex S_n in the parse state edge graph, given latest committed parse state edge SE_{n-1} (or null edge if S_n is initial), current goal concept G and latest word graph vertex W_n:

1. **Syntactic Parse**: For each path-final tree in SE_{n-1}, attempt to apply all lexical actions Σl_k keyed by words Σw_k in the lexicon[4]. Apply all possible sequences of computational actions to the new trees. For each successful parse i `add` a hypothesis parse state edge SE_n^i to the parse state graph and `add` corresponding word edge WE_n^i to the word graph, making it *groundedIn* SE_n^i.
2. **Semantic Prune**: For each edge SE_n^i calculate maximal TTR representation T_n^i, and `revoke` SE_n^i from output buffer if T_n^i is not a valid supertype of G.
3. **Repair** IF all edges ΣSE_n are revoked, `repair`[5]: return to vertex S_{n-1} and repeat step (1) for *committed* edge SE_{n-2} that SE_{n-1} is *groundedIn* ELSE Continue.
4. **Update output buffer**: `commit` all remaining edges ΣSE_n. For each word edge candidate WE_n^i in the output buffer word graph, `commit` if *groundedIn* committed parse state edge SE_n^i.
5. **Halt**: If for some i, T_n^i and G are *type matched.*

4 Self-Repairing Capability

Due to Jindigo's constantly updating system threads, a goal concept may be revised shortly

[3]While not being fully addressed here, it is worth noting that our generation module and `DyLan` both maintain the same parse state edge graph in their output buffers, effecting an interleaving of the two modules.

[4]Work towards addressing the computational cost of testing each lexical action in the lexicon is currently being worked on.

[5]Optional commitment of interregnum filler such as "uhh", dependent on generation time taken.

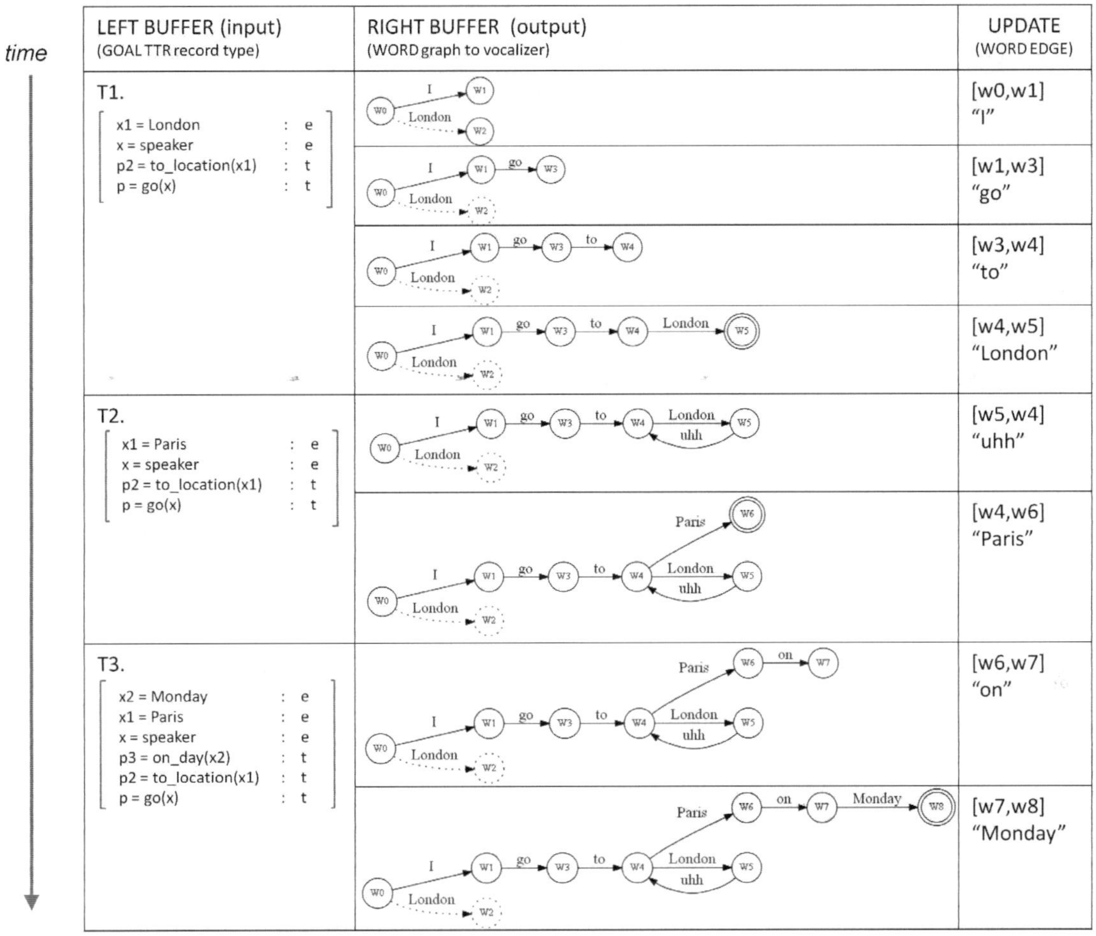

Figure 3: Incremental DS-TTR generation of a repair at time point T2 and extension at T3. Type-matched paths are double-circled nodes and uncommitted nodes and edges are dotted

after, or even during, the generation process, so trouble in generation may be encountered. Our `repair` function explained above operates if there is an empty state, or no possible DAG extension, after the semantic pruning stage of generation (resulting in no candidate succeeding word edge) by restarting the generation procedure from the last committed parse state edge. It continues backtracking by one vertex at a time in an attempt to extend the DS DAG until successful.

Our protocol is consistent with Shriberg and Stolcke (1998)'s empirical observation that the probability of retracing N words back in an utterance is more likely than retracing from N+1 words back, making the repair as local as possible. Utterances such as "I want to go, uhh, leave from Paris" are processed on a semantic level, as the repair is integrated with the semantics of the part of the utterance before the repair point to maximize re-use of existing semantic structure.

A subset of self-repairs, *extensions*, where the repair effects an "after-thought", usually in a transition place in a dialogue turn, are dealt with straight-forwardly in our system. The DS parser treats these as monotonic growth of the matrix tree through LINK adjunction (Kempson et al., 2001), resulting in subtype extension of the root TTR record type. Thus, a change in goal concept during generation will not always put demands on the system to backtrack, such as in the case of generating the fragment after the pause in "I go to Paris ...from London". It is only a semantics/syntax mismatch, where the revised goal TTR record type does not correspond to a permissible extension of a DS tree in the DAG, where overt repair will occur (for a comparison see figure 3).

In contrast to Skantze and Hjalmarsson (2010)'s string-based *speech plan* comparison approach, there is no need to regenerate a fully-formed string from a revised goal concept and compare it with the string generated thus far to characterize self-repair. Instead, repair here is driven by attempting to extend existing parse paths to construct the new target record type, backtracking through the parse state in an attempt to find suitable departure points for restarting generation, *retaining* the semantic representation already built up during the DS-TTR generation process.

5 Conclusion and Future Work

A prototype NLG module has been described that utilizes incremental semantic construction of TTR record types constrained by incremental Dynamic Syntax tree extension and TTR supertype relation checking to generate on a word-by-word basis. Although yet to undergo thorough evaluation, the system is capable of generating test-set self-repairs given manually induced goal TTR record type changes in the input buffer. The coming evaluation will not only involve a computational analysis, but an interactional one, involving human judges and experimental measures along the lines proposed by Schlangen (2009).

In terms of future development, the conceptual and phonological levels of the model could be expanded upon to get even finer granularity and consequently allow more natural system responses. A possible immediate extension could be the incorporation of a TTR subtyping process in the construction of goal concepts during generation by the dialogue manager, so as to incorporate incrementality into the conceptualization process (Guhe, 2007) as well as in surface realization.

Acknowledgments

Thanks go to my supervisor Matthew Purver and the RANLP reviewers for their helpful comments.

References

Patrick Blackburn and Wilfried Meyer-Viol. 1994. Linguistics, logic and finite trees. *Logic Journal of the Interest Group of Pure and Applied Logics*, 2(1):3–29.

Robin Cooper. 2005. Records and record types in semantic theory. *Journal of Logic and Computation*, 15(2):99–112.

Koenraad De Smedt. 1990. IPF: An incremental parallel formulator. In *Current research in natural language generation*, pages 167–192. Academic Press, London.

Markus Guhe. 2007. *Incremental Conceptualization for Language Production*. NJ: Lawrence Erlbaum Associates.

Gerard Kempen and Edward Hoenkamp. 1987. An incremental procedural grammar for sentence formulation. *Cognitive Science*, 11(2):201–258.

Ruth Kempson, Wilfried Meyer-Viol, and Dov Gabbay. 2001. *Dynamic Syntax: The Flow of Language Understanding*. Blackwell.

W.J.M. Levelt. 1989. *Speaking: From intention to articulation*. Mit Pr.

Matthew Purver and Ruth Kempson. 2004. Incremental context-based generation for dialogue. In A. Belz, R. Evans, and P. Piwek, editors, *Proceedings of the 3rd International Conference on Natural Language Generation (INLG04)*, number 3123 in Lecture Notes in Artifical Intelligence, pages 151–160, Brockenhurst, UK, July. Springer.

Matthew Purver, Arash Eshghi, and Julian Hough. 2011. Incremental semantic construction in a dialogue system. In J. Bos and S. Pulman, editors, *Proceedings of the 9th International Conference on Computational Semantics*, pages 365–369, Oxford, UK, January.

Yo Sato. 2011. Local ambiguity, search strategies and parsing in Dynamic Syntax. In E. Gregoromichelaki, R. Kempson, and C. Howes, editors, *The Dynamics of Lexical Interfaces*, pages 205–233. CSLI.

David Schlangen and Gabriel Skantze. 2011. A general, abstract model of incremental dialogue processing. *Dialogue and Discourse*, 2(1):83–111.

David Schlangen. 2009. What we can learn from dialogue systems that dont work. In *Proceedings of DiaHolmia (Semdial 2009*, pages 51–58.

Elizabeth Shriberg and Andreas Stolcke. 1998. How far do speakers back up in repairs? A quantitative model. In *Proceedings of the International Conference on Spoken Language Processing*, pages 2183–2186.

Gabriel Skantze and Anna Hjalmarsson. 2010. Towards incremental speech generation in dialogue systems. In *Proceedings of the SIGDIAL 2010 Conference*, pages 1–8, Tokyo, Japan, September. Association for Computational Linguistics.

Gabriel Skantze and David Schlangen. 2009. Incremental dialogue processing in a micro-domain. In *Proceedings of the 12th Conference of the European Chapter of the ACL (EACL 2009)*, pages 745–753, Athens, Greece, March. Association for Computational Linguistics.

Initial Experiments with Multilingual Extraction of Rhetoric Figures by means of PERL-compatible Regular Expressions

Daniel Devatman Hromada
Lutin Userlab – ChART – Paris 8 – EPHE - Slovak Technical University
hromi@kyberia.sk

Abstract

A language-independent method of figure-of-speech extraction is proposed in order to reinforce rhetoric-oriented considerations in natural language processing studies. The method is based upon a translation of a canonical form of repetition-based figures of speech into the language of PERL-compatible regular expressions. Anadiplosis, anaphora, antimetabole figures were translated into the form exploiting the back-reference properties of PERL-compatible regular expression while epiphora was translated into a formula exploiting recursive properties of this very concise artificial language. These four figures alone matched more than 7000 strings when applied on dramatic and poetic corpora written in English, French, German and Latin. Possible usages varying from stylometric evaluation of translation quality of poetic works to more complex problem of semi-supervised figure of speech induction are briefly discussed.

1 Introduction

During middle ages and before, the discipline of rhetoric composed - along with grammar and logic - a basic component of so-called trivium. Being considered by Platon as the "one single art that governs all speaking" (Plato, trans. 1986) in order to be subsequently defined by Aristotle as "the faculty of observing in any given case the available means of persuasion" (Aristotle, trans. 1954), the basic postulates of rhetoric are still kept alive by those being active in domains as diverse as politics, law, poetry, literary theory (Dubois, 1970) or humanities in general (Perelman & Olbrechts-Tyteca, 1969)

When it comes to more "exact" scientific disciplines like that of informatics or linguistics , rhetoric seems to be somewhat ignored - definitely more than its "grammar" and "logic" trivium counterparts. While contemporary rhetoric disposes with a strong theoretical background - whether in the form of the Rhetorical Structure Theory (Taboada, Mann, & Back, 2006), "computational rhetoric" (Grasso, 2002) or computational models of natural argument (Crosswhite & Fox, 2003); a more practically-oriented engineer has to nonetheless agree with the statement that "the ancient study of persuasion remain understudied and underrepresented in current Natural Language systems" (Harris & DiMarco, 2009) .

The aim of this article is to reduce this "under-representation" gap and in a certain sense augment the momentum of the computational rhetoric not by proposing a complex model of argumentation, but by proposing a simple yet efficient and language-independent method for extraction of certain rhetoric figures (RF) from textual corpora.

RFs, also called "figures of speech", are one of the basic means of persuasion which an orator has to his disposition. Traditionally, they are divided into two categories : tropes - related to deeper, i.e. semantic features of the phrasal constituents under consideration; and schemes - related to layers closer to actual material expression of the proposition, i.e. to the morphology, phonology or prosody of the generated utterance.

The method proposed within this article shall deal only with reduced subset of the latter - that is, with detection of rhetoric schemes anadiplosis, anaphora, antimetabole and epiphora which are based on a repetition or reordering of a given word, phrase or morpheme across multiple subsequent clauses. While such a stylometric approach was currently implemented with encouraging results by (Gawryjolek, 2009), his system is operational only when combined with probabilistic context-free grammar parser adapted to English language, and hence dysfunctional when applied upon languages for which such a parser does not exist.

In the following paragraphs of this article we shall present a system of rhetoric figure extraction which tends to be language-independent, i.e. applicable upon a textual corpus written in any language. Ideally, no antecedent knowledge about the grammar of a language is necessary for successful extraction by means of our method, the 1) prescriptive form of the figure-to-be-extracted and 2) the symbol representing phrase and/or clause boundaries is the only information necessary.

More concretely, our proposal is based on a fairly simple translation of a canonical form of a rhetoric figure under question into a computer language, namely into the language of PERL-compatible regular expressions (PCREs). PCREs are, in their essence, simply strings of characters which describe the sets of other strings of characters, i.e. they are a matching form, a template, for many concrete character strings. As many other regular expressions engines, PCREs make this possible by reserving special symbols - "the metacharacters" - for quantifiers and classes. But in addition to these features common to many finite state automata, PCREs offer much more (Wall & Loukides, 2000). These are the reasons why we consider the PCREs to be appealing candidates for a translation of rhetorical figures into a computer-readable symbolic form:

- by implementing "back references" (Friedl, 2006) , PCREs make it possible to refer to *that which was already matched,* hence allowing to construct automata able to match repetitive forms
- by implementing (from PERL version 5.10 on) "recursive matching", PCREs make it possible to match very complex patterns without a need to have recourse to other means, external to PCREs
- since the language of PCREs is very concise, the resulting PCRE describing a rhetorical figure under question is usually a string of few dozens of characters which could be eventually constructed not by means of human intervention, as was the case in this article, but by means of unsupervised genetic programming (Koza, 1992) or other means of grammar induction engine (Solan, Horn, Ruppin, & Edelman, 2005)

Element	Meaning
W	word
...	arbitrary intervening material
< ... >	phrase or clause boundaries
Subscripts	identity (same subscripts), nonidentity (different subscripts)

Table 1: part of RF-representation Formalism (RFRF)

2 Method

2.1 PERL-Compatible Rhetoric Figures

Four figures were chosen - namely anadiplosis, anaphora, epiphora and antimetabole – in order to demonstrate the feasibility of the "rhetoric stylometry" approach. We have adopted the Rhetoric Figure Representation Formalism (RFRF) - initially concieved by (Harris & DiMarco, 2009) - and reduced it in order to describe only the four figures of interest. Basic symbols of RFRF and their associated meanings are presented in Table 1.

Since the goal of this article is primarily didactic, i.e. we shall start this *exposé* with very simple anadiplosis involving just one back-reference, and end up our proposal with somewhat more complex recursive PCRE matching epiphorae containing arbitrary number of constituents.

2.1.1 Anadiplosis

Anadiplosis occurs when a clause or phrase starts with the word or phrase that ended the preceding unit. It is formalized by RFRF as :

$$< \ldots \mathbf{W}_x >< \mathbf{W}_x \ldots >$$

We have translated this representation into this PERL-Compatible Rhetoric Figure (PCRF):

/((\w{3,})[.?!,] \2)/sig

The repetition-matching faculty is assured by a backreference to an initial n-gram composed of at least three word characters. Therefore, this PCRE makes it possible to match utterances like the one in Cicero's *De Oratore* :

Sed genus hoc totum orationis in eis causis excellit, in quibus minus potest inflammari animus iudicis acri et vehementi quadam incitatione; non enim semper fortis oratio quaeritur, sed saepe placida, summissa, lenis, quae maxime commendat ***reos. Reos*** *autem appello non eos modo, qui arguuntur, sed omnis, quorum de re disceptatur; sic enim olim loquebantur.*[1]

This is the simplest possible anadiplosis figure since it matches only string with two occurences of a repeated word. Therefore we label this figure as **anadiplosis{2}**.

2.1.2 Anaphora

Anaphora is a rhetoric figure based upon a repetition of a word or a sequence of words at the beginnings of neighboring clauses. It is formalized by RFRF as :

$$< \mathbf{W_x} \ldots >< \mathbf{W_x} \ldots >$$

We have translated this representation into the following PCRE form:

```
/[.?!;,] (([A-Z]\w+) [^.?!;,]+[.?!;] \2 [^.?!;,]
+[.?!;,] (\2 [^.?!;,]+[.?!;,])*)/sig
```

As all RFs presented in this article, this anaphora is also based on back-reference matching. In contrast with anadiplosis where dependency was of very *short-distance* nature, in case of anaphora, the second occurrence of the word can be dozens of characters distant from the initial occurrence. What's more, this RF takes into account possible third repetition of a W_x which makes it possible to match utterances like Cicero's:

Quid *autem subtilius quam crebrae acutaeque sententiae?* ***Quid*** *admirabilius quam res splendore inlustrata verborum?* ***Quid*** *plenius quam omni genere rerum cumulata oratio?*[2]

Since this PCRFs allows us to match anaphorae with two or three occurences of a repeated word, it is seems to be appropriate to label it as **anaphora{2,3}**.

2.1.3 Antimetabole

Antimetabole is a rhetoric figure which occurs when words are repeated in successive clauses in reversed order. In terms of RFRF, one can formalize it as follows:

$$<\mathbf{W_A\, W_B\, W_c \ldots W_C\, W_B\, W_A}>$$

We have translated this representation into following PCRE form:

```
/((\w{3,}) (.{0,23}) (\w{3,})[^\.!?]{0,23} \4 \3 \
2)/sig
```

Differently from previous examples when there was only one element matched and back-referenced, three elements - A, B, C- are determined in initial phases of matching this chiasmatic antimetabole. Subsequently, the order of A & C is switched while B is considered to be identic intervening material intervening between A and C and C and A. Since possible occurrence of other material intervening between ABC and CBA (i.e. ABCxCBA) is also taken into account, this PCRF has successfully matched expressions like:

Alle wie **einer**, **einer** wie **alle.**[3]

2.1.4 Epiphora

Epiphora or epistrophe is a RF defined as "ending a series of phrases or clauses with the same word or words". It is formalized by RFRF as:

$$< \ldots \mathbf{W_x} >< \ldots \mathbf{W_x}>$$

We have translated this representation into following PCRE form:

```
/([A-Z][^\.\?!;]+ (\w{2,}+)([\.\?!;] ?[A-Za-z]
[^\.\?!;]+ (?:\2|(?-1))*)\2[\.\?!;])/sig
```

In contrast with anaphora{2,3} figure presented in 2.1.2, the epiphora figure hereby proposed exploits the "recursive matching" properties of latest versions of PCRE (Perl 5.10+) engines. In other words, the expression *(?:\2|(?-1))* match any number of subsequent phrases or clauses which end with W_x and not just three, as was the case in case of epiphora. Hence, a quadruple epiphora :

---

[1] *"For vigorous language is not always wanted, but often such as is calm, gentle, mild: this is the kind that most commands the* ***parties****. By '* ***parties*** *' I mean not only persons impeached, but all whose interests are being determined, for that was how people used the term in the old days. "*

[2] *"* ***Is there something*** *more subtle than a rapid succession of pointed reflections?* ***Is there something*** *more wonderful than the heating-up of a topic by verbal brilliance,* ***something*** *richer than a discourse cumulating material of every sort? "*

[3] *" All as one, one as all. "*

*Je te dis toujou la même **chose**, parce que c'est toujou la même **chose**, et si ce n'était pas toujours la même **chose**, je ne te dirais pas toujou la même **chose**.*[4]

was detected by this recursive PCRF when it was applied upon corpus of Molière's works.

Since the recursive matching allows us to create a sort of "greedy" epiphora, we propose to label it as **epiphora{2,}** in possible future taxonomy of PCRFs.

2.2 Corpora

In order to demonstrate the language-independence of the rhetoric stylometry method hereby proposed, we confronted the matching faculties of initial "PERL Compatible Rhetoric Figures" (PCRF) with the corpora written in diverse languages.

More precisely, we have performed the rhetoric stylometry analysis of 4 corpora written by poets and orators who are often considered as exemplary cases of mastering their respective languages.

For English language, complete works of William Shakespeare had been downloaded from project Gutenberg (Hart, 2000). The same site served us as the source of 40 works of Johann Wolfgang Goethe written in German language. When it comes to original works of Jean-Baptiste Molière, 39 of them where recursively downloaded from French site *toutmoliere.net*. Finally, the basic Latin manual of rhetoric, Cicero's "De Oratore" was extracted from the corpus of Perseus Project (Crane, 1998) in order to demonstrate that PCRF-based approach can yield interesting results when applied even upon corpora written in antique languages.

Corpora from Project Gutenberg was downloaded as pure utf8-encoded text. No filtering of data was performed in order to analyze the data in their rawest possible form. The only exception was the stripping away of possible HTML tags by means of standard HTML::Strip filter.

Before the matching, the totality of the corpus was split into *fragments* whenever frontier **\n[^\w+]** (i.e. new-line followed by at least one non-word character) was detected. Shakespeare's corpus were splitted into 109492 fragments, Goethe's into 46597 fragments , Cicero's into 970 fragments while works of Moliere yielded 6639 fragments.

3 Results

In total, more than 7000 strings were matched by 3 PCRFs within 4 corpora containing in 17 Megabytes of text splitted into more than 163040 textual fragments.

	Anadiplosis{2}	**Anaphora{2,3}**	**Antimetabole {abcXbca}**	**Epiphora{2,}**
Cicero	0.00309	0.2711	0	0.0144
Goethe	0.00242	0.0717	0.0003	0.0042
Molière	0.01129	0.1634	0.000602	0.0210
Shkspr	0.00087	0.008	0.000219	0.008

Table 2: Relative frequencies of occurence of diverse PCRFs within diverse corpora (PCRF per fragment)

As is indicated in Table 2, the instances of anadiplosis, anaphora, antimetabole and epiphora were found in all 4 corpora involved in this study, the only exception being the absence of antimetabole in Cicero. In general, anaphora{2,3} seems to be the most frequent one: number of cases when this PCRFs succeeded to match highly surmounts the other two figures especially in case of Romance language authors – i.e. almost every sixth fragment from Moliere and every fourth from Cicero was matched by anaphore{2,3}.

The only exception to this "dominance of anaphora" seems to be Shakespeare whose complete works yielded exactly the same frequency of epiphora and anaphora occurences.

	Anadiplosis{2}	**Anaphora{2,3}**	**Antimetabole{abcXbca}**	**Epiphora{2,}**
Cicero	20	1	4	19
Goethe	44	3	33	287
Molière	57	1	29	65
Shkspr	7	2	17	64

Table 3: Elapsed time (in seconds) of different PCRF/corpus runs on average PC desktop

As is indicated in Table 3, computational demands of PCRF-based are not high in case of anaphora{2,3}. On the contrary, the recursive epiphora{2,} is much more demanding. As the recursive structure of this PCRF indicates, the speed of matching process is growing non-polynomially with the length of the textual fragment upon which the PCRF is applied and therefore the choice of correct fragment separator

[4] *"I always tell you the same **thing** because it is always the same **thing** and if it wasn't always the same **thing** I would not have been telling you the same **thing**."*

token (c.f. 2.2) seems to be of utmost importance.

4 Discussion

We propose a language-independent parse-free method of extracting instances of rhetoric figures from natural language corpora by means of PERL-compatible regular expressions. The fact that PCREs implement features like back-references or recursive matching make them good candidates for the detection & extraction of rhetoric figures which cannot be matched by simpler finite state automata or context-free languages.

In order to demonstrate the feasibility of such an approach, we have therefore "translated" the *canonical* definitions of anadiplosis, anaphora and epiphora into four *PERL-compatible rhetoric figures* - namely anadiplosis{2}, anaphora{2,3}, epiphora{2,} and antimetabole{abcXbca} - and applied them upon Latin, English, French and German corpora. All four PCRFs successfully matched some strings in at least three of four corpora, indicating that repetition-based rhetoric figures can possibly belong to the set of *linguistic universalia* (Greenberg, 1957). Anaphora{2,3} surpassed in frequency of occurrences all the other figures, the only exception being Shakespeare in whose case the number of matched epiphorae was equal to the number of matched anaphorae.

We do not pretend that PCRFs presented hereby are the most adequate translations of traditional anadiplosis, anaphora, antimetabole or epiphora into an artificial language. Since PCREs can contain quantifiers and classes, it is evident that for any set of strings – which is one our case the set F of all the occurences of a given figure within its respective corpus – more than one possible regexp could be constructed in order to match all members of the set F. Therefore it may be the case that PCRFs that we have proposed in this "proof of concept" article are not the most specific ones nor the fastest ones.

When it comes to specificity, it may be stated that the closer look upon the extracted data indicates that PCRFs proposed hereby have proposed some "false positives", i.e. have matched strings which are not rhetorical figures (for example an expression "*FIRST LORD. O my sweet lord*" was matched by epiphora{2,} when applied upon Shakespeare's corpus, but is definitely not a rhetoric figure since the substring in capital letters simply denotes the name of dramatic persona pronouncing the following statement and not the clause of the statement itself).

When it comes to speed, it is established that PCREs with unbounded number of back-reference are NP-complete (Aho, 1991) and verily this may be the reason of very high run-times of a recursive epiphora{2,} in contrast to its non-recursive PCRF counterparts. From practical point of view it seems therefore more suitable – especially in case of analysis of huge corpora - to stick to non-recursive PCRFs. The other possible solution how to speed up the parsing – and in certain cases even to prevent the machine to fell into "infinite recursion loop" is the tuning of the "splitting parameter" so that the corpus is split in fragments of such a size that the *NP-complexity of the matching PCRE shall not have observable implications* upon a real run-time of a rhetoric figure detection process.

There are at least three different ways how PCRFs could be possibly useful. Firstly, since PCRFs are very fast and language-independent, they can allow the scholars to extract huge number of instances of rhetoric figures from diverse corpora in order to create an exhaustive compendium of rhetoric figures. For example, the corpus of >7000 strings which were extracted from corpora mentioned in this article (downloadable from http://www.lutin-userlab.fr/rhetoric/) could be easily put to use not only by teachers of language or rhetoric, but possibly also by those who aim to develop a semi-supervised system of *rhetoric figure induction* (c.f. last paragraph). Manual annotation of such a compendium and subsequent tentatives of such a figure of speech induction shall be presented in our forecoming article.

Secondly, the extracted information concerning the quantities of various PCRFs within different corpora could serve as an input element (i.e. a feature) for classifiying or clustering algorithms. PCRFs could therefore facilitate such stylometric tasks like authorship attribution, author name disambiguation or maybe even plagiate detection.

Thirdly, due to their language independence, PCRFs presented hereby can be thought of as a means for evaluation of differences between two different languages, or two different states of the same language. One can for example apply the PCRFs upon two different translations T1 and T2 and see that the distribution of PCRFs within T2 is more similar to the distribution of PCRFs in the original than the distribution in T2. Therefore, one could possibly state that from rhetoric, stylistic or even poetic standpoint, T1 is more adequate translation of the original text than T2. On the other hand, when we speak about comparing two different states of the same language , we propose to perform PCRF-based analysis not only upon a corpus representing the *l'état de l'art* state of the language - like that of a Shakespeare, for example – but also to compare such a state with more initial states of the language development, as is represented by CHILDES (MacWhinney & Snow, 1985) corpus.

Finally, by considering PCRFs to be a method which could possibly be used as a tool of analysis of the development of language faculties in a human baby, we come closer to its third and somewhat "cognitive" implementation. This implementation - which is the subject of our current research - is based upon a belief that it is not unreasonable to imagine that PCRFs could possibly be constructed not manually, but automatically by means of genetic programming paradigm (Koza, 1992). Given the fact that PCRE-language is one of the most concise programming languages possibles and conceivables, and given the fact that the 1) speed of execution 2) the specifivity 3) the sensitivity could possibly serve as the input parameters of a function evaluating the fitness of a possible PCRF candidate, it is possible that the research initiated by our current proposal could result in a full-fledged and possibly non-supervised method of rhetoric figure induction. In such a way could our PCRFs possibly become something little bit more than just another tool for stylometric analysis of textual corpora – in such a way they could possibly help answering a somewhat more fundamental question: "*What is the essence of figures of speech and how could they be represented within&by an artificial and/or organic symbol-manipulating agent?*"

Acknowledgments

The author wishes to express his gratitude to University Paris8 – St. Denis and Lutin Userlab for support without which the research hereby presented would not be possible, as well as to thank philologues and comparativists of École Pratique des Hautes Études and ÉNS for keeping alive the Tradition within which the Language is considered to be something more than just an object of parsing and POS-tagging.

References

Aho, A. V. (1991). *Algorithms for finding patterns in strings, Handbook of theoretical computer science (vol. A): algorithms and complexity*. MIT Press, Cambridge, MA.

Aristotle. (1954). *Rhetoric*. 1355b.

Crane, G. (1998). The Perseus Project and Beyond: How Building a Digital Library Challenges the Humanities and Technology. *D-Lib Magazine*, 1, 18.

Crosswhite, J., Fox, J., Reed, C., Scaltsas, T., & Stumpf, S. (2003). Computational models of rhetorical argument. *Argumentation Machines—New Frontiers in Argument and Computation*, 175–209.

Dubois, J. (1970). *Rhétorique générale: Par le groupe MY*. Larousse.

Friedl, J. (2006). *Mastering regular expressions*. O'Reilly Media, Inc. Sebastopol, CA, USA.

Gawryjolek, J. (2009). *Automated annotation and visualization of rhetorical figures.*

Grasso, F. (2002). Towards computational rhetoric. *Informal Logic, 22*(3).

Greenberg, J. H. (1957). The nature and uses of linguistic typologies. *International Journal of American Linguistics*, 23(2), 68–77.

Harris, R., & DiMarco, C. (2009). Constructing a Rhetorical Figuration Ontology. *Persuasive Technology and Digital Behaviour Intervention Symposium*.

Hart, M. (2000). *Project gutenberg*. Project Gutenberg.

Koza, J. R. (1992). *Genetic programming: on the programming of computers by means of natural selection*. The MIT press.

MacWhinney, B., & Snow, C. (1985). The child language data exchange system. *Journal of child language*, *12*(02), 271-295.

Perelman, C., & Olbrechts-Tyteca, L. (1969). *The new rhetoric: A treatise on argumentation*.

Plato. (1986). *Phaedrus*. 261e.

Solan, Z., Horn, D., Ruppin, E., & Edelman, S. (2005). Unsupervised learning of natural languages. *Proceedings of the National Academy of Sciences, 102*(33), 11629.

Taboada, M., Mann, W. C., & Back, L. (2006). Rhetorical Structure Theory. Citeseer.

Wall, L., & Loukides, M. (2000). *Programming perl*. O'Reilly Media, Inc. Sebastopol, CA, USA.

Is Three the Optimal Context Window for Memory-Based Word Sense Disambiguation?

Rodrigo de Oliveira, Lucas Hausmann and Desislava Zhekova
University of Bremen
(rdeoliveira, lhausmann, zhekova) @uni-bremen.de

Abstract

In this work we research the effect of micro-context on a memory-based learning (MBL) system for word sense disambiguation. We report results achieved on the data set provided by the English Lexical Sample Task introduced in the Senseval 3 competition. Our study revisits the belief that the disambiguation task profits more from a wider context and indicates that in reality system performance is highest when a narrower context is considered.

Keywords

word sense disambiguation, memory-based learning, supervised learning

1 Introduction

Back in the 50's since the first efforts in computational linguistics, it has been said that more context information leads to a stronger guiding in resolving the problem of ambiguity (Weaver, 1955). Yet, there are different kinds of ambiguity (e.g. structural vs. lexical ambiguity). Word sense disambiguation (WSD), as reviewed by Ide and Véronis (1998), is targeting the problem of lexical ambiguity. In general, it aims to find the correct sense of a given word depending on the context in which it is found. According to the authors, context can also be defined in different ways: micro-context, constructed by a window of n (e.g. 1, 2, 3, etc.) number of words before and after the target word; topical-context, making use of substantive words typical of the given sense in a window of several sentences; domain, concerned with the domain specificity of the used corpus and a disambiguation approach using this knowledge for the selection of senses. Depending on the data sources that are used for the disambiguation pipeline, it is not certain that topical-context or domain information will always be provided. Thus, in our work, we are interested in the context as asserted by micro-context, since it is easiest to obtain and, as Ide and Véronis (1998) also commented, highly informative in respect to the sense the target word is used with in the given surrounding.

In this paper, we investigate the effect of context window size on a machine learning system that makes use of memory-based learning (Daelemans and van den Bosch, 2005), explained further in section 3. As Daelemans and van den Bosch (2005) note, memory-based learning is highly sensitive to the amount of considered data in the form of features and their respective informativeness. Yet, Weaver (1955) claims that in order to disambiguate a given word, a wider context should be considered for the performance of the system to rise overall. However, a wider context implies more data and thus further features, which, as a whole, closes the circle of an endless loop over the trade-off between amount and informativeness of the used data.

Based on the presented problem, our assumption is that, for a memory-based learning approach, extending the context will lead to system performance improvement. Since the local context of a word, or its micro-context, has been the most often used source of information in the state-of-the-art word sense disambiguation approaches, we revise the findings in the field relevant to our work in section 2. Further, in section 3, we introduce the data that we employed in our study as well as the word sense disambiguation system that was developed specifically for this investigation arrangement. In section 4, we describe the experimental setup as well as the results we achieved and discuss the findings overall. In the last section of the paper, section 5, we sum up our investigation and review possible future directions.

2 Related Work

The optimal size of the context window that needs to be considered during memory-based WSD has been an important problem in the field for a long time (Wang, 2005). The diversity of algorithms

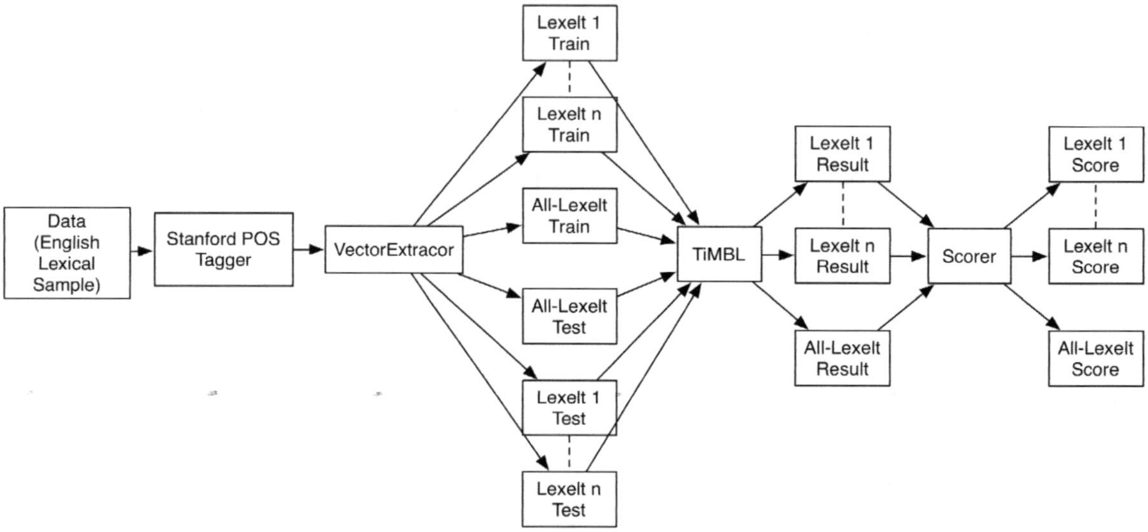

Figure 1: Overview of the WSD pipeline

used for the process, the data and ambiguity found in it, the language, that the final system is applied on as well as the variations in the distinct parameter optimization settings, constitute an immense pool of possibilities that can lead to a specific context window preference.

As Yarowsky and Florian (2002) find, the different methods and algorithms can benefit from the choice of the context size in a distinct way, which means that the optimal size of the micro-context can depend on the used method and that the selection of the size of the context leads to a variation of the WSD pipeline output. It was again Yarowsky (1994) that also claimed that the different types of ambiguity occurring in the data can be captured by a different size of the micro-context. In their work, Leacock et al. (1998) consider topical context as less informative than the immediate context around the target word. The authors look at various local context windows and suggest that a range of n=3 or n=4, meaning a context window of three, respectively four words before and after the target lemma, provide enough information from the local context. Based on his empirical study, Yarowsky (1994) also concludes that a window of 3 words around the target lemma leads to the optimal results. The latter findings became a default setup for multiple systems over the last few decades since a smaller context window is computationally more feasible than a bigger one (Decadt et al., 2004). Li et al. (2009), on the other side, use the Chinese Senseval[1] data set to look at a variation of the context window going beyond the idea of symmetric combination of lemmas before and after the target one.

Right in the beginning of machine translation, Weaver (1955) expressed a hope that not only the most optimal context window can be discovered but also the smallest one such that the correct sense of the target word is still selected. Yet, almost six decades later, there is still no specification of which size of the window needs to be used in which experimental setup. This provides a clear motivation for further investigation in the area.

3 The System

The data used in our research is retrieved from the WSD competition Senseval 3 (Mihalcea and Edmonds, 2004), namely the test and train files of the English Lexical Sample Task (Mihalcea et al., 2004). Lexical sample tasks use a small set of words and corpus instances of these words. Due to the reduced size of the data, a supervised machine-learning approach was applicable, in which we extract context information surrounding the ambiguous word.

The disambiguation pipeline (an overview of which is shown in figure 1) starts with a preparation process of the sentences, in which we tag every word with its part of speech (POS). This first pre-processing was carried out with Stan-

[1] http://www.senseval.org/senseval3/data.html

Feature	Description	Example
CT_{-5}	TP -5 from TW	,
CT_{-4}	TP -4 from TW	and
CT_{-3}	TP -3 from TW	I
CT_{-2}	TP -2 from TW	'd
CT_{-1}	TP -1 from TW	once
CT_0	TW	decided
CT_1	TP 1 from TW	to
CT_2	TP 2 from TW	wash
CT_3	TP 3 from TW	all
CT_4	TP 4 from TW	his
CT_5	TP 5 from TW	clothes
CP_{-5}	POS of TP -5 from TW	,
CP_{-4}	POS of TP -4 from TW	CC
CP_{-3}	POS of TP -3 from TW	PRP
CP_{-2}	POS of TP -2 from TW	MD
CP_{-1}	POS of TP -1 from TW	RB
CP_0	POS of target word	VBD
CP_1	POS of TP 1 from TW	TO
CP_2	POS of TP 2 from TW	VB
CP_3	POS of TP 3 from TW	PDT
CP_4	POS of TP 4 from TW	PRP$
CP_5	POS of TP 5 from TW	NNS
NA	first noun after TW	clothes
NB	first noun before TW	cleanliness
VA	first verb after TW	wash
VB	first verb before TW	had
PA	first preposition after TW	to
PB	first preposition before TW	for

Table 1: The pool of features used for classification (TP n is the token at position n and TW is the target word) and the values in the respective vector

ford's POS-tagger[2] (Toutanova et al., 2003). After the original files are tagged, the output is further used from the next component in our WSD system, which extracts the desired information in the form of features building up a feature vector. It is also important to state, that the output of this second step is one separate file for each lexelt in the data, as well as one file containing data for all lexelts. A lexelt consists of a lemma and its word class. Out of a total of 57 lexelts, we then end up with 57 pairs of single-lexelt test and train files and 1 pair of all-lexelt test and train files.

In the extraction of vectors, we started with the feature set used in (Kübler and Zhekova, 2009), which is composed of tokens and POS-tags of the ambiguous word and its surrounding words, plus the first verb, noun and preposition before and after the ambiguous word, as shown in table 1.

For the actual classification process, we used TiMBL[3] (Daelemans et al., 2007), which is a considerably efficient decision-tree implementation of the *k*-nearest neighbor classification algorithm. We used the IB1-IG algorithm to process each of our train and test file pairs. We did not approach a parameter optimization, since we investigate the pure effect of the context window on the system performance and not the system's best possible performance. Again the output of this step is a file for each lexelt as well as a combined file including all lexelts, with both the feature vectors from the test set and the newly added senses assigned to each of them. Our system transforms this output in the format needed by the scoring software integrated in the pipeline. For this purpose we used the scorer provided by Senseval 3. Additionally, to score each lexelt based on TiMBL's prepared output file, an answer key file for each lexelt and a sense map (also provided in the data package from Senseval 3) were used.

[2]http://www-nlp.stanford.edu/software

[3]http://ilk.uvt.nl/timbl

4 Experiments

In order to investigate the actual effect of the micro-context on the IB1-IG algorithm, we approached several experiments, the setup of which we describe further in section 4.1. The results that we obtain are listed and discussed in section 4.2.

4.1 Experimental Setup

The features CT and CP are optimizable, in the sense that one can increase the value of n and expand the n-gram window to extract vectors. Thus, we approached altogether the following six experimental system runs: EX0 ($n = 0$), EX1 ($n = 1$), EX2 ($n = 2$), EX3 ($n = 3$), EX4 ($n = 4$) and EX5 ($n = 5$). In the EX0 setting, with $n = 0$, vectors are composed of CT0 and CP0 only (i.e no more than the target word itself is regarded) plus the non-optimizable features (NA,NB,VA,VB,PA and PB), for which the n value is irrelevant. With this initial feature set, we obtain the system performances, register them in a table and terminate EX0. For subsequent experiments we increment n simultaneously and symmetrically, i.e. for each $-x$ included (where x = some feature), a $+x$ is also included. In EX1, that results in the inclusion of the features CT+1, CT-1, CP+1 and CP-1 to the previous set used in EX0. The largest feature set in this study, namely that used in EX5 with $n = 5$, is demonstrated in table 1. This vector was extracted from the following corpus instance:
"...I had a mania for cleanliness, and I'd once decided to wash all his clothes...".

Once we have extended the context until $n = 5$

POS	EX0		EX1		EX2		EX3		EX4		EX5	
	fine	coarse	fine	coarse	fine	coarse	fine	coarse	fine	coarse	fine	coarse
a	39.4	**55.1**	40.3	51.0	**41.9**	52.7	36.8	44.9	36.0	46.4	37.3	47.6
n	56.1	64.4	**59.1**	**67.1**	56.0	64.0	56.9	64.1	55.8	63.5	57.4	65.40
v	59.2	62.4	**64.6**	**68.0**	63.8	67.1	62.7	66.5	62.2	65.7	62.5	66.2

Table 2: System results across word types.

and obtained all results for each separate lexelt, for all lexelts together, and for every experiment, we analyze the evolution of performances. According to the assumption that more context yields better performance, we expected to conclude that:

- The larger the context-window we have in the system, the better the performance;
- From a certain point onwards, this gain is either irrelevant or reduces system performance, since too much information tends to mean more noise in the automated learning process.

4.2 Experimental Results

The scoring software provided by Senseval 3 allowed for the scoring step to be carried out in fine-grained scoring mode and in coarse-grained mode as well. The scores that we obtained are listed in table 3 in the form of the harmonic mean (F-score) of precision and recall for both modes. As *total* scores we report the average scores of all separate word experts and as *combined* we list the scores that the single classifier working with data for all words obtained. Table 2 offers an averaged performance of the system per word type. What the figures show is that for virtually all experiments (except partially in EX0), for both fine- and coarse-grained scores, ambiguity on verbs is better resolved than ambiguity on nouns with our system. The linguistic feature used in the vectors is mainly POS, which indicates that such a feature has more relevance in the disambiguation of verbs in comparison to other word types.

What we find is that there is a direct correlation between the amount of possible senses for the same word and the accuracy of the system. Words with 10 or more senses, for instance, had scores ranging from 20.8 to 80.6. In respect to words with 5 or less senses where scores ranged from 38.5 to 96.9. This is another indicator that factors as the feature set employed, the learning algorithm used as well as the level of ambiguity of the given word have a direct influence on the system performance.

There is a difference in performance when granularity is changed. Fine-grained scoring methods tend to lead to lower scores if compared to coarse-grained scores. In our case, regardless of context window size, coarse-grained scores were indeed higher than fine-grained scores for the same experiment. In both cases, fine- and coarse-grained, the context window from experiment 1 results in the majority of best scores. Nonetheless, it is important to note, that with the few lexelts for which larger context windows worked better, namely in 6 percent of the cases for window 3, and 10 percent for window 5, granularity does play a role. In those rare cases, context window 3 displayed the best average performance for a fine-grained disambiguation. Whereas window 5 functioned best for a coarse-grained disambiguation. This suggests, that in case the lexelt scores are not sufficient a context window of $n \geq 3$ can be considered.

A similar irregularity in performance gain or loss between fine- and coarse-grained disambiguation is visible for one specific word class, namely adjectives as shown in table 2. We should, however, note that the data for adjectives is not representative enough, since we only have 5 instances and, thus, more data is needed in order to be sure that this variation is indeed relevant.

Comparing the *total* and *combined* performance, it is surprising to see that the classifier that was trained on the whole data set performed better in all experimental settings and modes than the average performance of all separate word experts. We believe this is due to the fact that TiMBL uses an information gain algorithm, allowing it to evaluate features better if it has more data. This implies that in a setting, in which no per word classifier optimization is approached, a single classifier is indeed sufficient.

Overall, we see that the context window size used in EX1, which is $n = 1$, results in the best performance in the majority of cases. This leads to the fact that, in the simple setting of our system, a micro-context of one word before and after the target one performs best. Our findings then contradict our expectations in the sense that we estimated an increase of system performance with a context window of 3 or 4, since such a distance has been common practice in the area for the last few decades and was proposed as optimal by Leacock et al. (1998). A possible explanation for this outcome stands behind the features extracted from a wider context, which can bring more noise than helpful information for a memory-based classifier.

5 Conclusion and Future Work

We have shown that the default size for a context window in memory-based word sense disambiguation, used for more than a decade, is hardly still optimal. We now find that a window of ± 1 yields the best possible averaged results over all ambiguous words. This work also raised some issues which should be investigated further, for instance why the disambiguation of certain words works so much better with bigger windows. Another point of interest is the fact that the average score achieved from all separate word experts is lower than the score achieved from the classifier working with all lexelts simultaneously. Lastly, it might be beneficial to investigate if these findings hold true for more than just the English language. As R.Martin (1992) has indicated, English tends to keep relevant context information very close to the word in question, which would explain why our small window of ± 1 worked so well.

References

Walter Daelemans and Antal van den Bosch. 2005. *Memory Based Language Processing*. Cambridge University Press.

Walter Daelemans, Jakub Zavrel, Ko van der Sloot, and Antal van den Bosch. 2007. TiMBL: Tilburg Memory Based Learner – version 6.1 – Reference Guide. Technical Report ILK 07-07, Induction of Linguistic Knowledge, Computational Linguistics, Tilburg University.

Bart Decadt, Véronique Hoste, Walter Daelemans, and Antal V. den Bosch. 2004. In Rada Mihalcea and Phil Edmonds, editors, *Proceedings of the Third International Workshop on the Evaluation of Systems for the Semantic Analysis of Text (Senseval-3)*, pages 108–112.

Nancy Ide and Jean Véronis. 1998. Introduction to the Special Issue on Word Sense Disambiguation: The State of the Art. *Computational Linguistics*, 24(1):1–40.

Sandra Kübler and Desislava Zhekova. 2009. Semi-Supervised Learning for Word Sense Disambiguation: Quality vs. Quantity. In *Proceedings of the International Conference RANLP-2009*, pages 197–202, Borovets, Bulgaria, September. ACL.

Claudia Leacock, George A. Miller, and Martin Chodorow. 1998. Using corpus statistics and WordNet relations for sense identification. *Computational Linguistics*, 24:147–165, March.

Gang Li, Guangzeng Kou, Ercui Zhou, and Ling Zhang. 2009. Symmetric Trends: Optimal Local Context Window in Chinese Word Sense Disambiguation. In *Proceedings of the 2009 Ninth International Conference on Hybrid Intelligent Systems - Volume 03*, HIS '09, pages 151–154, Washington, DC, USA. IEEE Computer Society.

Rada Mihalcea and Philip Edmonds, editors. 2004. *Proceedings of Senseval-3: Third International Workshop on the Evaluation of Systems for the Semantic Analysis of Text*, Barcelona, Spain.

Rada Mihalcea, Timothy Chklovski, and Adam Kilgarriff. 2004. The SENSEVAL–3 English Lexical Sample Task. In *SENSEVAL-3: Third International Workshop on the Evaluation of Systems for the Semantic Analysis of Text*, pages 25–28, Barcelona, Spain. Association for Computational Linguistics.

James R.Martin. 1992. *English text: system and structure*. Benjamins, Philadelphia [u.a.]. XIV, 620 S. : graph. Darst.

Kristina Toutanova, Dan Klein, Christopher D. Manning, and Yoram Singer. 2003. Feature-rich part-of-speech tagging with a cyclic dependency network. In *Proceedings of HLT-NAACL*, pages 252–259.

Xiaojie Wang. 2005. Robust utilization of context in word sense disambiguation. In *CONTEXT*, pages 529–541.

Warren Weaver. 1955. Translation. In William N. Locke and A. Donald Boothe, editors, *Machine Translation of Languages*, pages 15–23. MIT Press, Cambridge, MA. Reprinted from a memorandum written by Weaver in 1949.

David Yarowsky and Radu Florian. 2002. Evaluating sense disambiguation across diverse parameter spaces. *Natural Language Engineering*, 8:293–310.

David Yarowsky. 1994. Decision lists for lexical ambiguity resolution: application to accent restoration in Spanish and French. In *Proceedings of the 32nd annual meeting on Association for Computational Linguistics*, ACL '94, pages 88–95, Stroudsburg, PA, USA. Association for Computational Linguistics.

LEXELT	POS	senses	EX0		EX1		EX2		EX3		EX4		EX5	
			fine	coarse	fine	coarse	fine	coarse	fine	coarse	fine	coarse	fine	coarse
activate	v	5	77.4	77.4	71.0	71.0	68.8	68.8	63.4	63.4	63.4	63.4	65.6	65.6
add	v	6	54.9	54.9	78.9	78.9	81.5	81.5	79.8	79.8	80.6	80.6	78.0	78.0
appear	v	3	66.9	66.9	71.0	71.0	68.5	68.5	69.4	69.4	70.2	70.2	70.2	70.2
argument	n	5	44.7	55.2	47.9	52.1	39.4	44.8	44.7	51.0	46.8	52.1	51.1	56.2
arm	n	6	84.7	84.7	87.0	87.0	84.7	84.7	83.2	83.2	83.2	83.2	82.4	82.4
ask	v	6	32.9	32.9	59.9	59.9	55.9	55.9	55.9	55.9	51.9	51.9	51.9	51.9
atmosphere	n	6	56.7	54.8	55.0	53.2	40.0	40.3	43.3	43.5	41.7	41.9	43.3	43.5
audience	n	4	69.1	97.4	70.2	96.4	71.3	96.4	72.3	95.4	69.1	95.4	71.3	96.4
bank	n	10	72.2	79.1	68.3	78.3	70.6	79.1	71.4	78.3	73.8	80.6	67.5	79.1
begin	v	4	47.9	47.9	51.1	51.1	51.1	51.1	52.7	52.7	44.7	44.7	44.7	44.7
climb	v	5	44.5	44.5	56.9	56.9	59.9	59.9	59.9	59.9	61.5	61.5	61.5	61.5
decide	v	4	73.8	73.8	72.1	72.1	70.5	70.5	70.5	70.5	75.4	75.4	77.0	77.0
degree	n	7	62.9	78.6	68.1	82.5	70.7	85.7	68.1	82.5	69.0	82.5	65.5	81.0
difference	n	5	54.1	63.4	55.1	60.4	48.0	53.5	48.0	54.5	44.9	53.5	48.0	55.4
different	a	5	45.8	62.0	47.9	62.0	45.8	62.0	41.7	56.0	47.9	62.0	41.7	60.0
difficulty	n	4	39.1	87.0	52.2	87.0	43.5	82.6	47.8	82.6	39.1	87.0	47.8	87.0
disc	n	4	39.6	39.6	45.1	45.1	44.0	44.0	40.7	40.7	38.5	38.5	40.7	40.7
eat	v	7	83.5	83.5	87.1	87.1	82.4	82.4	75.3	75.3	76.5	76.5	76.5	76.5
encounter	v	4	58.5	93.8	55.4	96.9	58.5	96.9	60.0	96.9	61.5	96.9	60.0	96.9
expect	v	3	65.2	65.2	71.0	71.0	75.4	75.4	75.4	75.4	75.4	75.4	73.9	73.9
express	v	4	54.7	61.8	56.6	65.5	54.7	61.8	49.1	61.8	50.9	60.0	56.6	67.3
hear	v	7	43.8	50.0	53.1	59.4	56.2	62.5	56.2	62.5	53.1	59.4	53.1	59.4
hot	a	22	71.4	71.4	78.6	78.6	78.6	78.6	71.4	71.4	71.4	71.4	69.0	69.0
image	n	7	58.9	58.9	50.7	50.7	49.3	49.3	50.7	50.7	52.1	52.1	54.8	54.8
important	a	5	38.5	66.7	23.1	46.7	30.8	53.3	23.1	33.3	23.1	33.3	15.4	33.3
interest	n	7	69.2	69.6	70.3	70.7	68.1	68.5	69.2	69.6	65.9	66.3	70.3	69.6
judgment	n	7	34.4	40.6	40.6	46.9	53.1	56.2	53.1	53.1	53.1	53.1	53.1	56.2
lose	v	9	47.2	47.2	36.1	36.1	47.2	47.2	33.3	33.3	33.3	33.3	33.3	33.3
mean	v	7	50.0	50.0	70.0	70.0	67.5	67.5	72.5	72.5	70.0	70.0	70.0	70.0
miss	v	8	40.0	40.0	50.0	50.0	43.3	43.3	46.7	46.7	43.3	43.3	43.3	43.3
note	v	3	60.6	60.6	60.6	60.6	60.6	60.6	62.1	62.1	60.6	60.6	63.6	63.6
operate	v	5	44.4	55.6	72.2	88.9	72.2	77.8	66.7	83.3	61.1	77.8	61.1	77.8
organization	n	7	69.1	76.8	67.3	78.6	72.7	83.9	78.2	89.3	70.9	85.7	76.4	92.9
paper	n	7	43.9	51.4	45.9	59.5	38.8	50.5	38.8	51.4	39.8	52.3	41.8	53.2
party	n	5	63.6	63.6	64.5	64.5	64.5	65.4	63.6	64.5	64.5	64.5	62.6	63.6
performance	n	5	25.3	41.2	28.9	44.7	28.9	44.7	33.7	44.7	31.3	37.6	31.3	36.5
plan	n	3	76.8	77.8	73.9	76.4	72.5	75.0	72.5	75.0	75.4	75.0	81.2	81.9
play	v	11	44.2	44.2	42.3	42.3	38.5	38.5	42.3	42.3	32.7	32.7	38.5	38.5
produce	v	6	55.9	57.4	55.9	57.4	55.9	57.4	50.5	51.1	51.6	54.3	50.5	53.2
provide	v	6	85.1	92.8	85.1	94.2	88.1	95.7	95.5	98.6	95.5	98.6	95.5	97.1
receive	v	9	85.2	85.2	88.9	88.9	81.5	81.5	88.9	88.9	85.2	85.2	88.9	88.9
remain	v	3	82.6	82.6	82.6	82.6	87.0	87.0	89.9	89.9	88.4	88.4	89.9	89.9
rule	v	5	60.0	60.0	66.7	66.7	56.7	56.7	60.0	60.0	63.3	63.3	56.7	56.7
shelter	n	4	49.4	49.4	60.5	60.5	51.9	51.9	48.1	48.1	51.9	51.9	55.6	55.6
simple	a	7	25.0	58.8	31.2	47.1	37.5	52.9	31.2	47.1	25.0	52.9	43.8	58.8
smell	v	7	55.6	57.4	66.7	70.4	64.8	68.5	70.4	74.1	66.7	70.4	70.4	72.2
solid	a	14	16.1	16.7	20.8	20.8	16.7	16.7	16.7	16.7	12.5	12.5	16.7	16.7
sort	n	4	59.0	67.9	71.1	85.7	66.3	78.6	66.3	78.6	67.5	79.8	66.3	79.8
source	n	6	48.3	51.7	58.6	62.1	41.4	44.8	44.8	44.8	37.9	37.9	37.9	41.4
suspend	v	7	53.1	53.1	45.3	45.3	45.3	45.3	51.6	51.6	50.0	50.0	46.9	46.9
talk	v	9	67.1	67.1	72.6	72.6	76.7	76.7	72.6	72.6	71.2	71.2	71.2	71.2
treat	v	9	56.1	61.4	56.1	57.9	56.1	57.9	45.6	45.6	45.6	47.4	50.9	52.6
use	v	5	71.4	71.4	78.6	78.6	71.4	71.4	64.3	64.3	64.3	64.3	71.4	71.4
wash	v	12	67.6	73.5	64.7	70.6	58.8	76.5	58.8	79.4	55.9	76.5	52.9	76.5
watch	v	7	60.8	80.4	82.4	88.2	78.4	86.3	74.5	86.3	72.5	82.4	72.5	82.4
win	v	7	59.0	61.5	51.3	56.4	56.4	64.1	43.6	53.8	56.4	61.5	51.3	56.4
write	v	8	43.5	43.5	56.5	56.5	52.2	52.2	47.8	47.8	56.5	56.5	52.2	52.2
total			56.3	62.5	60.6	66.2	59.1	64.7	58.4	63.7	57.6	63.3	58.5	64.2
combined			59.2	64.2	61.9	66.9	61.0	65.8	61.6	66.2	60.6	65.1	60.3	65.0

Table 3: System results.

Heterogeneous Natural Language Processing Tools via Language Processing Chains

Diman Karagiozov
Tetracom IS Ltd.
diman@tetracom.com

Abstract

One of the most recent developments in NLP is the emergence of linguistic annotation meta-systems which make use of existing processing tools and implement pipelined architecture. In this paper we describe a system that offers a new perspective in exploiting NLP meta-systems by providing a common processing framework. This framework supports most of common NLP tasks by chaining tools that are able to communicate on the basis of common formats. As a demonstration of the effectiveness of the system to manage heterogeneous NLP tools, we developed an English processing chain, pipelining OpenNLP-based and C++ NLP implementations. Furthermore, we conducted experiments to test the stability and measure the performance of the English processing chain. A baseline processing chain for the Bulgarian language illustrates the capabilities of the system to support and manage processing chains for more languages.

1 Introduction

Increasingly complex digital content needs to be retrieved, stored and aggregated for future access. In addition, it should be organized, annotated and structured. However, it is difficult to manage the information flow because of its volume, rapidly evolving structure and its multilinguality.

The usage and integration of natural language processing and understanding tools (NLP and NLU) is vital for processing digital content. The different input and output formats, supported operating systems and programming languages determine the existence of the wide range of NLP tools. Furthermore, the choice of available tools makes their integration in content management systems, analytical tools and in-house systems very difficult.

One of the latest developments in NLP is the emergence of linguistic annotation meta-systems which make use of existing processing tools and implement pipelined processing architecture (Cristea and Pistol, 2008). This paper describes a system that exploits NLP meta-systems and provides a common processing framework capable to host a variety of tools for different natural languages that are able to communicate on the basis of common formats. Furthermore, our system provides a well-defined integration API, so that 3rd party software components can use the NLP services provided by the system.

The paper is organized as follows: Section 2 overviews related work, Section 3 describes system architecture, Section 4 presents the language processing chains method, Section 5 discusses implementation, evaluation and results, Section 6 describes the scope of LPC for Bulgarian and Section 7 sketches further work and conclusion.

The work reported in sections 3 (NLP System Architecture), 4 (Language Processing Chain) and 5 (UIMA Implementation of LPC) was designed, developed, evaluated and analyzed by the author of this paper.

2 Related Work

Several standardization approaches have been made towards the interoperability of the NLP tools (XCES[1], TEI[2], GOLD[3]). None of the proposed standards have been universally accepted, leading to the development of resources and tools according to the format of each research project.

[1] http://www.xml-ces.org/
[2] http://www.tei-c.org/index.xml
[3] http://www.linguistics-ontology.org/gold.html

More notably, two systems that facilitate the access and usage of existing processing tools have emerged. GATE (Cunningham et al., 2002) is an environment for building and deploying NLP software and resources that allows integration of a large amount of built-ins in new processing pipelines.

UIMA (Unstructured Information Management Application) (Ferrucci and Lally, 2004) offers the same general functionalities as GATE but once a processing module is integrated in UIMA it can be used in any further chains without any modifications (GATE requires wrappers to be written to allow two or more modules to be connected in a chain). Currently, UIMA is the only industry OASIS standard [4] (Ferrucci et al., 2006) for content analytics.

3 NLP System Architecture

The processing of unstructured text in system is split into three independent subtasks, executed sequentially.

Pre-processing – at this stage the text is extracted from the input source (documents in OpenOffice, PDF, MS Office, HTML, ePub, FB2 and other formats). Details of the implementation of the pre-processing engine are not in the scope of this article.

Processing – at this stage the text is annotated by several NLP tools, chained in a sequence. We call the implementation of the processing engine for a specific language a 'Language Processing Chain' (LPC).

Post-processing – at this stage the annotations are stored in a data store, such as file system, relational or NoSQL database. Details of the implementation of the post-processing engine are not in the scope of this article.

The overall performance of an NLP task depends on the performance of the atomic NLP tools, used in the processing engine and the size of the input text. As the classical request-response chain cannot be used for such tasks because the response time cannot be predicted, we use an asynchronous, message-based, communication channel between the components in the system.

A pre-processing engine detects the mime type of the input source, extracts the text from it, detects the language of the text and sends it to a language-specific queue.

One (of the several) language processing chains checks-out a message, processes it and sends the annotated text to an output queue where a post-processing engine stores the text annotations in a data store.

"Figure 1" depicts the top-level architecture of the NLP components in the system.

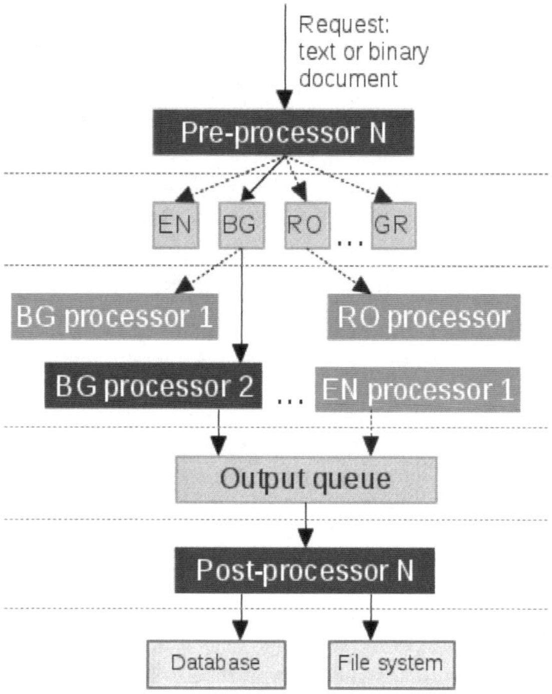

Figure 1. Top-level architecture.

4 Language Processing Chain

In order to achieve a basic set of low-level text annotations the following atomic NLP tools have to be executed in sequence (Cristea and Pistol, 2008): *Paragraph splitter* (splits the raw text in paragraphs) → *Sentence splitter* (splits each paragraph in sentences) → *Tokenizer* (splits each sentence into tokens) → *POS tagger* (marks up each token with its particular part of speech tag) → *Lemmatizer* (determines the basic form of each token) → *Word sense disambiguation* (disambiguates the meaning of each token and assigns a sense to it) → *NounPhrase Extractor* (marks up the noun phrases in each sentense) → *NamedEntity Extractor* (marks up named entities in the text).

"Figure 2" overviews the components and the sequence of execution of the atomic NLP tools, which are part of a LPC.

[4] http://www.oasis-open.org/committees/uima/

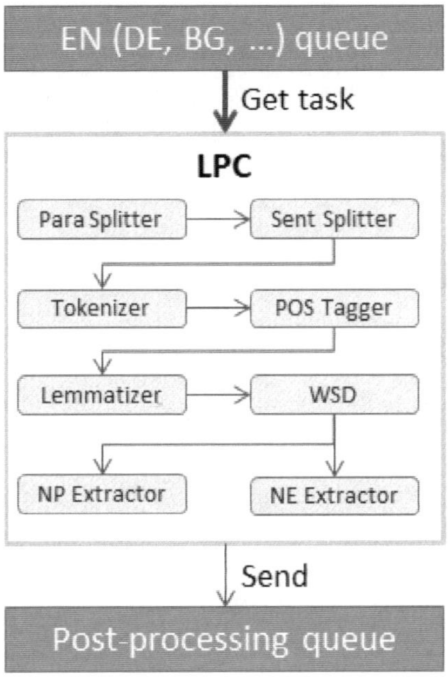

Figure 2. Components of a language processing chain.

The key requirements to our system are the possibility to use heterogeneous NLP tools for different languages, transparent horizontal scalability, and transparent hot-swap of linguistic components. Last but not least is the requirement of a minimal installation footprint.

After evaluating both GATE and UIMA meta-systems, in respect to the above requirements, we based the implementation of the processing engine on the UIMA framework (JAVA version). We wrapped the UIMA base framework with an OSGi shell (OSGi Alliance, 2009), making it available to the rest of the components in the system. The horizontal scalability of the NLP functionalities and the transparent hot-swap of the linguistic components are empowered by a network-distributed architecture based on ActiveMQ[5].

5 UIMA Implementation of LPC

A typical UIMA application consists of: *a Type System Descriptor*, describing the annotations that will be provided by the components of the application; one or more *Primitive Analysis Engines*, each one providing a wrapper for a NLP tools and adding annotations to the text; *an Aggregate Engine*, defining the execution sequence of the primitive engines (Gordon et al., 2011).

[5] http://activemq.apache.org/

5.1 Type System Descriptor

In order to put the atomic NLP tools in a chain, they need to be interoperable on various levels. The first interoperable level, the compatibility of formats of linguistic information, is supported by a defined scope of required annotations, described as a UIMA Type System Descriptor.

The uniform representation model, required by the UIMA type system, provides normalized heterogeneous annotations of the component NLP tools. Within our system, it covers properties that are critical for the further processing of annotated data, e.g. lemma, values for attributes such as gender, number and case for tokens necessary to run coreference module to be subsequently used for text summarization, automatic categorization and machine translation.

In order to facilitate the introduction of further levels and types of annotation, a general *markable* type has been introduced, carrying subtype and reference to another *markable* object. In this way we can test and later include new annotation concepts into the core annotation model.

"Table 1" enlists the annotations which are available in the Type System Descriptor of the system. The parameters of each annotation type, listed in "Parameters" column, extend the standard UIMA annotation set of parameters (begin offset, end offset and covered text).

Annotation type	Parameters
Paragraph	–
Sentence	–
Token	POS; MSD (lemma, gender; number, case); Word sense
Noun Phrase	Head, Lemma
Named Entity	Type (one of: date, location, money, organization, percentage, person, time); Normalized value
Markable	Type; Reference

Table 1: Summary of the text annotations and their parameters

5.2 UIMA LPC Components

We have built a reference LPC for English in order to illustrate the integration of English NLP tools into a processing chain.

Tool type	Based on
Paragraph Splitter	Regular expressions
Sentence Splitter	OpenNLP[6]
Tokenizer	OpenNLP
Lemmarizer	RASP[7]
POS tagger	OpenNLP
Word sense disambiguation	C++ LESK (Banerjee, 2002)[8]
NP extractor	Rules engine
NE recognizer	OpenNLP

Table 2: Tools, wrapped into UIMA primitive engines, contained in the English LPC.

We have successfully pipelined JAVA-based NLP tools and external C++ tools into a single LPC. A challenge, solved during the integration process, was the different sets of POS tags used by the OpenNLP and RASP tools. We created a rule-based converter between the Penn Treebank and CLAWS tagsets in order to achieve the interoperability of the tools.

5.3 Evaluation

Furthermore, we extended the standard UIMA functionalities to measure the performance of the whole LPC and each individual primitive engine. We based the current evaluations on the processing of a corpus of 27'085 EU law documents from EUR-Lex[9]. "Table 3" gives an overview of the contents of the processed corpus.

	Number of tokens (N)	Docs	Avg tkns[10]
C1	N ∈ [1,1000)	8'900	520
C2	N ∈ [1000,2500)	4'863	1'600
C3	N ∈ [2500,7500)	7'589	4'600
C4	N ∈ [7500,12500)	2'485	9'600
C5	N ∈ [1250,25000)	2'082	17'300
C6	N ∈ [25000,50000)	834	34'800
C7	N ≥ 50000	332	82'600

Table 3: Distribution by number of tokens of documents in the processed corpus.

[6] http://incubator.apache.org/opennlp/

[7] http://www.informatics.sussex.ac.uk/research/groups/nlp/rasp/

[8] We managed to achieve 30 time better performance of the C++ version compared to the initial Perl LESK tool.

[9] http://eur-lex.europa.eu/

[10] Average number of tokens in a document in a class

"Figure 3" depicts the average processing time (in milliseconds) of documents belonging to each of the above categories (C1-C7). The performance of the English LPC is linearly related to the number of tokens in the processed documents.

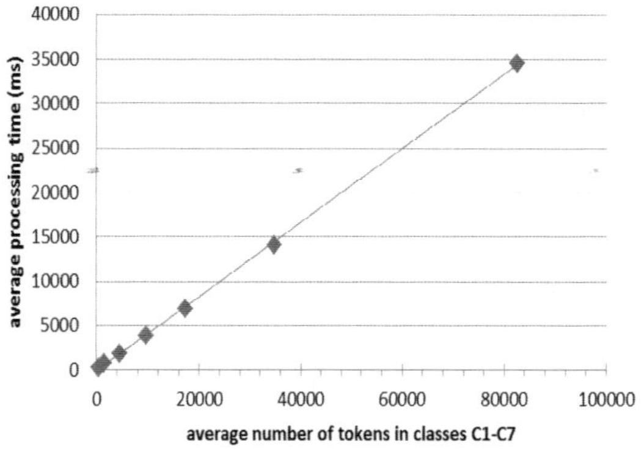

Figure 3. Average processing time of a document compared to the average number of tokens in documents in categories C1 to C7.

"Figure 4" shows the average processing time (in milliseconds) for each UIMA primitive engine (PE) for documents in categories C3 and C4. The performance of each PE is also linearly related to the number of tokens in the processed documents. The UIMA overhead time, caused by the CAS flow controller, is less than 1% of the total execution time and thus it is not represented at the "Figure 4".

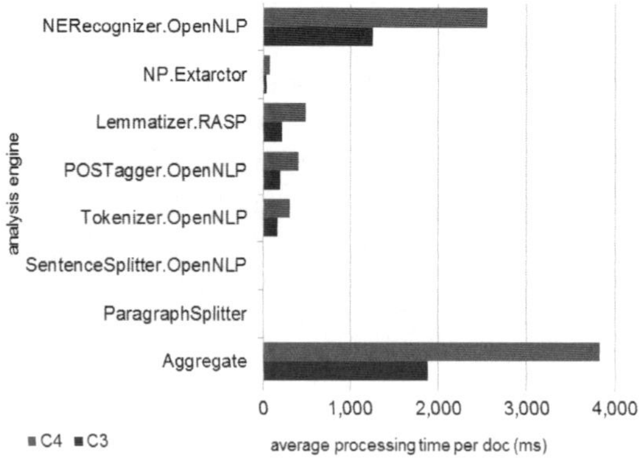

Figure 4. Average processing time of the primitive engines in the English LPC.

The results show that the Named Entitiy (NE) Recognizer (NERecognizer.OpenNLP) is a bottleneck in the English LPC mainly because the recognitions of the 7 different NE types (date, location, money, organization, percentage, person, and time) are executed sequentially.

Possible solution to this problem is to run the recognition process in parallel for all 7 NE types. Another approach that will be evaluated in the process of further development of the English LPC is to replace the OpenNLP statistical NE recognizer with a solution, using language specific rules and lexicons.

6 Bulgarian LPC

We developed a Bulgarian language processing chain in order to demonstrate the ability of the system architecture to support more languages. The UIMA primitive engine wrappers, within the Bulgarian LPC, are the same as in the English one. The baseline NLP tools are developed by the Department of Computational Linguistics[11] at the Bulgarian Academy of Sciences. The Bulgarian NLP tools, integrated in our system, are based on the theory of finite-state language processing (Komani, 1999). The tools are implemented in C++ and are external for the JAVA-based UIMA environment.

The evaluation of the Bulgarian LPC was based on the processing of 200 Bulgarian fiction books, resulting in an average number of 100'000 tokens per document. The data, however, cannot be compared with the English LPC in terms of performance (average processing time per document) because of the different platforms, available tools and implementation approaches. The evaluation only demonstrates the capabilities of our system to support and manage LPCs for different languages.

7 Conclusion and Further Work

The described architecture of a language processing chain and its implementation in our system goes towards the direction of standardized multilingual online processing of language resources. The framework can be extended by integration of new types of tools and new languages and thus providing wider online coverage of linguistic services in a standardized manner.

A future extension of our system is the implementation of processing chains for other languages. The final version of German, Greek, Polish and Romanian LPCs will be available by the end of 2011.

The core LPC annotation set will be extended to support annotation of coreference chains by anaphora resolution tools and the results will be effectively used to improve text summarization and recognition process of named entities.

Last but not least, the LPC framework will be made available to a wider range of platforms and programming languages such as PHP and .Net via API implementation. Furthermore, we will provide a LPC engine web service in order to enable the integration with 3rd party systems in other languages, such as Python, Ruby, and Perl.

The source code of the pre-processing, processing and post-processing engines, as well as the core annotation schema, will be released as open-source under the GPL3 license as soon as it becomes mature enough for the open-source community.

Acknowledgements

The work reported in this paper laid the foundation of the "Applied Technology for Language-Aided CMS" project co-funded by the European Commission under the Information and Communications Technologies (ICT) Policy Support Programme (Grant Agreement No 250467). We would like to thank to consortium members for their guidance and valuable feedback for refinement, extensions and standardization of the NLP architecture of system.

References

A. Kornai, 1999. *Extended Finite State Models of Language.* Cambridge University Press. ISBN 0-521-63198-X.

Banerjee, Satanjeev. 2002. *Adapting the Lesk algorithm for word sense disambiguation to WordNet.* University of Minnesota, Duluth. Master's thesis.

H. Cunningham, D. Maynard, K. Bontcheva, V. Tablan. 2002: *GATE: A framework and graphical development environment for robust NLP tools and applications.* In Proceedings of the 40th Anniversary Meeting of the ACL (ACL'02). Philadelphia, US.

D. Ferrucci, A. Lally. 2004: *UIMA: an architectural approach to unstructured information processing in the corporate research environment.* Natural Language Engineering 10, No. 3-4, 327-348.

D. Ferrucci, A. Lally, D. Gruhl, E. Epstein, M. Schor, J.W. Murdock, A. Frenkiel, E. Browm, T. Hampp. 2006, *Towards an Interoperability Standard*

[11] http://dcl.bas.bg/en/home_en.html

for text and Multi-Modal Analytics, IBM Research Report, RC24122 (W0611-188).

Cristea D., Pistol, I. 2008. *Managing Language Resources and Tools using a Hierarchy of Annotation Schemas.* In Proceedings of Workshop 'Sustainability of Language Resources and Tools for Natural Language Processing', organized in conjunction with LREC 2008

OSGi Alliance., *OSGi Service Platform, 2009 Core Specification, Release 4, Version 4.2.*

I. Gordon, A. Wynne, Y. Liu. 2011, *Engineering High Performance Service-Oriented Pipeline Applications with MeDICi*, ICSOC 2010 Workshops, LNCS 6568, pp. 88-99.

Pattern-Based Ontology Construction from Selected Wikipedia Pages

Carmen Klaussner
University of Nancy 2
carmen@wordsmith.de

Desislava Zhekova
University of Bremen
zhekova@uni-bremen.de

Abstract

In this paper, we describe how ontologies can be built automatically from definitions obtained by searching *Wikipedia* for lexico-syntactic patterns based on the hyponymy relation. First, we describe how definitions are retrieved and processed while taking into account both recall and precision. Further, concentrating only on precision, we show how a consistent and useful domain ontology can be created with a beneficial precision of 80%.

1 Introduction

Knowledge bases are created to depict models of the world in the way we perceive it (Lacy, 2005). Nowadays, the general concern about the representation and communication of information increases the need to do the latter in a more meaningful and structured way (Brachman, 1983). Natural Language Processing (NLP) is a task, which is relatively easy for humans, but presents a complex computational challenge, as machines need carefully structured and well-designed content to unambiguously interpret information (Lacy, 2005). Ideally, one creates hand-crafted thesauri, such as *WordNet*[1], which are more reliable, but with information constantly changing, their coverage falls behind and costs of maintenance remain high. Thus, the possibility of creating knowledge bases from regularly updated knowledge sources, such as *Wikipedia*[2], which offers a vast amount of information on a wide variety of topics, seems to be a desirable solution for this difficult situation.

In this paper, we present the *Ontology creator (Oc)*[3], which extracts articles from *Wikipedia*, searches them for definitions and transfers the results into an appropriate knowledge representation using the ontology language *OWL*[4]. For this purpose, we use lexico-syntactic patterns that were reported to enable successful extraction of semantic relations (Hearst, 1992; Hearst, 1998; Mititelu, 2006; Mititelu, 2008). We evaluate the overall system performance and concentrate on successful hyponymy patterns in order to improve the resulting ontology's precision. Our hypothesis is that, by searching *Wikipedia* for the hyponymy relation, one can create consistent domain ontologies that can be easily used as good knowledge bases.

Thus, section 2 gives an overview of related projects. In section 3 we introduce the *Ontology creator* and describe how patterns are built and represented in the knowledge base. Further, in section 4 we evaluate the system performance and describe the most common errors that we observed. Section 5 closes with a concluding comment.

2 Related Work

In order to be able to extract definitions from domain-independent, unrestricted text, methods for discovering lexico-syntactic patterns are generally used, employing English corpora (Hearst, 1992; Hearst, 1998; Mititelu, 2006; Mititelu, 2008), such as the British National Corpus. Lexico-syntactic patterns can model semantic relations, such as hyponymy (the notion of hyponym–hypernym in the sense that if L_0 is a (kind of) L_1, then L_1 is hypernym to L_0 (Hearst, 1992)). As reported by Mititelu (2008), some patterns' success rates reach 100%. Suchanek et al. (2008) also used *Wikipedia* as the information base. The authors extract facts from *Wikipedia*'s infoboxes and combine these with the category structure of *WordNet* into an ontology. In this way, they maintain a clearly-structured hierarchy of word senses, enriched by *Wikipedia*'s vast amount of information with a final precision of 95%.

[1] http://wordnet.princeton.edu/
[2] http://en.wikipedia.org/wiki/
[3] http://sourceforge.net/projects/ontocreation/
[4] http://www.w3.org/TR/owl-ref/

3 Ontology Creation

In order to examine our hypothesis, we designed a system, the *Ontology creator*, that extracts definition relations from *Wikipedia* and converts them into a representation in *OWL*. Thus, in section 3.1 we introduce the system module that collects the articles. Further, in section 3.2, we introduce the parser that is used to assign grammatical structure to the individual sentences. Section 3.3 focuses on the lexico-syntactic patterns and section 3.4 explains how a pattern match is represented in *OWL*.

3.1 Extracting from Wikipedia

For the purpose of building a domain-specific ontology that concentrates on only one area of knowledge, it is necessary to collect articles that are highly topically-interlinked. Consequently, for the acquisition of articles from *Wikipedia*, we use a webcrawler, that starts with a given article and collects pages that have a referring link to it. We employ the open-source webcrawler *JSpider*[5], which is a highly configurable Web Spider engine. It allows to limit the search to only one website, to set the depth into its structure as well as the MIME type and to restrict the number of resources to be fetched per site. These features are all important to keep the articles' topics as closely related as possible. Currently, the depth level is set to two, which will produce a fair number of connected pages.

3.2 Parsing Articles

To gain a more accurate basis for the pattern search, the *Oc* uses the *Stanford parser* (Klein and Manning, 2003) to derive grammatical structures for each sentence. To bridge the stages from the HTML article to a usable list representation for the parser, we used the *DocumentPreprocessor*[6].

3.3 Building Lexico-Syntactic Patterns

For extracting definitions from text, we make use of lexico-syntactic patterns indicative of the hyponymy relation. Since definitions represent statements about the world, they are often expressed in terms of each other, where one concept is used to define another one (Brachman, 1983). Hyponymy, or the *IS-A* link, is one of the most basic types of conceptual relations for categorising classes of things in the world represented, carrying with it the notion of an explicit taxonomic hierarchy (Brachman, 1983). One deterministic characteristic of a taxonomic hierarchy is that all members inherit the properties of their respective superclass by virtue of being an instance of that class (*inheritance of properties*) (Brachman, 1983). Classes can be made up of subclasses or individuals. Classes may be viewed as classifying types, since they are abstract concepts of physical or virtual objects in the world. If a class is a subclass to another one, it will introduce a more specific concept than its superclass. Members of a class are instantiations of a particular class concept.

(1) *An apple is a fruit.*

Example (1) is the explicit version of ordinary hyponymy, which allows the inheritance of lexical semantic properties. There are lexico-syntactic patterns for different semantic relations, although hyponymy seems to yield the most accurate results. Yet, in order to use a specific pattern, one has to define how its variables are realised in natural language (exemplified in (2)) (Hearst, 1992):

(2) $NP_0\ such\ as\ NP_1, NP_2..., (and \mid or) NP_n$
$for\ all\ NP_i,\ 1 \leq i \leq n, hyponym(NP_i, NP_0)$

Building a search pattern for the above example is realised when an NP_0 (indicating the superclass) is represented by a single noun phrase consisting of a proper noun or a determiner, a noun and an optional adverbial phrase, whereas $NP_1, NP_2..., (and \mid or) NP_n$ may consist of more than one of the above noun phrases. Using these specifications to search for definitions in the sentence: *"Other forms of deception, such as disguises or forgeries, are generally not considered lies, though the underlying intent may be the same."*, one obtain matches as: *hyponym("forgery","deception")*, *hyponym("disguise","deception")*.

The patterns that were integrated into the *Oc* (listed in table 1) were suggested by Hearst (1992) and extended by Mititelu (2008). We used a subset of them, consisting of those rated the highest (discarding patterns for lack of results or for performance reasons). We also modify pattern 11 to admit plural matches and synonyms. In order to optimise the pattern search, we use the *JRegex*[7] li-

[5]http://j-spider.sourceforge.net/

[6]http://www.koders.com/java/

[7]http://sourceforge.net/projects/jregex/files/

No.	Pattern
1.	NP_0 *including* NP_{1+i}
2.	NP_0 *such as* NP_{1+i}
3.	*by such* NP_0 *as* NP_{1+i}
4.	NP_0 *(mainly | mostly | notably | particularly | usually | especially | principally)* NP_{1+i}
5.	NP_0 *in particular* NP_{1+i}
6.	NP_0 *like | except* NP_{1+i}
7.	NP_0 *for example* NP_{1+i}
8	NP_0 *other than* NP_{1+i}
9.	*state(=*NP_0*) of *ment(=*NP_{1+i}*)*
10.	NP_0 *i.e. | e.g.* NP_{1+i}
11.	NP_0, *(a) kind(s) | type(s) | form(s) of* NP_{1+i}

Table 1: Patterns for the acquisition of definitions

brary as well as *Commons Lang*[8].

3.4 Data Processing

In order to depict obtained definitions, we use an ontology representation. In the context of computer and information sciences, ontologies are meant to formally describe the terminological concepts and relationships that constitute a domain and generally provide a more common understanding of it as well as one that can be communicated between humans and machines. Thus, an ontology is a formally described, machine-readable collection or vocabulary of terms and their relationships and is used for knowledge sharing and reuse. Ontologies are encoded into files using ontology languages. A taxonomical ontology is the most common form of an ontology. It consists of a hierarchy of concepts which are related with specialisation *IS-A* relationships (Lacy, 2005). *OWL* is one of the languages that can be used to define ontologies and the associated individual data. For this project, we use the *OWL DL* dialect, as it supports consistency checks and reasoning and thus allows us to infer new facts from existing ones. The hyponymy relation in *OWL* can be expressed through the use of the relation between a superclass and its subclasses or members. Since we have only general indications of what the various matches can look like, we use a processing approach that is appropriate for most entities. The first decision to be taken is whether to make a noun phrase into a new class or an individual. This, however, is only relevant for NP_{1+i} since NP_0 always has instances and therefore always constitutes a class. An individual is only created if all its substrings have been classified as proper nouns by the *Stanford parser*, otherwise the current string is processed as a subclass. All modifiers are set to become subclasses of the predefined `characteristicValues` class and are linked to the respective class through the `hasCharacteristic` property. The number of superclasses/subclasses in a match is also dependent on the number of modifiers of both NP_0 and NP_{1+i}. If we consider as an example the following: *"... primitive animals, such as starfish ..."* that leads to the relation: *hyponym("starfish"-*NP_1*,"primitive animal"-*NP_0*)*, where a modifier of NP_0 is present , there will be a class `Animal`, which will be superclass to `PrimitiveAnimal` in an intersection with `hasCharacteristic some Primitive` and `Animal`. This in turn will be superclass to the `Starfish` class. We assume that nouns that are modified by some adjective would constitute an own concept and will only be more specific through this addition.

[8]http://commons.apache.org/lang/

Vanilla ⊂ Flavour
&
SubstanceWithFlavour:hasFlavour some Flavour
∩
Substance

Figure 1: Complex subclass example in OWL

Superclasses that consist of multiple nouns will not be subdivided any further, since one cannot assume that each noun by itself will actually constitute an own class or convey a separate concept in the same way. Figure 1 depicts the conversion of NP_0 featuring a head with an of-complement as in *"... flavour of substance, such as vanilla,..."*. In this case `Flavour` is made into a class with subclasses: `Vanilla,...etc.` and linked through a new property called `hasFlavour`, which has `Flavour` as its range, to the new `SubstanceWithFlavour` class, which will be subclass to a general `Substance` class.

This representation may not always be the most suitable, but concepts introduced by an of-complement[9] do present a difficult case. The processing of NP_{1+i} featuring an of-complement cannot be done in the same way, since there is no range for a possible property relation as in the previous example. Furthermore, the concept introduced by it is usually already rather specific. Although *OWL* allows defining distinct members and disjoint classes to mark mutual distinctness, we cannot in general make all classes or individuals

[9]Apart from "of", "for" and "in" were also allowed in the relation.

relations	count	detailed	
matched	65	ideal	52
		incomplete	7
		parser error	6
not matched	122	missing pattern	73
		parser error	2
		ambiguity	47
total	187		

Table 2: System results.

Precision	0.80
Recall	0.32
F_1-Measure	0.46
$F_{0.5}$-Measure	0.62

Table 3: Precision, recall and f-measures of *Oc*.

of a match mutually distinct/disjoint, since tests showed that two names, for instance, in an enumeration sometimes refer to the same individual.

4 Experiments

In order to investigate the system performance in regard to recall and precision, in section 4.1, we look at the performance overall and in section 4.2, we attempt to fine-tune the system to obtain the highest possible results in regard to precision.

4.1 System Evaluation

For the purpose of evaluating *Oc*'s performance, its final output was compared to a gold-standard. Therefore, we let the program process 20 topically-related *Wikipedia* article extracts (a total of 641 sentences) and compare the results to the gold-standard analysis of the same sentences. The manual analysis was subject to various criteria. A definition relation was only recognised as relevant or correct if the subclass/individual clearly translated into a sub-concept/instance of the superclass. Moreover, it was also evaluated how useful or appropriate the match is. We do not count more complex concepts that consist of a head with more than one of-complement or relations where subclass and superclass are separated by extra nested relative clauses. A match, whether successful or not, consists of a superclass and its subclass/individual. Relations that are obtained by simple derivation of the system are not counted, for example "... *snacks such as nuts, dried fruit,* ..." results in: *hyponym("Nut","Snack")*, *hyponym("DriedFruit","Snack")* and *hyponym("DriedFruit","Fruit")*. Yet, the third relation is derivative from the entity itself and is therefore not counted.

Table 2 lists all matched relations and the ones that are appropriate but were not matched. Of 187 relations in the sample, 65 were captured and 122 were not retrieved. Further, we show detailed distribution of all matched relations, of which 52 were matched ideally, 7 incompletely (parts were missing) and 6 incorrectly. We also show the various categories of relations that were not found. 73 are not retrieved because there is no appropriate capturing pattern yet, 2 are due to incorrectly-assigned parser tags and 47 matches are not found because of missing patterns. Thus, the *Oc* manages to reach a recall of 32% and precision of 80%. The F_1 measure with recall and precision weighed equally lies at 46%. Yet, using an abundant source, such as *Wikipedia*, takes the burden from the general lack of data, which allows us to rate precision twice as high as recall. Thus, $F_{0.5}$ marks a 62% overall system performance. A more systematic representation of the figures is shown in table 3.

4.1.1 Reasons for Non-Retrieval

Table 2 divides not matched relations into different categories:

Missing Patterns: If we consider the sentence: *"Piquance is considered another such basic taste in the East."*, we see that a pattern, such as $NP_1\ VP * \textit{another such}\ NP_0$ is needed. Similarly, in 73 of the 122 cases where relations are not captured a new pattern can be added.

Ambigious Patterns: Further, in 39% of the cases the appropriate pattern was also missing, but not as easy to replace as in the aforementioned scenario. For example in: *"Couverture is a term used for chocolates rich in cocoa butter..."* the range, *"term used for chocolates rich in cocoa butter"*, is a complex concept that is difficult to convert into one distinct superclass. An additional problem is that the mechanism would go as far as *"term"* and then stop, resulting only in Couverture $\subset$ Term. Although it is technically possible to check that there is no identifying clause following the prospective superclass, this has proved even for smaller cases to be extremely time-consuming and since the classic *IS-A* pattern did not account for many cases, it seemed wiser to forgo this option and leave out the pattern entirely. An even more difficult matter is presented by *"The word cacao itself derives from the* `Nahuatl, Aztec`

$$\text{Food,Poison} \subset \text{Flavour}$$
$$\text{SubstanceWithFlavour:hasFlavour} \quad \text{some} \quad \text{Flavour} \sqcap \text{Substance}$$

Figure 2: False processing example

category	count	%
Matched Relations	1706	100%
Correct Relations	1389	81%
Incorrect Relations	317	19%

Table 4: Ontology evaluation system results.

`language`, *word cacahuatl..."* leading to *hyponym("Nahuatl","Aztec language")*. There is little in regard to distinguishing environment to seperate results of mere enumerations from one of two terms that are in a hyponymy relationship and separated by a comma. Such examples lead to a drastic reduction in precision. Thus, it seemed sensible to process more articles on the topic to compensate for potential matches of these cases.

4.1.2 Captured Relations Issues

Having described frequent issues connected to definitions that were not captured, we now examine the ones that were retrieved. Even though with 80% the overall precision is reasonably satisfactory, we now also consider whether the respectively assigned representation in *OWL* is appropriate.

Patterns not Exclusive to Hyponymy: In some cases incorrect processing is due to the fact that the pattern is not exclusive to hyponymy, but covers simple non-hyponymy sentences as well, as in *"The majority of the Mesoamerican people made chocolate beverages, including Aztecs, who made..."* Yet, there are patterns that are more reliable to produce hyponymy and for the benefit of higher precision, one can concentrate on those.

Incomplete: The question of the appropriate representation in *OWL* is more difficult to evaluate. Most issues concern heads with an of-complement as superclass, where it is not clear what the subsequent clause is referring to. In most cases the *OWL* results are not wrong, but in at least 2 cases they seem awkward. For example: *"It refers to the ability to detect the flavour of substances such as food, certain minerals, and poisons, etc."* results in the structure in figure 2, while it should have processed as Food, Poison... $\subset$ Substance. This is partly due to the ambiguity resulting from the scope of the noun phrase referenced, for which the parser did not make any difference in structure. Thus, it is worthwhile to reconsider the way the of-complement is processed.

Creating an ontology from a small set of sentences, as was done here, is bound not to yield a large ontology. Our system obtained a total of 52 correct relations from searching 641 sentences. Most relations are topically-related, although there are some which are not, since referring links sometimes bear only a remote relation. In this ontology, which started on the term "chocolate", we also find facts about dialectologists. Creating larger ontologies may circumvent such problems which *Wikipedia*'s ample resources would also allow. Yet, what is essential and of primary interest to us, is the ontology's correctness and appropriateness.

4.2 Ontology Evaluation

After both a quantitative and qualitative analysis of the *Oc*, which were able to highlight the more frequent issues in connection to pattern-based ontology construction, we now concentrate on further enhancing precision. Recall can be increased by adding new patterns or widen the scope of the existing ones, although in our case it is essential not to compromise precision in any way. In this context, we choose to give precision a clear priority, since we are not looking for as many relations as possible, but for as many correct ones as possible. In order to further precision we concentrate on more successful hyponymy patterns and use a larger sample to obtain more accurate results. The articles were collected across a couple of different topics to also test for the patterns' suitability independent of the genre. Since this is a larger sample, we are not able to make a close analysis of whether the match yielding a relation is appropriate, as we had done during the first test. Important is only whether the final relation in the ontology is correct and appropriate in terms of content, superclass/subclass relation and processing, as we aim to determine the usefulness of the ontology overall. For the current experiment, we retained patterns: 2, 3, 4, 5, 8 and 9 (table 1). Table 4 depicts the final system results from it. The first row displays the number of retrieved relations overall (1706), followed by the number of correct ones (81%) and incorrect ones

$Tomato \subset Fruit$
$Tomato \subset Vegetable$

Figure 3: Contradictory facts

(19%). The of-complement matches appeared in 6% of all matched relations. The final system precision based on the ontology evaluation is slightly higher than the precision we achieved by evaluating the general system performance, which is not surprising since building larger ontologies also leads to a more accurate evaluation as well as to more overlaps of facts, where incorrect ones sometimes compromise correct ones. In the following part, we look at the different issues the resulting ontology poses and how they can be addressed in future research.

General Issues One of the general issues that can be observed is a classification problem. A specific entity is sometimes classified as two slightly controversial things. The facts in figure 3 both appear in the ontology, resulting from a more biological classification of tomato (fruit) and a maybe slightly more practical one (vegetable). Both facts are correct for their scope, but e.g. make it impossible to have fruit and vegetable as disjoint classes. At the moment, there is no component that deals with this issue, as a relative correctness would maybe also depend on the application area. Issues with of-complements, as have already been described in 4.1, remain. In the current set, 6% of the matches had an of-complement. In general, the easiest option is to disregard matches with these grammatical structures completely, however, if genuine they do express a particular kind of relationship that would not be captured in quite the same way otherwise.

Necessary Additions Until now, we had not included past participle in verb phrases. However, there are examples which show that this decision should be re-assessed: *"...NP JJ alcoholic NNS beverages, RB especially NP VBN distilled NNS beverages..."*. Since "distilled" is disregarded, this yields the relations *hyponym("alcoholic beverage","beverage")*, which is derived from the superclass: "alcoholic" modifying "beverage", and *hyponym("beverage","alcoholic beverage")* and consequently, every "beverage" is also per definition an "alcoholic beverage".

In addition, it would be beneficial to create more disjunct members or disjoint classes which would provide a possibility for a self-check in the *Oc*. Although, as has already been pointed out, classification issues may render this difficult.

5 Conclusion and Future Work

The overall aim of this project is to build consistent domain ontologies from facts obtained from websources, such as *Wikipedia*. In our work, a large number of relations remained unmatched, but the high precision encourages further research in this area. Since *Wikipedia* is an extremely big resource, one can afford losing prospective facts for the benefit of obtaining a more correct and hence more useful knowledge base. In order to enhance the *Oc*, it would be necessary to put more work towards the idea of disjointness and disjunct members in *OWL*. This way the resulting ontology would be more alert to irregularities. Further, one could evaluate the different patterns in regard to their respective ambiguity dimensions.

References

Ronald J. Brachman. 1983. What IS-A Is and Isn't: An Analysis of Taxonomic Links in Semantic Networks. *Computer*, 16(10):30–36, Oct.

Marti A. Hearst. 1992. Automatic acquisition of hyponyms from large text corpora. In *Proceedings of the 14th conference on Computational linguistics - Volume 2*, COLING '92, pages 539–545, Stroudsburg, PA, USA. ACL.

Marti A. Hearst. 1998. Automated discovery of WordNet relations. In *C. Fellbaum, WordNet: An Electronic Lexical Database*, pages 131–153. MIT Press.

Dan Klein and Christopher D. Manning. 2003. Fast Exact Inference with a Factored Model for Natural Language Parsing. In *Advances in Neural Information Processing Systems*, volume 15. MIT Press.

Lee W. Lacy. 2005. *Owl: Representing Information Using the Web Ontology Language*. Trafford Pub.

Verginica B. Mititelu. 2006. Automatic Extraction of Patterns Displaying Hyponym-Hypernym Co-Occurence from Corpora. In *Proceedings of CESCL*.

Verginica Barbu Mititelu. 2008. Hyponymy Patterns. In *Proceedings of the 11th international conference on Text, Speech and Dialogue*, TSD '08, pages 37–44, Berlin, Heidelberg. Springer-Verlag.

Fabian M. Suchanek, Gjergji Kasneci, and Gerhard Weikum. 2008. YAGO: A Large Ontology from Wikipedia and . *J. Web Sem.*

Lexico-Syntactic Patterns for Automatic Ontology Building

Carmen Klaussner
University of Nancy 2
carmen@wordsmith.de

Desislava Zhekova
University of Bremen
zhekova@uni-bremen.de

Abstract

In this paper, we evaluate different lexico-syntactic patterns in regard to their usefulness for ontology building. Each pattern is analysed individually to determine its respective probability to return the hyponymy relation. We also create different ontologies according to this accuracy criteria to show how it influences the resulting ontology. Using patterns with a success rate over 80% leads to an approximate accuracy of 77% in the final ontology.

1 Introduction

Computers have become increasingly important in the communication and usage of information. Therefore, also the way in which information is prepared for processing by computers has gained in interest, since machines do not possess human-comparable skills in regard to Natural Language Processing, when, for instance, solving issues of ambiguity (Lacy, 2005). Machines need knowledge bases that offer clearly structured and meaningful representation of information. However, information is not static, but instead constantly changing. This makes hand-crafted, reliable knowledge bases, such as *WordNet*[1] not feasible, since its constant extensions to ensure a continuing coverage would result in exceedingly-high costs. Automatic ontology building is one approach to address this issue. An ontology is a type of knowledge representation that is understandable to both humans and computers. It is populated by definitions or facts that are organised into hierarchies. These thereby model relationships of and dependencies between entities in the world. Automatic ontology building can be realised in different ways. One approach is pattern-based extraction of definition relations, which are then converted into the respective ontology representation. Pattern-based extraction has shown quite reasonable success rates, while it is easy to implement and can be applied to unrestricted text (Hearst, 1998). Although using lexico-syntactic patterns for ontology building is reasonably successful, ambiguous patterns, which return correct as well as incorrect results, remain problematic since they can lead to an overall decrease in accuracy for the whole ontology.

In the present paper, we assess various lexico-syntactic patterns that model the semantic relation of hyponymy in order to identify those, which are both frequent and reliable to return this relation. These patterns have been classified as successful in connection with other knowledge sources, whereas we aim to measure their reliability with *Wikipedia*. Our hypothesis is, that the usage of reliable lexico-syntactic patterns indicative of hyponymy, return relations that can create useful, widely-applicable ontologies. The latter are suitable as knowledge bases in many computational linguistic applications (e.g. Machine Translation, Information Extraction, Text Generation, etc).

Thus, section 2 gives a short overview of related work projects and approaches. In section 3, we introduce the system that we use for the automatic ontology building – the *Ontology creator (Oc)*[2]. We also describe how patterns are employed, while further, in section 4, we evaluate the different lexico-syntactic patterns in regard to their accuracy and describe the most common issues that we observed during our experiments. We create different ontolgies in order to effectively investigate to what extent using successful/unsuccessful patterns influences the overall accuracy of the final outcome. In section 5 we conclude and suggest further approaches for the advancement of our work.

[1] http://wordnet.princeton.edu/

[2] http://sourceforge.net/projects/ontocreation/

2 Related Work

There has been considerable work in regard to pattern-based extraction of information. Hearst (1992), for instance, identified a method for discovering new lexico-syntactic patterns. This entails searching corpora for specific terms that are connected through a semantic relation and deriving possible patterns from the results. If they prove to successfully return the same relation, these patterns can be applied domain-independently in order to identify and extract definitions. Lexico-syntactic patterns can model various semantic relations, although hyponymy seems to yield the most accurate results (Hearst, 1992). Moreover, they have the advantage of a frequent occurrence across many different text genres, and a reasonable overall accuracy even with little or no pre-encoded knowledge (Hearst, 1998). Mititelu (2006) also pursued the same aim and applied a slightly different method for discovering patterns, while working with English corpora. For some patterns, the subsequent success rates were as high as 100% (Mititelu, 2008).

Another approach very similar to ours is the one presented by Maynard et al. (2009). The authors also use lexico-syntactic patterns for the automatic creation of ontologies, but since they do not restrict their set of extracted relations only to hyponymy, the final ontology hardly reaches 50% precision. The authors conclude that the achieved results are very promising, however, they see the need for further improvement and refinement of the used lexico-syntactic patterns.

3 Pattern-Based Ontology Construction

The *Oc*, which was conceived for automatic ontology building, consists of different parts, that are presented in the following section. Section 3.1 introduces ontologies and the hyponymy relation, that forms the basis for the lexico-syntactic patterns. We show how different definition types, that were returned by the patterns, are transformed into an ontology representation using the web ontology language *OWL*. Section 3.2 describes the outer modules that were integrated into the *Oc* to obtain a knowledge source for the definition search.

3.1 Patterns in Ontology Building

In the context of computer and information sciences, an ontology is a machine-readable collection of terms and is used in knowledge sharing and reuse. Ontologies can encode models of the world, that is: objects, concepts, entities and the relationships that hold between them. Ontologies can be constructed on a textual basis and encoded into files using ontology languages. *OWL*[3] is one of the languages that can be used for this purpose. Relationships between entities in *OWL* exist between superclasses and subclasses or superclasses and individuals/members. Classes may have subclasses, which introduce more specific concepts than their superclass, or members/instantiations of a particular class concept. Their relation is generally one of hyponymy (in the sense that: If NP_i is a (kind of) NP_0, then for $1 \leq i$, hyponym (NP_i, NP_0) (Hearst, 1998)) or the *IS-A* link. This represents one of the most basic types of conceptual relations carrying with it the notion of an explicit taxonomic hierarchy, which allows all members of a particular superclass to inherit the properties of that class (Brachman, 1983). In *OWL*, these attributes of class members are introduced by the property relation and can be restricted through the superclass.

Lexico-syntactic patterns are suitable for automatic ontology building, since they model semantic relations. These display exactly the kind of relation between their parts that makes them easily translatable into an ontology representation. The lexico-syntactic pattern in (1) (Hearst, 1992) corresponds to the classic hyponymy relation:

(1) If $(NP_0 \; such \; as \; NP_1, NP_2 ..., (and \mid or) NP_n)$
$for \; all \; NP_i, \; 1 \leq i \leq n, hyponym(NP_i, NP_0)$

The pattern specification as in (1) is able to identify and match sentences, as for example: *"The other major European powers, such as the UK, still had high fertility rates..."* Consequently, a lexico-syntactic pattern is a reoccuring environment that is indicative of a certain relationship between two or more entities. Having identified a lexico-syntactic pattern for a particular relation, it can usually be applied to unrestricted text and across different genres. When these relations are then transferred into *OWL*, there are different issues to be considered. First of all, there is the decision of whether to make a new entity an individual rather than a class. In this context, where there are only general indications of how the results will look like, the processing approach has to

[3] http://www.w3.org/TR/owl-ref/

NightTerrors

$\sqcap$

ParasomniacDisorder

$\sqcap$

(Disorder $\sqcap$ hasCharacterisitic some Parasomniac)

$\sqcap$

Disorder

Figure 1: Simple subclass example in OWL

be one that is likely to be suitable in most cases.

All NP_0s become superclasses, since all of them will have either members or subclasses and should therefore constitute a class. A NP_{1+i}, on the other hand, will only be an individual, when all its substrings have been classified as proper nouns by the parser, otherwise it will be a subclass. Modifiers are generally set to become subclasses of the predefined `characteristicValues` class and linked to its class through the `hasCharacteristic` property. Modifiers to both NP_0 and NP_{1+i} also determine the number of superclass/subclass levels that are created. For example, if we consider the match *"....night terrors other than parasomniac disorders ..."* (leading to the relation: *hyponym("night terrors"-NP_1, "parasomniac disorders"-NP_0))*, where a modifier of NP_0 is present (as visualised in figure 1). First a general class `Disorder` is created. Through an intersection with `hasCharacteristic some Parasomniac` and `Disorder`, it will be indirect superclass to `NightTerrors`. It is generally assumed, that nouns that are modified by some adjective would otherwise constitute an own concept and will only be more specific through this addition. For two joined nouns, we could not make the same generalisation, since not all of them share this construction, where one concept modifies another and each convey a separate concept.

The conversion of NP_0s featuring a head with a complement leads to multiple problematic cases, such as varying scope and irregularities in processing. Yet, it is not our goal to discuss them here, since they are presented in more detail in (Klaussner and Zhekova, 2011).

The *Oc* uses the *OWL DL dialect*, which supports reasoning and thus inference of new facts from existing ones. It also allows to determine whether an ontology is consistent (inconsistency is then the case when an individual is a member of two mutually disjoint classes, e.g. an instance that is young and old at the same time). Although *OWL* allows to mark this mutual distinctness of members or classes, we cannot make all classes or individuals of a match mutually distinct/disjoint, since two names can often refer to the same individual. Only patterns that specifically indicate different subtypes can be processed in this way.

3.2 Knowledge Resource

For the purpose of testing our patterns and the later building of ontologies, we used articles obtained from *Wikipedia*, which has the advantage of being a regularly-updated knowledge resource, that contains articles on a wide variety of topics, although without an explicit hierarchy. The articles were extracted by a webcrawler, which is given a specific search term, which it will then use to further collect pages that have a referring link to it. Building a domain-specific ontology on possibly only one area of knowledge, requires a collection of articles of which as many as possible will be topically-interlinked. For this project, we chose the open-source webcrawler *JSpider*[4], which is a highly configurable Web Spider engine. It allows to limit the search to only one website, set the depth into its structure as well as the MIME type and the number of to be fetched resources per site. These features are all important to keep the articles' topics as closely related as possible. In order to be able to search and process the data, so that specific patterns can be identified, the data itself has to be transformed into a format that allows us to recognise those patterns. Such a transformation can be achieved by the application of a syntactic parser. The *Oc* makes use of the *Stanford parser* (Klein and Manning, 2003) to derive grammatical structures for each sentence, which then form a more accurate basis for the later pattern search. The *Stanford parser* is a freely available lexicalised PCFG (probabilistic context-free grammar) parser, that allows the user to employ a specific configuration. When extracted, the articles need to be transformed from their original HTML format to an appropriate sentence list representation. For this purpose, we use the *DocumentPreprocessor*[5]. After obtaining the articles and letting each sentence be processed by the parser, the *Oc* starts searching for specific patterns.

[4] http://j-spider.sourceforge.net/

[5] http://www.koders.com/java/

4 Experiments

More ambiguous patterns tend to introduce accuracy issues to the resulting ontologies and will compromise the ontolgies' reliability and thus also its usefulness overall. For this reason, it is necessary to separate more reliable patterns from those, which will be of very little value given a majority of ambiguous results. Thus, in section 4.1, we describe the evaluation of different lexico-syntactic patterns and afterwards discuss the most common errors that were observed. In section 4.2, we show how the respective successfulness/accuracy of a pattern influences the value of the ontology.

4.1 Pattern Evaluation

In order to evaluate a pattern's usefulness for automatic ontology creation, we assess each pattern's success rate individually. All patterns are tested on a corpus containing 733 *Wikipedia* articles (a sample consisting of 161585 sentences), that were collected across different areas to also ensure a pattern's applicability across genres. In the ideal case, patterns are both successful and frequent. A given lexico-syntactic pattern is considered to have matched correctly, if its results (hypernym/hyponym(s)) can be rephrased into a structure as the one presented in example (2).

(2) $NP_1, NP_2 ..., (and \mid or)\ NP_n\ is\ a\ NP_0$
$for\ all\ NP_i,\ 1 \leq i \leq n, hyponym(NP_i, NP_0)$

Hence, the following sentence: *"The other major European powers, such as the UK, still had high fertility rates..."*, which leads to the relation: *hyponym("UK","MajorEuropeanPower")*, needs to be rephrasable into: `UK is a MajorEuropeanPower`.

Another important point is the "one-directionality" of the respective pattern, meaning the position of hyponym and hypernym in relation to the pattern is not arbitrary. A match to a pattern should always display the same order of hyponym/hypernym: $hyponym\ (pattern - specific\ part)\ hypernym$, since otherwise processing can create false results.

The patterns used for the *Oc* (shown in table 1) were suggested by Hearst and Mititelu (Hearst, 1992; Mititelu, 2008). Some of the patterns were discarded for lack of results or performance reasons (more ambiguous patterns, such as the classic *IS-A* were not used here as the results were altogether too erroneous). Pattern grouping under the same number indicates a similarity in the pattern, that allows for a group search.

No.	Pattern
1.	NP_0 *including* NP_{1+i}
2.	NP_0 *such as* NP_{1+i}
3.	*by such* NP_0 *as* NP_{1+i}
4.	NP_0 *like* NP_{1+i}
5.	NP_0 *except* NP_{1+i}
6a.	NP_0 *e.g.* NP_{1+i}
6b.	NP_0 *i.e.* NP_{1+i}
7a.	NP_0, *(a) kind(s) | type(s) | form(s) of* NP_{1+i}
7b.	NP_0: *(a) kind(s) | type(s) | form(s) of* NP_{1+i}
8.	NP_0 *other than* NP_{1+i}
9.	*There (are | is) (could | would) be two types of* NP_0 *(: | ,)* NP_{1+i}
10a.	NP_0 *especially* NP_{1+i}
10b.	NP_0 *notably* NP_{1+i}
10c.	NP_0 *particularly* NP_{1+i}
10d.	NP_0 *usually* NP_{1+i}
10e.	NP_0 *mostly* NP_{1+i}
10f.	NP_0 *mainly* NP_{1+i}
10g.	NP_0 *principally* NP_{1+i}

Table 1: *Patterns for the acquisition of definitions*

No.	Overall occurrence	% of success	one-directional
1.	601	409 (68%)	No
2.	2389	2107 (88.2%)	Yes
3.	9	9 (100%)	Yes
4.	401	330 (82%)	Yes
5.	18	10 (56%)	Yes
6a.	170	134 (79%)	Yes
6b.	no occur.	nil	nil
7a.	48	31 (65 %)	Yes
7b.	7	6 (85%)	Yes
8.	19	16 (84 %)	Yes
9.	4	4 (100%)	Yes
10a.	61	9 (89%)	Yes
10b.	22	13 (59%)	Yes
10c.	29	23 (79%)	Yes
10d.	9	7 (78%)	Yes
10e.	5	4 (80%)	Yes
10f.	3	2 (67%)	Yes
10g.	no occur.	nil	nil

Table 2: *Pattern success rates*

Table 2 shows the results for the pattern evaluation. The number label indicates the specific pattern according to table 1. Column 1 displays overall occurrence in the whole corpus. Further, column 2 shows all successful ones out of all occurrences in both number and percent. The final column lists the directionality for each pattern. Only two patterns (1 and 2) obtained over 600 occurrences in the corpus. All others have results much lower than that. The most successful patterns (4 and 9), with a 100% accuracy, are also among the most infrequent. Patterns 6b and 10g did not occur at all in the used data.

4.1.1 Common Pattern Issues

In this section, we discuss the most common issues regarding the pattern search in our experiments.

Range A rather frequent issue is the one of range. Here, problems occur, when the extracted entities, NP_0 and NP_{1+i}, are not in a hypernym-hyponym(s) relationship, due to the fact that the hyponym(s) refer to another entity than the one extracted, as the pattern can vary in its scope. For example, let us consider the following sentence: *"Other foreign artists also settled and worked in or near Paris, like Vincent van Gogh..."* from which were extracted the relation: *hyponym("Vincent van Gogh","Paris")*, instead of the correct one: *hyponym("Vincent van Gogh", "ForeignArtist")*.

One-directionality of a pattern Some patterns are not only one-directional. Thus, a match as the following is also returned: *"The newspaper created a new children section covering children books, including both fiction and non-fiction, and initially counting only hardback sales."*. Although, here "non-fiction/fiction children books" is implied, this match instead results in the relations: *hyponym("Fiction","ChildrenBooks") hyponym("NonFiction","ChildrenBooks")*. The relation should be realised in the reverse order, as not all fiction or non-fiction books are children's books. If a pattern displays such a tendency, the latter can be particularly problematic, since even correct matches will produce incorrect results.

Pattern-specific issues An interesting case is the sentence: *"Lentil is also commonly used in Ethiopia as a stew like dish called Kik..."*. It shows a use of "like" other than in a construction, such as NP_0 *like* NP_{1+i}. Although the match does theoretically fit the pattern, its meaning does not entail the intended relationship of hyponymy.

Extra-embedded subclauses Another problem can be observed, namely that hypernym and hyponym(s) are not directly named after each other, but interrupted by a subclause, sometimes even containing another match as in *"There are two types of unsweetened cocoa powder: natural cocoa, like the sort produced by Hershey's and Nestlé using the Broma process, and Dutch-process cocoa, such as the Droste brand..."*

4.2 Ontology Creation

In the following part, we describe three different ontologies, that were created from the pattern matches. One is populated by the results for the patterns with an accuracy level of over 80%. The second features all remaining matches from the patterns with an accuracy of below 80%. The third combines all patterns. Since we cannot check the source for every relation in the ontology, we apply a more restrictive approach to the results. The aim is to determine the usefulness of the ontology overall. Therefore, it is only important, whether a relation in the ontology is correct and appropriate in terms of general content and the correctness of superclass/subclass relation.

Table 3 shows the results for the three ontology evaluations. In row 1 are the numbers for the more accurate patterns, below the less accurate ones and row 3 shows the combined ontology. The total number of the relations of the first setting is 4566, of which 3534 were correct and 1032 were incorrect. Respectively, the number of the relations from the second setting is 1508, of which 798 were found to be correct and 710 incorrect. The total number of the combined ontology with all patterns is 5823, of which 4140 were correct and 1683 incorrect.

Evaluation As this evaluation shows, there is little to be gained by using patterns with an accuracy of below 80%. Only 53.9% of the resulting ontology was correct. Whereas using more reliable patterns had an ontology accuracy of 77.4 %. For the ontology that used all patterns, an overall accuracy of 71.1% was achieved. Although, there is only about 6% difference between using only >80% accuracy patterns and using all patterns, this difference is mainly due to the fact, that the percentage of >80% patterns was overall much higher in the sample. Hence, using patterns with higher accuracy is likely to be effective in the long run. For simple class concepts, there are generally no problems. However, more complex concepts, as introduced by extra complements, do present difficulties in regard to scope, where a correct match will frequently be processed incorrectly. As *Wikipedia* is a relatively large resource, one may not have to rely on such problematic relations, since individual facts do occur more often. Another more general issue are "relational" words, such as: *different, related, nearby, comparable...* In most cases, these relate to a broader context and

setting	overall success	matched	successful match	unsuccessful match
1.	>80%	4566	3534 (77.4%)	1032 (22.6%)
2.	<80%	1508	798 (53.0%)	710 (47.0%)
3.	56-100%	5823	4140 (71.0%)	1683 (29.0%)

Table 3: *Ontology comparison*

bear less semantic relevance. It would therefore be worthwhile investigating their contribution to the ontology-building process. The question of making a new entity a class or an individual is also a complex issue, since there may be different semantic implications linked to it. Considering individual countries, there may be two possibilities; one is an interpretation for a country as an individual and the other as a class, which may have members itself: France $\in$ Country $\bigvee$ (Lorraine, Languedoc-Roussillon $\in$ France) $\subset$ Country.

For these reasons, also appropriate processing and representation of the results has to be considered.

Most errors are connected to issues as outlined in 4.1.1. Furthermore, it can be beneficial to analyse successful and frequent patterns more closely to see what grammatical constructions are most likely to occur in connection with them, so one can adapt the processing accordingly. As this rather superficial analysis is already able to effect a considerable increase in performance, looking at individual patterns in detail is reasonably worthwhile. In addition to using frequent and successful patterns, one can add the successful, but less frequent ones, as they do not put much strain on the system. Yet, their real accuracy level is questionable, since they do not occur often enough to confirm it.

5 Conclusion and Future Work

The overall aim of this project is to evaluate lexico-syntactic patterns in regard to their accuracy and reliability to match definitions in articles from online web sources, such as *Wikipedia*. Results are then transferred into an ontology representation using the language *OWL*. We show that using reliable patterns, one can create an ontology with an overall accuracy of 77%. However, some issues in connection to the incorrectly matched relations as well as processing remain. It is necessary to conduct larger experiments to find out how frequent a specific issue appears in text. Using lexico-syntactic patterns to extract definition relations has shown substantial success, which justifies a closer analysis of pattern ambiguity and other pattern-related issues. In general, since *Wikipedia* is a big resource with a vast amount of articles, one is able to afford losing some prospective facts for the benefit of precision and consequently to obtain a more accurate and thus also more useful knowledge base.

References

Ronald J. Brachman. 1983. What is-a is and isn't: An analysis of taxonomic links in semantic networks. *Computer*, 16(10):30–36, Oct.

Marti A. Hearst. 1992. Automatic acquisition of hyponyms from large text corpora. In *Proceedings of the 14th conference on Computational linguistics - Volume 2*, COLING '92, pages 539–545, Stroudsburg, PA, USA. ACL.

Marti A. Hearst. 1998. Automated discovery of wordnet relations. In *C. Fellbaum, WordNet: An Electronic Lexical Database*, pages 131–153. MIT Press.

Carmen Klaussner and Desislava Zhekova. 2011. Pattern-Based Ontology Construction From Selected Wikipedia Pages. In *Proceedings of RANLP 2011 Student Research Workshop*.

Dan Klein and Christopher D. Manning. 2003. Fast exact inference with a factored model for natural language parsing. In *Advances in Neural Information Processing Systems*, volume 15. MIT Press.

Lee W. Lacy. 2005. *Owl: Representing Information Using the Web Ontology Language*. Trafford Publishing.

Diana Maynard, Adam Funk, and Wim Peters. 2009. Using lexico-syntactic ontology design patterns for ontology creation and population. In *Proceedings of WOP2009 collocated with ISWC2009*, volume 516. CEUR-WS.org, November.

Verginica Barbu Mititelu. 2006. Automatic extraction of patterns displaying hyponym-hypernym co-occurence from corpora. In *Proceedings of the First CESCL*.

Verginica Barbu Mititelu. 2008. Hyponymy patterns. In *Proceedings of the 11th international conference on Text, Speech and Dialogue*, TSD '08, pages 37–44, Berlin, Heidelberg. Springer-Verlag.

Towards a Grounded Model for Ontological Metaphors

Sushobhan Nayak
Indian Institute of Technology, Kanpur, India
snayak@iitk.ac.in

Abstract

A novel approach to learning metaphors without any prior knowledge is proposed, in which ideas are acquired as concrete concepts and later on develop their abstraction. A grounded model of linguistic concepts and a hierarchical probability map is used to interpret/generate ontological metaphors.

1 Introduction

Consider the following sentences:

- You are *wasting* my time. (TIME IS MONEY)(Lakoff and Johnson(1980))
- We need to *combat* inflation. (INFLATION IS AN ENTITY)(Lakoff and Johnson(1980))

These usages are so ingrained in everyday conversation that we fail to recognize that they are actually metaphors that try to describe abstract concepts in terms of concrete ones(Lakoff and Johnson(1980)). A proper understanding of language and thought therefore calls for an increased and focused research into metaphors and the way they are acquired, interpreted and generated.

As such, there have been many attempts at interpreting metaphors over the years. The earlier works like Wilks(1975); Fass(1991) are based on a violation of selectional restrictions in a given context. Kintsch(2000) effectively uses LSA to interpret metaphors like "My lawyer is a shark". However, these models are incapable of handling Lakoff and Johnson(1980))'s view of metaphors. The works that are closest to the modern view, in their attempt at interpreting common text from financial or other domains, encompass Narayanan(1997); Narayanan(1999). Shutova et al.(2010) also show metaphor paraphrasing using noun-verb clustering. However, they both need a hand-coded seed set or metaphor repository to do further learning. The model proposed here assumes no prior knowledge. From multimodal input, we first ground some basic concepts and using them, exploit the language syntax to learn/interpret/generate metaphorical mappings in a natural way that emulates language learning in an early learner.

2 Proposed Model

The models till date have looked at metaphors as something that is acquired/interpreted differently than common language. However, the treatment by Lakoff and Johnson(1980)) suggests that we should look at metaphor acquisition as we look at language acquisition, and not something that is interpreted/acquired *after* we have acquired the basic nuances of the language. There is ample evidence in literature to suggest that basic linguistic forms can be grounded(Roy and Reiter(2005)). Consider an early learner who has acquired the grounded concepts of the verb *impale* and understands that, based on its experience till date, only a living entity is capable of executing it. Then it comes across this:"*Arrogance impaled him.*" Now based on this linguistic input only, in the absence of any other physical stimuli, what is to stop the learner from interpreting 'arrogance' as a living entity? It is only when it comes across other usages of the concept 'arrogance' that its initial idea that 'arrogance is an entity' might be modified to 'arrogance is an abstract concept'. However, as one might notice, 'arrogance is an entity' is actually a well established metaphor. This leads us to look at metaphor acquisition in a different light. Why look at 'arrogance' etc. as abstract concepts that *need* to be understood through grounded concepts *later*? Why not look at them as *grounded* concepts, which *later* acquire the abstractness, there by being imparted with metaphorical mappings, which is suggested by the example alluded to before? The proposed model takes this approach, where we start with grounding some very basic verbs/nouns and then go on to acquire/interpret/generate ontological metaphors (a metaphor in which abstract notions are projected through concrete concepts of objects/entities/substance etc., i.e. some physical entity.), just as we would do any other words/concepts.In the discussion that follows, it's assumed that language representation incorporates Langacker(1987))'s *image schema*, and that language understanding incorporates Embodied Construction Grammar(ECG) (Bergen et al.(2004)).

2.1 Grounded Forms

It is more or less established in literature that linguistic concepts are cognitively characterized in terms of *image schemas*, which are schematized recurring patterns from the embodied domains of force, motion, and space(Langacker(1987); Lakoff and Johnson(1980)). Before we go into learning ontological metaphors, we create a grounded system that helps modify/nurture image schemas of new concepts as they come along.

Almost all types of ontological metaphors come under three broad categories of an Object, a Substance or a Container. In fact, these concepts emerge directly for an early learner through physical experience(Lakoff and Johnson(1980)). A probable scenario for an artificial learner can be to try grounding concepts from multimodal inputs of image, sound and written transcripts. Consider the work by Mukerjee et al.(2011), where they try to discover coreference using image grounded verb argument structure. From multimodal input of a video, and associated narration, they have been able to learn the verb structure CHASE(A,B). This can be further extended to derive the image schemas of CHASE and the actors A and B. Mukerjee et al.(2011) use velocity features of the objects in the video to unsupervisingly cluster them to find the cluster of CHASE(A,B). This cluster that contains much of the velocity related information for concept CHASE can be presented as an image schema for CHASE(A,B); and since CHASE is a two-party interaction, learning CHASE means the concept of agents A and B are also learned. In the present model, the centroid, maxima, and minima of the feature cluster have been stored to represent CHASE[1], whereas A and B are being treated as *point objects*, i.e. entities whose behavior would remain unchanged if they are replaced by geometrical points in the visual space they act in. Storing maxima/minima also helps us create image schemas of adjectives SLOW() and FAST(). In this model, these functions take an action, say CHASE, as argument, and output the minimum or maximum of the action's velocity feature. With this sort of grounding at hand, we can handle the mental simulation part in ECG(Bergen et al.(2004)) used for understanding linguistic occurrences. A *fast(chase)* would mean the simulation runs with the image schema of CHASE, with the velocity features being maintained at their maximum.

We now have grounded forms of CHASE(A,B), SLOW(),FAST() and entities(point-objects). We next take cues from Mukerjee and Sarkar(2007) and learn IN(A,B), OUT OF(A,B), INTO(A,B) and the 'container'. Mukerjee and Sarkar(2007) use Voronoi-based features to distinguish space into the interior or exterior of an object. In this model, the image schemas of IN(A), OUT OF(A), INTO(A) and the 'container' are interpreted as being interconnected. While the boundaries of the object-container in the visual input are taken as the boundaries of concept 'container', IN(A,B) is represented by substance/entity A inside container B. INTO(A,B) and OUT OF(A,B) are schemas in two states, where the object/substance A is in/out of the container B in one state, and changes its position in the other. Substance is crudely grounded as something that can't be represented by a point object, i.e. something that is not executing rigid body motion. Essentially, combined with, say INTO(A,B), if in the motion schema simulation of action INTO(A,B), A can't be represented by a point, it is taken as a Substance. This further allows us to ground adjectives MORE(A) and LESS(A) for Substances, based on the change they bring about in the volume of the Voronoi interior.

To reiterate, the objective of this section is not to claim that a proper image schema has been developed for the above concepts. The goal here has been to show that even from a simple multimodal input like a video and the associated commentary, an intelligent agent can get a crude grounded model of linguistic concepts. This can only mean that an early human learner will be much better at this job. To summarize, the model has at its disposal, the grounded concepts of Entity/Object,

[1] This is just the chosen representation. One might well like to store the whole cluster for representing the action. The claim here is not that the present representation is the one that is actually there; the idea is just to demonstrate that even such a crude model works.

Substance, Container, CHASE(A,B), INTO(A,B), IN(A,B), OUT OF (A,B), MORE(A), LESS(A), SLOW() and FAST(). However, these alone are insufficient to show how metaphors are acquired ('chase' verb is sparsely used in general literature), and we therefore *assume* the availability of GIVE(AgentA, AgentB, Entity/Substance C), SOME(Substance A) and SPEND(Substance A) hereafter.

2.2 Concept Acquisition

The vast majority of our vocabularies are learned later purely from the linguistic input(Bloom(2000)). The goal from here-on will thus be to acquire language concepts with the help of the aforementioned grounded concepts and a text corpus. To determine how far language usage alone can help shape the concept of metaphors, we compiled a list of sentences from Lakoff and Johnson(1980)) and Lakoff et al.(1991) that correspond to the metaphor-mappings for Containers, Objects and Substances. The salient findings are:

- Of the 85 sentences denoting Container metaphors,in 65, the abstract idea was imparted the image schema of a container based only on the prepositions *in/out*. In the rest 20, adjectives (*full, empty*) and verbs (*explode, erupt, fill*) took the mantle.
- In all of the 63 sentences for Object metaphor, the Object property was imparted to the concept because VERB(A,B) took object arguments, i.e. verbs were the primary basis of metaphor mapping.
- Of the 42 sentences for Substance metaphors, 17 mappings were done based on adjectives (*more, less*) while the rest were of the type Container contains Substance, i.e. first the Container property was imparted, and then whatever was supposed to be inside the container was called a substance.

Based on this observation, we construct a model of concept acquisition which incorporates the following bold (unproven) claims:

Claim 1 Verbs, adjectives, nouns and prepositions all play roles in concept acquisition and have varying importance in different forms of concept acquisition

Claim 2 There are only a limited representative verbs/adjectives that are grounded (i.e. have stable and distinct image schema), and the rest import their schemas and modify them to suit themselves. So, this structure is hierarchically organized.

Claim 3 They can be represented in terms of a probability map, whence we can get an idea of the interplay between different concepts.

Claim 4 Abstract concepts are acquired as concrete concepts first, just like any other grounded concept, and later they acquire their abstraction due to emergence of future evidence.

Claim 1 is supported by the observation that precedes it. Claim 2 is somewhat self-explanatory, and better understood through examples. Consider verbs `impart`, `provide`, `shower`, `bombard`, `donate` etc. A close look will reveal that they can all be derived from GIVE(). For instance, SHOWER() (as in 'shower somebody with praises') can be a combination of verb GIVE() and adjective MORE(). In fact this kind of representation seems more memory-efficient. If we are required to store image schemas of the millions of words that we come across, our memory will be a mess. Storing only a select few and combining them to derive the others is a more structured, systematic and efficient mechanism. Furthermore, we should also notice that we had to take help of an adjective to describe a verb, which reinforces Claim 1. The first level of hierarchy consists of these grounded forms which are distinguishable. The second level is the derived one that draws from all the nodes of the first level. Claim 3 asserts that this interplay can be represented through a probability map. For instance, for a single verb GIVE(), the adjectives can be assigned probabilities based on how frequently they modify GIVE() to produce an understandable image schema, so that we have an idea of which ones are more probable of appending to the verb when a new concept involving the same emerges. We will later see how this map can incorporate many aspects of the metaphor acquisition task.

2.2.1 The Model

We now describe the metaphor acquisition model based on Claim 4. We first have a repository of grounded concepts. Then as the learner is exposed to more sentences, the sentences are searched for contexts similar to the ones already learned. The noun arguments, which might be new concepts, are assigned a dynamic probability of belonging to one of the classes of Object/Substance/Container. With more evidence, these probabilities are modified within a reward/penalty scenario. All concepts are treated concrete unless evidence to the contrary crops up.

The model is better understood through examples. Let the learner come across the sentence – 'I can't give you much time' ≡ GIVE(MUCH(`time`)). Now MUCH() takes a Substance as an argument. So `time` is assigned the schema of Substance with probability 1. Then GIVE(`time`), which takes either a Substance or an Object as its argument, dynamically changes the probabilities to $2/3$ for Substance and $1/3$ for Object. When it further comes across "In time, you will understand", i.e. IN(`time`), the probabilities are modified to 1/4, 2/4 and 1/4 for container, substance and object respectively. This assignment helps us in two ways – firstly, it prevents us from exclusively assigning the concept to any single class, thereby allowing us to model metaphors that contextually take up the properties of different classes. And secondly, it also gives us an idea of the affinity of the abstract concepts for different classes. To avoid confusion, as of now, from the above example, we can only assume that `time` is a concrete concept that has properties of Object, Container and Substance [2].

ACQUISITION: We next tackle the problem of distinguishing between abstract and concrete concepts. Consider an early learner who comes across the following:

- Llama is a four-legged animal.
- Anger is a red-eyed demon.

How does the subject distinguish between concrete Llama and abstract Anger? One way to look at it would be that as soon as the learner comes across these, it incorporates the features in the image schema of the concept. The schema field is then searched for possible conflicts. If two properties are in conflict, they are brought to the CONTEST field in the image schema, where 'voting' takes place between the conflicting scenarios. Voting is done to take care of two possibilities. First, the conflict that arises might be due to a false evidence. If one of the properties is discarded based on some false evidence, the schema might become erroneous. So both are kept, but they are assigned probabilities of expected occurrence. Secondly, it gives room for metaphorical descriptions. For instance, suppose Anger has been assigned Object and Substance properties before this occurrence. Now when it acquires the schema of 'red-eyed demon', the properties it assumes are, say, physical appearance and adjectives describing a demon. The conflict arises between physical appearance and Substance (because a substance can't have eyes). So they are brought to the CONTEST field. Based on how often these concepts occur in the corpus, they are assigned probabilities. For example, in this case, the probability previously assigned with Substance property is converted to the equivalent vote and red-eye is given vote 1. On next occurrence of 'anger is a substance', we follow a reward/penalty scenario [3], where the vote of Substance is increased by one, and that of 'red-eye' is reduced by one. When the vote of one concept is reduced to zero, the CONTEST field is cleared of the two. Assuming that false alarms are very less in number compared to correct usages, this process will reach stability. One might also note that this process doesn't in anyway harm the objective of the second sentence. The idea that it wanted to convey about Anger remains there inside Anger's image schema in the form of the adjectives – only the physical appearance schema is eliminated, which is the ideal behavior. Given enough time to settle down, the concrete concepts would thus have some sort of physical characteristic in their image schema that is NOT derived from Object/Substance/Container. The abstract concepts, on the other hand, would only be linked to the basic schemas, without any distinguishing and particular physical characteristics. For example, 'Box is a container' and 'Love is a Container'. Both will imbibe concepts of enclosure, boundary etc. from the container. But BOX would have additional schemas of a lid, wooden material etc. (which would actually vary subjectively). Since the concept of 'Love is a Container' is ingrained

[2] Which creates no conflict since Substances can act as agents/point-objects. Similarly containers and objects are interchangeable based on the context.

[3] It is to be noted that this scenario is only followed for schemas that are in the CONTEST class, not for all the schemas. This prevents unnecessary removal of non-conflicting schemas.

in the learner, we will say that the subject has *acquired* the metaphor. This method of metaphor acquisition eliminates any argument regarding a violation of selectional restrictions and the need for basic seed metaphors to understand others. In this scenario, metaphors are learned like any other linguistic concept. The 'concrete first-then abstraction' should thus score over 'abstract first-concrete grounding' approach.

INTERPRETATION: This representation also helps in understanding of metaphorical occurrences. Previous works like KARMA(Narayanan(1997)), when they come across a metaphorical occurrence, search in a repository of metaphorical mappings to understand the statement. Understanding in the present system can naturally flow through the ECG approach. The ECG asserts that when we are interpreting 'Harry fell in water', we actually simulate Harry falling in water to understand the utterance. In the present approach, the occurrence 'Harry fell in love', when simulated, will behave like this – the sentence will first be converted to concept FALL(Harry, love), then using FALL(Object,Container), HARRY and LOVE would import those schemas. HARRY would also import its own physical characteristic schemas while LOVE would have no such schema. Then motion schema of FALL() would be brought along and these three will be composited to produce the final simulation. Metaphorical mapping would thus be understood as any other linguistic concept, the only distinguishing factor would be that while concrete concepts would bring in their associated physical properties, abstract concepts will be described by a bare-bones schema. The idea of assigning probabilities of a concept's association to different base classes helps us in another elegant way. Previously, to understand 'Harry is in love' and 'Love led to his demise', the models had to invoke two different metaphorical mappings of 'Love is a container' and 'Love is an entity'. Wheres as, in the present model, the concept Love has already been assigned to both the Container and Object class, and based on the context one of the assignments gets highlighted. This reduces the memory inefficient and crude method of having a repository of metaphor-maps.

GENERATION: Claim 3 helps us generate new metaphors or use established metaphors just as natural language is used, without conscious effort. Once the system needs to convey an abstract idea, it has at its disposal a probability map through which the idea is connected to other concrete concepts. Those concepts are further connected to verbs/adjectives etc. with certain other probabilities. A path through this map, which can represent a coherent structure, would lead to a metaphorical mapping. Which metaphorical mapping is more culturally accepted would of course depend on the rating of the path (in this case, simply the multiplication of probabilities). This model however would be extremely good in interpretation of newly created metaphors. The understanding process would just involve simulating the ideas by ECG. The older models, since they rely on a metaphor list, would have a hard time understanding new metaphors because they might not fit into the established scenarios.

3 Experiments

The Brown Corpus was used to test the ideas and derive some possible metaphorical mappings. All the occurrences of the grounded concepts, viz. CHASE(A,B), INTO(A,B), IN(A,B), OUT OF (A,B), MORE(A), LESS(A), SLOW() and FAST() were found out and the sentence structure was converted to these functional structures using a very crude method – the first occurrence of a singular or mass noun(NN) in the tagged corpus was assigned to the concept. For example, the sentence fragment 'into a hot cauldron' is converted to INTO(cauldron). Using this very basic method, some of the possible metaphor mappings that were found were:

Container The following concepts were common between IN(), INTO(), OUT OF(), leading to a strong Container metaphorical map–*future battle fight mission darkness violence chaos silence water mind religion language*

Substance The following concepts were common between GIVE() and MORE(), leading to a strong affinity for Substance mapping: *affection information emphasis interest protection time*

To have a flavor of how an abstract concept is connected to the base classes, we examined all occurrences of noun LOVE in the corpus. While 90% of the time it acted like Object/Substance, 10% of the time, it acted like container, hinting that the affinity of Love for Container is minimal. [4] The Object and Substance cases are almost indistinguishable except for when substance-specific adjectives like 'more/less' are used. Otherwise, Love is considered a physical material, and it is not usually distinguishable whether its an Object or a Substance.

To look into how deeper mappings like 'Time is Money' might be deciphered, we also looked into SPEND(), and WASTE(). 60% of usages of SPEND() were SPEND(Time)(in various forms like day/year etc.), while the rest were SPEND(Money), with very minimal(two or three occurrences of the 200 odd) SPEND(*other substance*). Similarly, of the 10 occurrences of verb WASTE(), 9 are concerning Time and the rest concerns Substance. The trend also points to one important assumption we have made – that is, abstract concepts are first learned as concrete. As we see, these verb usages correspond to abstract concepts much more readily than they do to their concrete counterparts. So it's but natural on the part of an early learner to assume them as concrete ideas.

4 Conclusion and Future Work

While the above description pointed towards a new approach of handling metaphors that is closer in spirit to the view that metaphors are an integral part of thought and language usage and not just poetic devices, the work might still look incomplete. This is so because even if the basic ideas and claims have been supported, the system is still not fully functional. To be precise, as of now we have the grounded concepts described in Section 2.1 and based on that extremely small test set, we have tried to learn some metaphorical mappings. As more concepts are grounded in some way or other, the system will be better equipped to handle other mappings.

The ultimate aim would be to finally simulate all this in an ECG framework to show that the model is capable of emulating human behaviour. However, this must again be reiterated that the aim of this paper was not to show a working model fully capable of handling ontological metaphors, which is under construction, but that the new approach might be better and more natural than previous works that depended on hand-coded knowledge in some form or other.

[4]The container metaphor arose almost exclusively in the usage 'in love'.

Acknowledgement

I would like to thank Dr. Amitabha Mukerjee for his constant guidance throughout this work.

References

Bergen, B, N Chang, and S Narayan. 2004. Simulated action in an embodied construction grammar. In *Proc. of the 26th Annual Meeting of the Cognitive Science Society*.

Bloom, Paul. 2000. *How Children Learn the Meanings of Words*. MIT Press, Cambridge, MA.

Fass, D. 1991. Met*: A method for discriminating metonymy and metaphor by computer. *Computational Linguistics* 17(1):49–90.

Kintsch, W. 2000. Metaphor comprehension: A computational theory. *Psychonomic Bulletin and Review* pages 257–266.

Lakoff, George, Jane Espenson, and Alan Schwartz. 1991. *Master metaphor list: 2nd draft copy*.

Lakoff, George and Mark Johnson, editors. 1980. *Metaphors We Live By*. University of Chicago Press.

Langacker, RW, editor. 1987. *Foundations of Cognitive Grammar I: Theoretical Prerequisites*. Stanford University Press.

Mukerjee, Amit, Kruti Neema, and Sushobhan Nayak. 2011. Discovering coreference using image-grounded verb models. In *Proceedings of RANLP*.

Mukerjee, Amitabha and Mausoom Sarkar. 2007. Grounded perceptual schemas: Developmental acquisition of spatial concepts. In *Spatial Cognition V Reasoning, Action, Interaction*, Springer Berlin / Heidelberg, volume 4387, pages 210–228.

Narayanan, S. 1997. *Knowledge-based Action Representations for Metaphor and Aspect (KARMA)*. Ph.D. thesis, CS, UC Berkeley.

Narayanan, S. 1999. Moving right along: A computational model of metaphoric reasoning about events. In *Proc. of NCAI*. pages 121–129.

Roy, Deb and Ehud Reiter. 2005. Connecting language to the world. *Artificial Intelligence: Special Issue on Connecting Language to the World* 167:112.

Shutova, E, L Sun, and A Korhonen. 2010. Metaphor identification using verb and noun clustering. In *Proc. of COLING*. pages 1002–1010.

Wilks, Y. 1975. A preferential pattern seeking semantics for natural language inference. *Artificial Intelligence* 6(1):53–74.

Automatic Acquisition of Possible Contexts for Low-Frequent Words

Silvia Necsulescu
IULA
Universitat Pompeu Fabra
Barcelona, Spain
silvia.necsulescu@upf.edu

Abstract

The present work constitutes a PhD project that aims to overcome the problem caused by data sparsity in the task of acquisition of lexical resources. In any corpus of any length, many words are infrequent, thus they co-occur with a small set of words. Nevertheless, they can co-occur with many other words. Our goal is to discover some more possible co-occurring words for low-frequent words relying on other co-occurrences observed in corpus. Our approach aims to formulate a new similarity measure, based on the words usage in language, to approve a transfer of co-occurring words, from a frequent word to a low-frequent word.

1. Introduction

The production of language resources (LR) is a bottleneck for the development of many Natural Language Processing applications. The development of language resources by humans is very expensive and time consuming. Currently, a mainstream line of research is working on the automation of this task by using Machine Learning classifiers. To create language resources, first and foremost, automatic systems are needed to induce information from selected co-occurrences among words.

Any corpus is characterized by Zipf's law which states that the frequency of words is inversely proportional to its rank in the frequency table (Zipf, 1935). Words in a text follow a power-law distribution and many words show a low-frequency of occurrence, causing the problem known as data sparsity. Low-frequent words do not provide enough information for automatic systems that rely on the distributional information of a target word, i.e. co-occurrences with other words in a context (Bel, et al. 2007). Therefore, the frequency of words is a pitfall in the automatic production of LRs.

To overcome it, the low-frequent words need additional information to be classified by an automatic system. Bybee (2010) suggests that in order to process low frequent words, we can take evidence from other similar words. Thus we want to define *"similar words"*. For this task, a similarity measure implies to gather co-occurring words from frequent words to be used as virtual input of non frequent ones.

The word co-occurrences vary from one domain to another. We aim to create a generic system that takes into account the domain in an automatic manner. Therefore, to be able to identify suitable co-occurring words for a specific domain, we use a list of examples classified a priori, which is the only external knowledge provided.

The present article contains examples in Spanish and English to highlight that the problem of data sparsity exists in any language. We aim to create a language independent system, developed over a Spanish corpus and later, tested over an English corpus.

The rest of the paper is organized as follows: section 2 shows that low-frequent words represented a pitfall in previous works. In section 3, we introduce our objective and the main hypothesis that motivates this work, while in section 4 we present the proposed methodology. In section 5 we emphasis the contribution of our work and we formulate our conclusion over the present proposal.

2. Related Work

There have been different proposals on word similarity, for instance the (Frakes and Baeza-Yates., 1992), Jaccard's coefficient (Salton and McGill., 1983), Kullback-Leibler divergence measure (Kullback and Leibler, 1951), the L_1 norm (Kaufman, and Rousseeuw, 1990), Lin's measure (Lin, 1998), etc. Each of these measures is based on a description of the distributional behavior of each word in terms of other co-occurring words. To calculate the similarity between two words, the similarity between these vectors of co-occurrences is calculated.

These proposals, however, are not useful to handle words that occur just a few times in a corpus, as they do not give enough evidence on their distributional behavior. Therefore, although they are the most numerous set of words, most of the research done in various sub-tasks of the extraction of LR simply ignores low frequent words because the information provided is not enough to be reliable. For instance, Lin (1998) applies his measure of similarity on words that occurred at least 50 times in corpus. Rapp (2002) eliminated all words with a corpus frequency less than 101 to extract word associations from text. In the creation of language models, Padó and Lapata. (2003) removed infrequent words with occurrences less than 100. Peirsman, et al. (2008) considered as valid co-occurring words, only words that occurred at least 5 times.

In a general evaluation of various similarity measures for LR extraction, Curran and Moens (2002) eliminates all words with a frequency lower than 5, while Weeds and Weir (2005) consider the co-occurrences of a word with a frequency lower than 27 do not provide reliable information to describe its distributional behavior.

For our project, we aim to find more possible co-occurrences for words whose frequency is lower than 100. We face up to two problems, one is to extract the significant information for a low frequent word and the second one is to find a new measure of similarity that can handle the reduced information attached to low-frequent words.

Weeds and Weir (2005) tackle the problem of finding unseen co-occurrences of words by using the existent co-occurrences in corpus. As they rely on existing standard similarity measures and use as features, syntactic related words, they do not overcome the data sparsity problem.

3. Objective and Hypothesis

As previous work proved, any corpus of any size contains many low-frequent words, which do not provide enough information about their distributional behavior in language. Nevertheless, any word in human language can co-occur with a large set of words, while the co-occurrences in text represent just a small sub-set of this set.

Our objective is to overcome data sparsity by discovering other possible co-occurring words for low-frequent words besides the co-occurrences observed in corpus. In this way, we provide to low-frequent words, additional contextual information that allows them to be correctly handled in a further task.

To attain this objective, we rely on the distributional hypothesis (Harris, 1954), i.e. similar words tend to be used in similar contexts, and on Bybee's (1988,2010) statement that there is a similarity between a frequent word and a low-frequent word induced abstraction process over language. Bybee suggested that low frequent words can be processed by taking or copying information of more frequent similar words.

The challenge for our project is to discover a new topological space where we can define a measure of similarity based on distributional behavior of words that can handle low-frequent words. We propose a topology based on a graph representation of the lexicon.

Geffet and Dagan (2005) proved that although two words are similar in their distributional behavior, they do not share all co-occurrences. Hence, after we declare two words similar in usage, we must determine what words can be transferred from one word to another.

Therefore, our hypothesis is that relying on the representation of words in a graph that models relations among them, we can define a similarity measure that allows to calculate the probability of success for the transfer of co-occurring words, from a frequent word to a low-frequent one.

In the next sentence the word "entangled" occurs just 53 times in the British National Corpus.:

```
Some horses become excited
and upset if something goes
a bit wrong when they are in
harness, such as chains or
ropes becoming entangled
around their feet.
```

But, its context contains frequent word, such as *harness* (841), *chain* (5181), *rope* (2186) and *feet* (13349). More, the pattern "*become [...] around*" occur 15 times in corpus. In this pattern, in the slot where *entagled* occurs, we find also *destructive* (778), *apparent* (5216), *wrapped* (1613), *unstable* (697), *millstones* (102), *known* (25176), *mobilized* (122), *centered* (31), *noticeable* (826), *compacted* (84), *deadlocked* (67). We suppose that some of these words are similar in their usage with the target word "*entagled*" and between their contexts we can find possible co-occurrences for the word "*entagled*"

4. Methodology

In an initial step, we aim to model IULA Spanish Corpus (Cabré et al. 2006) in a graph structure, to shed light over the relations that exist between words influenced by their context or by their lexical-morphological features.

Next, using the language topology created before, we aim to define a new measure of similarity between words to associate a low-frequent word with a frequent one, plausible for a transfer of co-occurring words.

Finally, a probabilistic model is created to calculate the probability of two words, unseen before together in context, to co-occur together.

4.1 Graph Model

To create the graph language model, we represent the corpus lexicon in nodes and there is an edge between two nodes, if they are contextual related or similar at lexical-morphological structure.

The contextual relations between words in our language topology are resulted from both *syntagmatic relations*, i.e. words that co-occur in the same context in the same time more frequently than expected by chance and *paradigmatic relations*, i.e. words that occur in the same context, but not in the same time. Thus, we will take advantage of all the information available.

Syntagmatic related words are the co-occurrences seen in corpus. The most key part in the graph design is to set up those syntagmatic relations that provide us with reliable information for low-frequent words i.e. words that co-occur in the same context and which manifest lexical-semantic affinities beyond grammatical restrictions (Halliday, 1966).

There are two mainstream lines to define syntagmatic related words: focused on the proximity in text or on the syntactic relations between them.

Besides, and differently to other authors, because we have very little information, we take into account all determiners and modifiers. The position in an area of text is not a strong enough constraint to extract exactly those words that are significant. For instance, word's modifiers or determinants can be outside of a fixed area of text while in the word proximity we can find useless information.

Meanwhile, to extract co-occurrences defined by syntactical relationships, a parser is needed to be applied. Nevertheless, the use of a parser has some drawbacks, such as a large preprocessing step and sparse information extracted. Therefore, for the extraction of the syntagmatic relations reliable for low-frequent words, we define heuristic rules, stronger than the simple presence in an area of text and looser than syntactic relations.

Ferrer i Cancho and Solé, (2001) stated that the most significant part of co-occurrences in sentence is due to syntactical relationships between words, e.g. head-modifier or dependency relationships, but also due to stereotyped expressions or collocations, e.g. take it easy, New York. More, Ferrer i Cancho et al. (2007) assumed the importance of the frequencies of word co-occurrences, while Choudhury et al. (2010) suggested the importance of the part-of-speech category in the language organization.

To define the syntagmatic relations, we aim to find statistical information that characterizes words syntactic related. We extract statistical information from corpus about word frequency, part-of-speech and co-occurring words in the same paragraph and we apply a parser. Finally, we mix the statistical information with the syntactic relationships, to formulate heuristic rules to be applied over raw text with the goal to extract those co-occurring words that are syntagmatic related with a target word.

Using reliable syntagmatic relations defined, we calculate paradigmatic relations to discover words that share the same context but in different moments. To determine paradigmatic related words, we compare their co-occurrences vector using one of the standard similarity measure, e.g. Lin's measure (Lin, 1998).

Syntagmatic or paradigmatic relations represent the syntactic behavior of a word. In human language, the interaction of words in an utterance is not separated by their lexical-morphological structure, e.g. in English, the verb *avoid* must be followed by a verb at *–ing* form. Therefore, we add in the graph structure an edge between words that are similar from the point of view of their lexical-morphological features, i.e. they present the same affixes or the same root.

4.2 The Structure Analysis

The graph model created previously represents the language topology. It contains linguistic relations, created from two points of view, first, relations that represent the combination of words in sentences and second, relations that connect similar words regarding their lexical-morphologic features. Relying on this topology, the next step is to define the measure of similarity between two words for a possible transfer of co-occurrences between them.

The previous studies over various models of language give us the intuition of the existence of common patterns in the large scale language organization. Language models created with co-occurrences (Ferrer i Cancho, et al., 2001) and syntactic relations (Ferrer i Cancho, et al., 2007) followed the same pattern of complex networks, characterized by a *small-world* structure (Watts, 1999) and a *scale-free* structure (Barabási, et al., 1999). The former presents a small average path length between vertices, a sparse connectivity (i.e. a node is connected to only a very small percentage of other nodes), and a strong local-clustering (i.e. the extent to which the neighborhoods of neighboring nodes overlap). The latter means that the number of vertices with degree *k* falls off as an inverse power of *k*, consequently, the majority of words have relatively few connections joined together through a small number of hubs with many connections.

To calculate the measure of similarity, first we want to extract general information over the graph structure, such as the type of words that are hubs and the type of words that are related with them, common properties of these words or what clusters of words are created and the common properties of them. Because, in our model, we use syntagmatic relations created in a heuristic manner, paradigmatic relations, and also similarity relations extracted from the internal word structure, first and foremost we have to verify if our topology keeps the complex network structure.

After we extracted the general information, to formulate the similarity measure, we focus on two axes. On one hand, we create clusters of words that occur in the same slot of a language pattern and we search similarities between the words structure from the same cluster (Bybee, 2006). On the other hand, we provide a list of words a priori classified and we search statistical similarities between the structures of words from the same class. To be able to analyze the importance of various structural features over the measure of similarity, such as the number of connections, the connection types or the connections with various classes of words, we search a response for the next questions:

- What are the features that characterize each word?
- What types of words are connected in topology with our words?
- What features have the structure that links two words from the same class/cluster?
- What is common in the structures of all the words from a class/cluster?

For a short illustration of our procedure, we created a graph using as corpus the sentences listed below, extracted from the IULA Spanish Corpus (Cabré, et al., 2006). The heuristic rule used to extract the syntagmatic related words is "*<noun> potential*". All the words that occur in the slot *<noun>* are related by a paradigmatic relation. For a better understanding of the graph, we do not draw these relations. The nouns ending with the suffix *–nte* are inter-connected with an edge for their lexical-morphological similarity. Analyzing the created graph, we observed that all nouns ended with the suffix *–nte* represent *human beings* and they are clustered by the lexical-morphological edges.

```
Carga Q se define como ## la
energía potencial ## que
posee una carga q […]

[…] juicio de los analistas,
## el precio potencial ## de
la sociedad en un  […]

El Consejo de Lisboa
incrementó ## el crecimiento
potencial ## de nuestras
economías.
```

```
[...] preservar, siquiera
mínimamente, ## el riesgo
potencial ## , pero cierto ,
de  [...]

Las inversiones son altas ,
unos 300 millones de dólares
, porque ## los clientes
potenciales ## se estiman en
20 millones .

Los demócratas intentan
asustar a ## los votantes
potenciales ## de Nader
asegurando que Bush pondría
en peligro

Las nuevas reglamentaciones
exigen examinar a ## los
donantes potenciales ## de
todo tipo de tejidos.
```

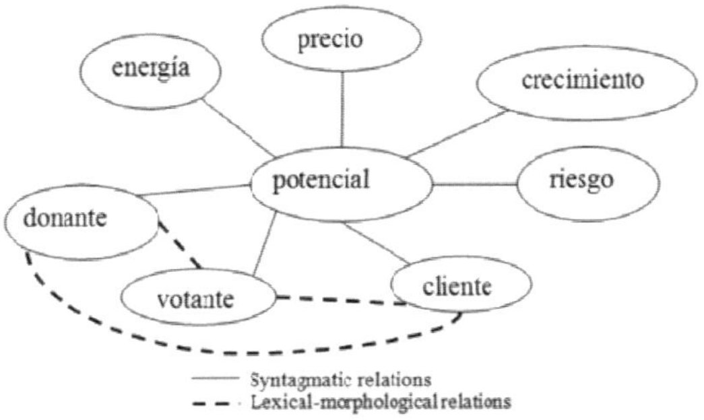

Figure 1: The graph language model created with the previous examples

The co-occurrences of a word are dependent on the domain. Therefore, we harvest on the one hand general features of the structure of the same corpus by comparing words that are used in the same language pattern and on the other hand, domain related co-occurrences by comparing words from the same class in that domain. By combining these two results, we define a measure of similarity appropriate for the given domain, wherever it is the general domain or a specialized one, and focused on the type of lexical resources that aim to be produced further.

4.3 The Probabilistic Model

Using the results of the previous stages, the graph language model and the similarity measure defined using the graph model, we create a probabilistic model.

We aim to calculate the probability that a target word w can occur with another word f, existent in corpus, in an utterance, even if this co-occurrence is not seen in context.

To calculate this probability we rely on each word similar in the topological model with w. We search between its co-occurring words f_i, a word that is similar with f. The final probability depends on the similarity between the word w and w_i, the similarity between f and f_{ij} and the probability that w_i occurs with f_{ij}. $P(f_{ij}|w_i)$ is 1 if this co-occurrence is seen in corpus. The next formula is the mathematical expression used to calculate the probability of co-occurrence.

$$P(f|w) = \frac{\sum_{i=1}^{|V(w)|}\sum_{j=1}^{|F(w_i)|} Sim(w,w_i)Sim(f,f_{ij})P(f_{ij}|w_i)}{\sum_f \sum_{i=1}^{|V(w)|}\sum_{j=1}^{|F(w_i)|} Sim(w,w_i)Sim(f,f_{ij})P(f_{ij}|w_i)}$$

Where

- w_i is a connected word with w
- f is a co-occurring word with w
- f_{ij} is a co-occurring word with w_i
- $V(w)$ is the set of similar words to w calculated using the relations from graph
- $F(w_i)$ is the set of co-occurring words with wi
- $Sim(x,y)$ is the similarity measure defined previously that calculates the similarity between the word x and y

Using the probabilistic model we decide which co-occurring words are transferred from one word to another. We provide, for the low-frequent words new possible co-occurring words. As a consequence, the context of low-frequent words is larger and therefore, they can be further classified by a system of automatic acquisition of lexical resources.

5. Contributions of the Work and Conclusions

The word frequency in a corpus is a bottleneck in the automatic acquisition of LRs based on corpus. In any corpus, there are many words whose context does not provide enough information to classify them. Our approach is based on the combination of words in valid utterances, to find a solution to overcome the data sparsity.

The importance of the work relies on our focus on low frequent words. As we showed previously, in different task of corpus analysis, a cutoff was applied over the words frequency to eliminate those words whose contextual information was small and consequently, not reliable. We aim to develop a new similarity measure, focused on low-frequent words, which differently than other standard measure of similarity is based on the graph model. This model contains edges that relate words from the same context, words that share the same context but in different moments and also words with a similar lexical-morphological structure.

Differently to previous work, our measure of similarity does not imply a semantic similarity, but a similarity at the distributional behavior that allows a transfer of co-occurring words from the most frequent word to the less frequent one.

If our hypothesis is valid, relying on the language topology created with various relation types, we induce more likely co-occurrences for low-frequent words. Further, our results can be used for the automatic acquisition of lexical resources to cover different domains and different languages.

Acknowledgments
I want to thank Nuria Bel and Muntsa Padró for their valuable indications in the development of the subject. This project is funded by the CLARA project (EU-7FP-ITN-238405).

References

Barabási, A.-L., and Albert, R. (1999). Emergence of scaling in random networks. Science , 286.

Bel, N., Espeja, S., and Marimon, M. (2007). Automatic Acquisition of Grammatical Types for Nouns. Human Language Technologies 2007: The Conference of the North American Chapter of the Association for Computational Linguistics;.

Bybee, J. (2006). From usage to grammar: the mind's response to repetition. Language 82(4). , pp. 711-733.

Bybee, J. L. (1988). Morphology as lexical organization. In M. H. Noonan, Theoretical morphology (pp. 119-141.). Academic Press.

Bybee, J. (2010). Language, usage and cognition.

Cabré, M. T., Bach, C., and Vivaldi, J. (2006). 10 anys del Corpus de l'IULA. Barcelona: Institut Universitari de Lingüística Aplicada. Universitat Pompeu Fabra.

Choudhury, M., Chatterjee, D., and Mukherjee, A. (2010). Global topology of word co-occurrence networks: Beyond the two-regime power-law. proceedings of COLING(10). Beijing, China.

Curran, J. R., and Moens, M. (2002). Improvements in automatic thesaurus extraction. PROCEEDINGS OF THE WORKSHOP ON UNSUPERVISED LEXICAL ACQUISITION .

Ferrer i Cancho, R., and Solé, R. (2001). The small-world of human language. Proceedings of the Royal Society of London .

Ferrer i Cancho, R., Mehler, A., Pustylnikov, O., and Díaz-Guilera, A. (2007). Correlations in the organization of large-scale syntactic dependency networks.

Frakes, W. B., and Baeza-Yates, R. (1992). Information Retrieval, Data. Prentice Hall.

Geffet, M., and Dagan, I. (2005). The Distributional Inclusion Hypotheses and Lexical Entailment. The 43rd Annual Meeting of the Association for Computational Linguistics.

Halliday, M. (1966). Lexis as a linguistic level. In memory of JR Firth , pp. 148–162.

Harris, Z. S. (1954). Distributional structure.

Kaufman, L., and Rousseeuw, P. J. (1990). Finding Groups in Data: An Introduction to Cluster Analysis. New York: JohnWiley.

Kullback, S., and Leibler., R. A. (1951). On information and sufficiency. Annals of Mathematical Statistics .

Lin, D. (1998). An information-theoretic definition of similarity. Proceedings of International Conference on Machine Learning. WI: Madison.

Padó, S., and Lapata, M. (2003). Constructing Semantic Space Models from Parsed Corpora. IN PROCEEDINGS OF ACL-03, (pp. 128--135).

Peirsman, Y., Heylen, K., and Speelman, D. (2008). Putting things in order. First and second order context models for the calculation of semantic similarity. Actes des 9es Journées internationales d'Analyse statistique des Données textuelles (JADT 2008). Lyon: France.

Rapp, R. (2002). The Computation Of Word Associations: Comparing Syntagmatic And Paradigmatic Approaches. coling.

Salton, G., and McGill, M. J. (1983). Introduction to Modern Information Retrieval. McGraw-Hill: New York.

Watts, D. J. (1999). Small Worlds: The Dynamics of Networks Between Order and Randomness. Princeton University Press.

Weeds, J., and Weir, D. (2005). Co-occurrence retrieval: A flexible framework for lexical distributional similarity. Computational Linguistics , 31.

Zipf, G. K. (1935). The Psychobiology of Language. Houghton-Mifflin.

Adapting Standard Open-Source Resources To Tagging A Morphologically Rich Language: A Case Study With Arabic

Hajder S. Rabiee
Royal Institute of Technology
hajder@kth.se

Abstract

In this paper we investigate the possibility of creating a PoS tagger for Modern Standard Arabic by integrating open-source tools. In particular a morphological analyser, used in the disambiguation process with a PoS tagger trained on classical Arabic. The investigation shows the scarcity of open-source tools and resources, which complicated the integration process. Among the problems are different input/output formats of each tool, granularity of tag sets and different tokenisation schemes.

The final prototype of the PoS tagger was trained on classical Arabic and tested on a sample text of modern standard Arabic. The results are not that impressive, only an accuracy of 73% is achieved. This paper however outlines the difficulties of integrating tools today and proposes ideas for future work in the field and shows that classical Arabic is not sufficient as training data for an Arabic tagger.

1 INTRODUCTION

It is estimated that about 220 million people are Arab speaking(Lewis, 2009) and that Arabic is the fourth most spoken language, thus it's a major international modern language. It is also recognised as one of the six major official languages of the United Nations. English on the other hand with 330 million speakers(Lewis, 2009), has received an unproportional attention when it comes to the development of open-source NLP tools and resources. The tools for Arabic are few and often miss certain features or do not live up to the same standard as their English counterpart (Atwell et al., 2004). The possible reasons for this are the non-Roman script and Arabic being a morphologically complex language.

The difficulties in integrating existing tools lie in the way each tool represents the texts. The morphological analysers use different encodings, e.g. CP-1256, UTF-8, ISO-8859-6 or different alphabets, e.g. transliteration scheme (Buckwalter) or the actual Arabic alphabet. The tokenisation algorithms are also different for each tool, leading to a different analysis granularity, hence a different tag set. As this is a basis for evaluation, the problem of evaluating tools on a common ground arises too. One of the fundamental parts of any linguistic application is the Part-of-Speech tagger (PoS tagger) which in turn is dependent on a morphological analyser which utilises dictionaries for lookup.

In this paper we investigate what open-source tools exist today for Arabic NLP, especially PoS taggers and morphological analysers. We compare them with regards to several aspects e.g. how easy it is to get hold of, which algorithm/model is used, how difficult it is to adapt into other tools, for which purpose it's suitable etc. For the purpose of building a prototype of a PoS tagger for Modern Standard Arabic (MSA), based on a Classical/Quranic Arabic (CA/QA) model. The problem is interesting because CA lacks many new (modern) words, e.g. *TV*; *computer*; *car*. QA has slightly different grammatical constructions than MSA. Moreover, in Arabic case endings are denoted by short vowels, these are usally omitted in written MSA; in contrast to QA which is fully diacritized.

2 BACKGROUND

In (Atwell et al., 2004) an outline of some of the most important tools is presented. Furthermore (Al-Sughaiyer and Al-Kharashi, 2004) report in their survey findings that many tools are only described generally with no measures of effectiveness and provide little in-depth investigation of available techniques. They also claim many researchers don't acknowledge the efforts of other and no systematic approach of evaluating algorithms exist either. Additionally the lack of standards is something criticised.

2.1 MORPHOLOGICAL ANALYSERS

Buckwalter Morphological Analyzer The Buckwalter Morphological Analyzer (BAMA) 1.0 (Buckwalter, 2002) was released in 2002, it can be obtained by sending an inquiry to LDC. There's also a Java port versioned 1.2 written by Pierrick Brihaye available online called *Aramorph*. The first version of BAMA has several shortcomings, as witnessed by (Altabba et al., 2010). The fact that all derivations are hard coded instead of relying on rules makes the runtime processing long. Furthermore, they state that it has a spelling problem where it converts between Arabic letters Aleph and Hamza. Problems exist with words like Hadramout

حَضرَمَوت

and problems when dealing with acts in the past tense and the pronoun is absent or past tense passive voice, e.g.

حَاول، أضرب

Many of the shortcoming mentioned by (Altabba et al., 2010) can probably be remedied if the lexical files would not apply a coarse representations of the affixes; collecting clitics together with prefixes or suffixes is not the best way. As argued by (Sawalha and Atwell, 2010) a more fine-grained representation of words in general is needed to account for the complexities of the Arabic language. The latest version, BAMA 2.0 and Standard Morphological Analyzer 3.1 (SAMA), which is based on BAMA 2.0, is only available through LDC membership though. Thus it was not possible for us to experiment with it.

Alkhalil The Alkhalil Morphological Analyzer is written in Java, the lexical resources consist of several classes, each representing a type of the same nature and morphological features. Analysis is carried out in the following steps: preprocessing, removal of diacritics; segmentation, each word is considered as (proclitic+stem+enclitic) too (Boudlal et al., 2011). According to (Altabba et al., 2010) the Alkhalil analyzer is the best one, although it has some problems with its database. It won the first prize at a competition by The Arab League Educational, Cultural Scientific Organization (ALESCO) in 2010. It has some limitations such as it does not provide PoS tags in good reusable format, e.g only in Arabic. Neither does it differentiate between clitics and affixes fully, it detects proclitics and enclitics but they are referred to either as prefix or suffix.

2.2 PART-OF-SPEECH TAGGERS

Stanford PoS tagger is originally developed for English at Stanford University and is described in (Toutanova and Manning, 2000). The tagger is based on the maximum-entropy model. The improved version, which is described in (Toutanova et al., 2003) adds support for other languages together with speed and usability improvements.

The latest version comes with trained models for Chinese, German and Arabic, it claims a 96.42% accuracy on Arabic. The tagger was trained on the training part of the Arabic Penn Treebank (ATB). It uses augmented Bies mapping of ATB tags(Bies, 2003). Which is not so fine-grain, as the authors also confirm, for example it does not tokenize clitics when tagging, e.g. the word

بسم

is tagged as noun, while it should be separated into the proclitic and noun as

ب + سم

tagging it as *preposition* and *noun* respectively. This smaller tag set makes it harder to assign a "wrong" tag, and probably one factor contributing to the high accuracy.

BrillTagger(Brill, 1995) combines the ideas of rule-based tagging with a general machine-learning approach which is *transformation-based.* The idea behind is to initially let the text pass through a annotator, in part-of-speech context this might be assigning each word its most likely tag. Then the text is compared to the gold standard, in order to create *transformations* that can be applied to improve the initial text as much as possible.

a rewrite rule - e.g. *change the word from modal to noun*

a triggering environment - e.g. *preceding word is a determiner*

TreeTagger is another language-independent tagger by (Schmid, 1994) and is based on decision trees. The tagger successfully tags many European languages, and it is adaptable to other languages if a lexicon and a manually tagged training corpus are available.

2.3 EVALUATION METHODS

Several methods for evaluating a tagger exist, among the most common are precision, recall and accuracy/success rate.

For a better understanding of how well a tagger performs, one can use tag-wise evaluation. Tag-wise measurement is a good way of evaluating a tagger, because by measuring one tag at a time one can get a better picture of what tags are harder to distinguish than others. The error measures are *precision* and *recall*. Precision is the fraction of tokens tagged T in the gold standard of those tagged T by the tagger. Recall is the fraction of tokens tagged T by the tagger of those tagged T in the gold standard.

2.4 OTHER RESOURCES

If we come to look at the situation of corpora or stemmers, the situation is similar (Al-Sughaiyer and Al-Kharashi, 2004), or even worse in the case of corpora. Not a single tagged MSA corpus exists freely or publicly. The only exception is Shereen Khoja who distributes her 50000 word tagged corpus for research purposes(Khoja, 2001). For our project, we were not able to obtain a copy.

3 METHOD

The first tools selected were the Alkhalil morphological analyser and the Stanford PoS tagger. The first one was selected because of its availability, portability and good support from the authors. The Stanford PoS tagger additionally seemed good as it belongs to a renowned NLP group and as the authors claim performs very well on Arabic. Furthermore it is written in the same language as the morphological analyser (Java), anticipating assembling the two would make it easy to create a prototype of a tagger.

The main aim of the PoS tagger is to see how well a tagger can perform on MSA text when trained on CA, i.e. tagging texts from a different lexicon than the tagger was trained on. We were further motivated by (Habash and Rambow, 2005) who reported positive results on using a morphological analyser during the tagging process, their work is based on (Hajič, 2000) who argues that a morphological analyser aids the morphological disambiguation process during tagging.

3.1 TRAINING CORPUS

The only corpus freely available to us was the Quranic Arabic Corpus (Dukes, 2009) for retraining the tagger. The corpus has 77430 words each annotated with tag, prefix, lemma and is fully diacritized. Only whitespace tokenisation was used, this has the drawback of the tagging not being very fine-grain. As Arabic is a highly inflectional language and many words have affixes that are discarded in the analysis. For the purpose of this investigation though, whose main goal is to tag MSA with a CA model, the decision was justified.

3.2 BUILDING A PROTOTYPE

The kind of flow we had in mind is illustrated in Figure 1. During the process it was discovered that the tagger didn't have a solution to tagging unknown words for a language, i.e. words that were not encountered during training. The tagger "only" develops rules from the training corpus and defines so called *extractors* internally that recognise morphological features, these are sufficient for English, but certainly not for a morphologically complex language as Arabic. The tagger also lacked a way of integrating a morphological analyser into it. There does not exist a way of getting a particular tag's confidence or any other useful measure.

In order to continue the investigation and build a prototype the Stanford tagger had to be abandoned. Instead the TreeTagger was selected, it allowed for the usage of the MA by constraining a word's possible tags in the text file. Thereby overriding the lexical information in the tagger parameter file, see Table 2 for an illustration of an input text file to be tagged. The Alkhalil analyser was abandoned at this stage too. Instead the BAMA 1.2 was chosen because it outputs the POS tags in English and not as Alkhalil, which outputs them only in Arabic. The Table 1 contains the exact mapping that is performed between the output from the MA to the Quranic corpus' tagset. The ABBREV and INTERJ from the MA, does not have any equivalent in the Quran corpus tag set, we mapped them to the common tag N (noun). A minor mapping issue occured with the tag ADV (adverb). From the MA it was ambiguous due to the fact that the Quran Corpus tag set actually distinguishes between T (time adverb) and LOC (location adverb), the output from the MA does not produce such a separation of the adverb. Therefore we mapped all ADV to T, which was the most common tag in the training corpus (T=1115 vs LOC=656 times). All morphological features were removed, e.g. N_3PERSON_PL, N_2PERSON_SG and collapsed to N. They both contribute to the count of the "N"-tag. This made the decision of choosing the most likely tag from the MA easier.

4 EVALUATION

The tagger was trained on Quranic Arabic (QA) which is both a smaller set than Modern Standard Arabic (MSA) and contains some more complex

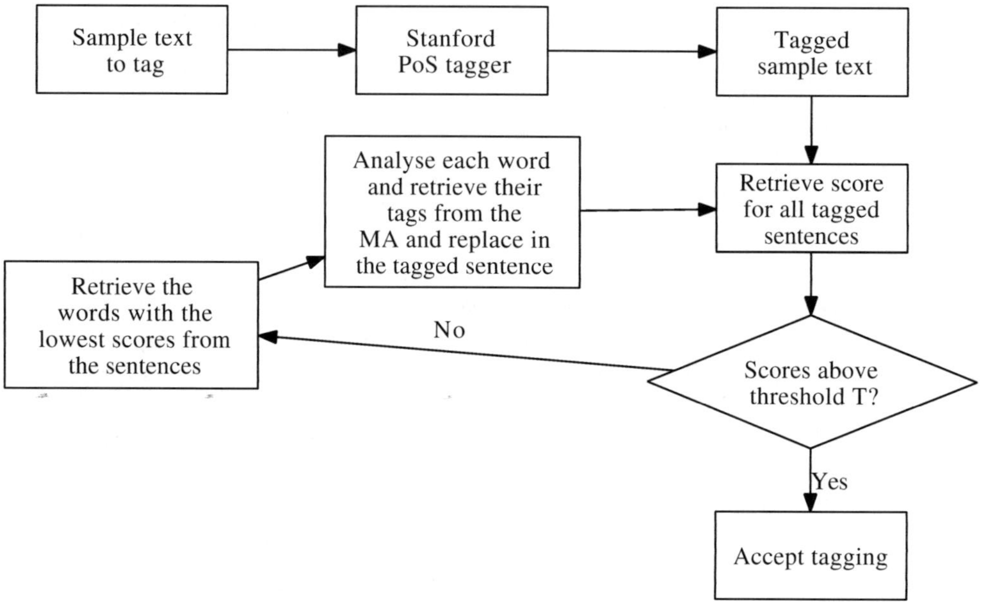

Figure 1: Initial thought of the integration between the MA and the PoS tagger

MA output	Quran Corpus equivalent
NOUN	N
N_PROP	PN
VERB.*[1]	V
PREP	P
REL_PRON	REL
ADV	T
INTERROG_PART	INTG
NEG_PART	NEG
EMPHATIC_PARTICLE	EMPH
INTERJ	N
ABBREV	N

Table 1: The mapping from BAMA's tag set to the Quran Corpus' tag set

WORD1	TAG1
WORD2	TAG1 TAG2 TAG3
WORD3	TAG1 TAG2
WORD4	TAG2 TAG3 TAG5
etc	...

Table 2: Sample input text with tag constraints of one tag

morphological and syntactic constructs, these are however much less in comparison to the words available in MSA, which includes *modern* words e.g. TV, mobile phone etc. From this perspective it would be interesting to see how the tagger - trained on QA - would perform on MSA together with the morphological analyser. The accuracy results from the initial tagging experiments are shown in Table 4. For the MSA sample text we chose an extract of an article from the Arabic BBC newspage[2] containing 66 words, they were manually annotated by an Arab speaker, and considered the "gold standard" during the evaluation. The tag set used is a very simple subset extracted from the training corpus (Quran corpus) and is described in (Dukes, 2009).

The tagger allowed for specifying the open class set and from the Quran Corpus those presented in Table 3 were extracted. *Baseline* was simply tagging each word as N (noun).

When more than one tag is appended to the sample text file, the tagger will be involved in making decisions between the different tags. If only one tag is chosen and input to the tagger, the tag's probability is implicitly 1; it is only the output from the MA that is considered. We experimented with both settings. Another configuration for our experiments was adding a probability to the tags, as well as setting an option to output maximum

[2] http://www.bbc.co.uk/arabic

Tag	Description
N	Noun
PN	Proper Noun
ADJ	Adjective
T	Time adverb
LOC	Location adverb
V	Verb
IMPN	Imperative Verbal Noun

Table 3: The open tag class

Experiment	Accuracy
Baseline on MSA	44%
Baseline on QA	36%
Stanford on QA	98%
TreeTagger on QA	96%
Stanford on MSA	39%
TreeTagger on MSA	35%
BAMA on MSA	69%

Table 4: Initial experiments accuracy

Tag	Precision	Recall	F-Measure	Accuracy
N	76%	89%	82%	
PRON	100%	25%	40%	
ADJ	0	0	0	
LOC	-	-	-	73%
T	-	-	-	
V	82%	60%	69%	
P	79%	100%	88%	
IMPN	-	-	-	

Table 5: MA tagging and tagger experiment with three appended tags on MSA text, no probabilities.

Tag	Precision	Recall	F-Measure	Accuracy
N	75%	86%	80%	
PRON	100%	25%	40%	
ADJ	0	0	0	
LOC	-	-	-	73%
T	-	-	-	
V	91%	67%	77%	
P	85%	100%	92%	
IMPN	-	-	-	

Table 6: MA tagging and tagger experiment on MSA text, three appended tags with frequency probability distribution

three tags to the appended file.

5 CONCLUSIONS

Using a training corpus with different characteristics than the text to tag, yielded expected results: very low. The results on the QA training text, were also expected: high. The *baseline* was tagging all words as a noun. It is interesting that both the Stanford tagger and the TreeTagger had a lower accuracy on MSA than the baseline. Changing parameters and settings for the appended tags leads to a slight improvement, see Table 6, which was the experiment with the highest accuracy and best values on the tags' error measures. The other experiment with no probability associated, in Table 5 also scored high. The accuracy remains the same as when choosing the frequency probability, see the results from Table 6. There's only a slight exchange of the error measures between the two. In general though, an accuracy of 70% is probably not good enough for many applications. It can be argued that a text with more words could have been used for tagging. Howevery, open-source tagged texts for gold standard, is a rare resource in Arabic NLP. Tagging a text manually is a time-consuming task and was not suitable for this case study. A high account of the accuracy is due to the morphological analysis, we see in Table 4 that the MA only achieves a 69% accuracy. While the usage of TreeTagger increases it to roughly 73%. By this we can draw the conclusion that the tagger contributes very little to the overall accuracy.

6 FUTURE WORK

First improvement is trying to experiment with a more fine-grain tag set. That would involve some more sophisticated methods on choosing the best solution from the MA, one way is to assign some sort of score to a solution that aids in the decision. This would open up for example building tools to adjust tagging granularity, depending on end application. The number of tagged corpora needs to increase. Our idea is to build on the work of (Sawalha and Atwell, 2010) and try to develop a corpora tagged with that new tag set.

Many resources are presented in (Nizar Habash, 2010), however many of those tools are licensed and/or not available publicly. This is a real impediment for those that wish to to take their steps into the area. Attracting new researchers requires having tools at hand easily. It is necessary if we wish to see more and better results. Finally, we believe it is only a matter of time until see more and better applications are being built for Arabic NLP.

ACKNOWLEDGEMENTS

I would like to thank my supervisor Dr. Eric Atwell. This work would has also been supported by my supervisor Viggo Kann from the Royal Institute of Technology.

References

[Al-Sughaiyer and Al-Kharashi2004] I. Al-Sughaiyer and A. Al-Kharashi. 2004. Arabic morphological analysis techniques: A comprehensive survey. *Journal of the American Society for Information Science and Technology*, 55:189–213.

[Altabba et al.2010] M. Altabba, A Al-Zaraee, and M A Shukairy. 2010. An Arabic morphological analyzer and part-of-speech tagger. Master's thesis, Arab International University, Damascus, Syria.

[Atwell et al.2004] E. Atwell, L. Al-Sulaiti, S. Al-Osaimi, and B. Abu Shawar. 2004. A review of Arabic corpus analysis tools. In *Bel, B and Marlien, I (editors) Proceedings of TALN04: XI Conference sur le Traitement Automatique des Langues Naturelles*, volume 2, pages 229–234.

[Bies2003] Ann Bies. 2003. http://www.ircs.upenn.edu/arabic/Jan03release/arabic-POStags-collapse-to-PennPOStags.txt.

[Boudlal et al.2011] A. Boudlal, A. Lakhouaja, A. Mazroui, A. Meziane, and M. Bebah. 2011. Alkhalil morpho sys: A morphosyntactic analysis system for Arabic texts. azze.mazroui@gmail.com.

[Brill1995] E. Brill. 1995. Transformation-based error-driven learning and natural language processing: A case study in part-of-speech tagging. *Computational Lingustics*, 21(4):543–566.

[Buckwalter2002] T. Buckwalter. 2002. *Buckwalter Arabic Morphological Analyzer 1.0*. Linguistic Data Consortium.

[Dukes2009] K. Dukes. 2009. The Quranic Arabic Corpus. http://corpus.quran.com/.

[Habash and Rambow2005] N. Habash and O. Rambow. 2005. Arabic tokenization, part-of-speech tagging and morphological disambiguation in one fell swoop. In *Proceedings of the 43rd Annual Meeting on Association for Computational Linguistics*. ACL.

[Hajič2000] J. Hajič. 2000. Morphological tagging: data vs dictionaries. In *Proceedings of the 1st North American chapter of the Association for Computational Linguistics conference*.

[Khoja2001] S. Khoja. 2001. Shereen khoja. http://zeus.cs.pacificu.edu/shereen/research.htm#corpora. Accessed 2011-08-30.

[Lewis2009] M. Paul (ed.) Lewis. 2009. *Ethnologue: Languages of the World*. SIL International, Dallas, Texas, sixth, edition. Online version: http://www.ethnologue.com/.

[Nizar Habash2010] Y. Nizar Habash. 2010. *Introduction to Arabic natural language processing*. Morgan and Claypool.

[Sawalha and Atwell2010] M. Sawalha and E. Atwell. 2010. Fine-grain moprhological analyzer and part-of-speech tagger for Arabic text. In *Language Resources and Evaluation Conference*.

[Schmid1994] H. Schmid. 1994. Probabilistic part-of-speech tagging using decisions trees. In *International Conference on New Methods in Language Processing*.

[Toutanova and Manning2000] K. Toutanova and C D. Manning. 2000. Enriching the knowledge sources used in a maximum entropy part-of-speech tagger. In *Proceedings of the Joint SIGDAT Conference on Empirical Methods in Natural Language Processing and Very Large Corpora (EMNLP/VLC-2000)*, pages 63–70.

[Toutanova et al.2003] K. Toutanova, D. Klein, C. Manning, and Y. Singer. 2003. Feature-rich part-of-speech tagging with cyclic dependency network. In *Proceedings of HLT-NAACL*, pages 252–259.

Towards Cross-Language Word Sense Disambiguation for Quechua

Alex Rudnick
School of Informatics and Computing, Indiana University
919 E. 10th St., Bloomington, Indiana, USA 47408
alexr@cs.indiana.edu

Abstract

In this paper we present initial work on cross-language word sense disambiguation for translating adjectives from Spanish to Quechua and situate CLWSD as part of the translation task. While there are many available resources for training Spanish-language NLP systems, linguistic resources for Quechua, especially Spanish-Quechua bitext, are quite limited, so some ingenuity is required in developing Spanish-Quechua systems. This work makes use of only freely available resources and compares a few different techniques for CLWSD, including classifiers with simple word context features, features from a Spanish-language dependency parser, a multilingual version of the Lesk algorithm, and a distance metric based on the Spanish wordnet.

1 Introduction

Quechua is an indigenous American language spoken by roughly ten million people in the Andes mountain range. While this population of speakers is larger than that of some well-studied European languages, NLP work on Quechua is constrained by the paucity of available training data, and especially of bitext for training machine translation systems. As part of our work on building MT systems for such under-resourced languages, we are developing cross-language word sense disambiguation software [1].

The major contribution of this work is that we have, with well-understood techniques and publicly available resources, developed a cross-language word-sense disambiguation system suitable for integration into an MT system for this under-resourced language. In this initial work, we have only addressed adjectives due to their lack of inflection in Quechua, but the techniques should be generally applicable, given the use of a morphological analyzer for Quechua. Our best approaches perform only slightly better than the "most frequent sense" baseline, but that baseline is fairly high to begin with, reaching roughly 75% classification accuracy.

Cross-language word-sense disambiguation (CLWSD) is a formulation of the more general word-sense disambiguation task that is concerned with making distinctions between possible translations of a given word. Instead of taking our sense inventory from a monolingual ontology such as WordNet or a dictionary, we are given a word in context in some *source language* text and want to predict the appropriate translation of that word in the given *target language*. CLWSD thus differs from the more general WSD task by taking the possible lexical choices in the target language to be the only relevant sense distinctions. Notably, many senses distinguished by more fine-grained sense inventories may map to the same word in the target language. For example, two distinct senses of the English word "bank", the abstract financial institution and the physical building, are both rendered in Spanish as the word *banco*, but the bank of a river is an *orilla*. For our purposes, we may treat the first two senses as identical.

In the rest of the paper, we will discuss some related work, describe the resources available to us for Quechua-Spanish translation tasks, outline the techniques we have applied, and present experimental results.

2 Related Work

Recent years have seen a resurgence of interest in the integration of word-sense disambiguation techniques into machine translation. We suspect that WSD will be especially useful for translat-

[1] The software for experiments in this paper is available at http://code.google.com/p/hltdi-l3/wiki/RANLP2011

ing into under-resourced and morphologically rich languages, for which good language models are likely to be sparse. Before the work of Carpuat and Wu (2007b), it was apparently unclear whether WSD was necessary or helpful for a state-of-the-art statistical MT system; lexical choice among possible translations for a given word can often be handled by the language model for the target language, simply due to collocations of appropriate words in the training data.

Interestingly, while Carpuat and Wu presented their work as the first time CLWSD has been integrated into a machine translation system such that it reliably improved the translation quality, an early paper by IBM researchers (Brown et al., 1991), outlines the CLWSD task in a strikingly similar way, as a WSD task where the possible senses of a word are extracted from statistical alignments learned over a bitext corpus. Brown *et al.* report significant translation quality improvements through the use of their WSD system, over a small hand-evaluated set of test sentences.

Dinu and Kübler (2007) have addressed the problem of monolingual WSD for a lower-resourced language, particularly Romanian. In their work, they describe an instance-based approach in which a relatively small number of features is used quite effectively. In other work on lower-resourced languages, Sarrafzdadeh *et al.* have investigated a version of the Lesk algorithm for Farsi.

Lefever *et al.* recently described a novel approach to WSD, making use of evidence from several languages at once to disambiguate English-language source sentences. This is done by building artificial parallel corpora in several languages, on demand, with the Google Translate API. They outperform the previous state-of-the art systems on the SemEval 2010 shared task 13 (Lefever et al., 2011).

3 Linguistic Resources for Translating Spanish to Quechua

There are many available bilingual dictionaries for Quechua, both in paper and electronic form. For this project, we made use of two different dictionaries. The first one was published by the *Academia Mayor de la Lengua Quechua* (2005) and distributed by the Runasimipi Qespiqa Software group[2] as an ODT document. We converted this to flat text, then wrote a custom parser to extract the translations of each word, both from the Spanish-Quechua and Quechua-Spanish sections of the dictionary. The second dictionary was compiled by `runasimi.de` and released as a large Excel spreadsheet, then later converted to XML by Michael Gasser. We extracted the desired entries with XPath.

3.1 Wordnet for Spanish

Wordnet [3] is a publicly available ontology of concepts in the English language, developed at Princeton. Similar resources, broadly called wordnets, are available for many languages, including a fairly large one for Spanish. Unfortunately the full version requires fees and a license to access. However, a subset of this resource is available for free, distributed by the FreeLing project (Padró et al., 2010).

Typically, wordnets contain information about a number of different relationships among the words in the database, including hypernymy, antonymy, meronymy, etc.; this version only contains information mapping from Spanish words to their "synsets" (sets of synonyms), which are unique ID numbers representing a single concept in the ontology, and also information about the hypernymy relationships between the synsets. Hypernymy relationships express which concepts are more general than others. For example, the synset for *perro* ("dog") has as a hypernym the synset "animal", which in turn has the hypernym "organism".

While one might expect these hypernymy relationships to form a tree, or at least an acyclic graph, there seem to be a few cycles in the graph represented by this wordnet, perhaps due to human error; care must be taken not to loop. Also, not every synset represented in the hypernymy graph corresponds to a word in Spanish, due to the limited nature of the freely available version of the resource.

3.2 Bitext

One of the most important resources for building a modern machine translation system is bitext, and hopefully sentence-aligned bitext. In our case, the largest aligned bitext that we have been able to find for is the Catholic Bible. This contains just over 31 thousand parallel verses, which are roughly sentence-length chunks. The Spanish text contains

[2]http://runasimipi.org

[3]http://wordnet.princeton.edu/

723 thousand tokens, and the Quechua text is 484 thousand; we expect Quechua sentences to contain fewer tokens due to Quechua's rich morphology. Each verse has a unique numeric identifier, which is consistent across languages, allowing us to easily find corresponding text in the Spanish and Quechua versions.

Another interesting available bitext corpus was collected by CMU's AVENUE project (Monson et al., 2006), although it contains many fewer sentences and thus is not as useful for learning lexical information, since its original intent was to illustrate the syntactic structure of the language. Thus the vocabulary covered is much less broad, and we report results from our experiments with the biblical text.

4 Approaches

In this section, we will discuss the various methods we tried, and in the next, we will compare their performances. For each method discussed here, we accounted for the inflections of Spanish nouns and adjectives and made use of the Snowball stemmer, available for Spanish in NLTK (Bird et al., 2009): in general, before words were compared, we normalized them by removing Spanish diacritics and inflection.

4.1 Extracting Ambiguous Words from Bilingual Dictionaries

Having parsed the dictionaries, we extract the relevant ambiguous words from both of them, which we define as all of the Spanish words sw, such that sw translates to at least two different Quechua adjectives, qw_1 and qw_2 – every case where, to generate a Quechua adjective from a given Spanish word, we must make a lexical choice.

Having discovered from the two dictionaries which Spanish words translate ambiguously, we then find examples of those Spanish words that translate to the Quechua words in question. We find each example of the target Quechua adjective in the target-language text and note the numbers of the verses that contain them. We then go through the corresponding verses in the Spanish text, and for the cases where the previously-noted relevant Spanish word is present in the verse, and only one of the corresponding Quechua words is present on the target side, we record the Spanish verse, the Spanish source word, the Quechua verse, and the Quechua target word as a training instance. Additionally, we record the head verbs of the verses and their direct object, when the FreeLing parser can identify them.

Filtering this process to only include Spanish-language adjectives for which we observe at least two distinct Quechua translations, and at least three instances of each of these target words, we collected 19 distinct Spanish adjectives that fit all of these criteria. They occurred from 7 (for *quemado*, "burned"), up to 346 (for *todo*, "every/all") times, for a total of 1156 instances in the data set.

4.2 KNN with Distances Over Wordnet

For our first attempt at disambiguating the Spanish adjectives, we tried a metric that measures distances over the wordnet hypernym graph, searching for matches among the words in the surrounding contexts for the adjective in the query instance and in the training set.

Given a graph of the hypernyms, we can measure semantic relatedness between two words based on the distance along the shortest path between two nodes, which goes through their closest common hypernym ancestor, if one exists. This is in effect a distance version of the "Path Length" similarity metric available in the Wordnet::Similarity module [4].

To generate the features for a given instance, we look up all of the wordnet entries for the words in a window of three tokens around each source Spanish adjective. Those entries and all of their transitive hypernyms are recorded, and then the distance between two instances, say between the instance we would like to classify and a given instance in the training set, is calculated based on the smallest "Path Length" distance between words in either instance's context window. If no matches are found within wordnet, we simply guess the most frequent sense within the training set, but if some matches are found, we guess the most frequent Quechua word within the $K = 3$ nearest neighbors.

4.3 Simplified Lesk Algorithm

A traditional approach to WSD proposed by Lesk (1986), is to make use of the available electronic dictionaries. The original Lesk algorithm looks up the dictionary entries for the words in a sentence and picks the sense of a word whose entry has the

[4] http://wn-similarity.sourceforge.net/

greatest overlap with the entries for the context word.

In our work, we adapted the Simplified Lesk algorithm, described in (Kilgarriff and Rosenzweig, 2000), to a cross-lingual setting. Here, to pick a target Quechua word, we look at the Quechua-Spanish entries for each candidate Quechua sense, then count occurrences of all of the Spanish words from that entry in the sentence surrounding the adjective in question. A score is then calculated, where matches between the dictionary entry and the surrounding context are weighted by the idf of each word, which is calculated such that each entry in the dictionary is considered a document.

4.4 Classification with Word Context Features, Synsets, and a Parser

Stepping away from the ontological features, we also tried training classifiers over more traditional word-context features. Here we make use of a context window of five words around a given Spanish-language adjective, marking the presence or absence of a given content word.

At training time, a feature is created for each content word within the context window for any item in the training set, and at classification time, we look for those content words around the instance's adjective, setting the feature values to 1 if the word is present, and 0 otherwise, and also marking whether the word appears to the left or right of the adjective. Marking whether each word is on the left or right of the adjective adds about two percentage points of accuracy, which may be due to the fact that the head noun typically comes before the adjective in Spanish.

Other features that we experimented with included the synsets from the Spanish wordnet for the words in the context window (up to three levels of hypernyms from the context words), also marked with the side of the adjective, the head verb of the sentence, and the object of that head verb, if present. Parses of the sentences were obtained automatically using the default settings for the dependency parser from FreeLing, which conveniently extracted and lemmatized them. All of these features were used with a KNN classifier with feature weighting based on information gain, decision trees, and a simple naïve Bayes classifier. Our decision tree classifier implementation is from NLTK (Bird et al., 2009).

5 Experimental Results

In Table 1, we report classification accuracy as a percentage of times the system predicted the correct Quechua adjective. We also report the percentage of the time that a non-baseline classifier disagreed with the most frequent sense baseline, and in instances where it did so, its accuracy. Performance gains are to be made in deciding when to go against the safe most frequent sense bet, and doing so accurately. The results reported here are all over roughly ten-fold cross validation: the exact number of folds depends on the size of the data set. In this chart, by "wn" we mean the synset features, and by "parse", we mean the main verb and its object.

In earlier experiments, we also limited the features to those that occur in exactly one of the classes – Spanish words that, within a particular training set, only occur in sentences that generate a specific Quechua adjective. This causes much worse performance for the instance-based learner, dropping down to 55.1% for the KNN classifier.

5.1 Baseline: Most Frequent Sense

A good baseline strategy for WSD tasks is to always guess the most frequent sense (MFS). In the cross-language setting this the most common relevant word in the target language. While very simple, this results in surprisingly high accuracy, since some words are much more common than others. It turns out that some fairly sophisticated systems do not beat this baseline, including most of the entries to the SemEval 2010 Task 13 evaluation (Lefever and Hoste, 2010), although to be fair the task of disambiguating nouns, as in that task, may be more difficult than that of adjectives. However, for the Quechua adjectives covered in this work, the most common alternatives are quite common. For comparison, assuming a uniform distribution over the possible classes would give an accuracy of 38.9%.

For the data set we extracted, guessing the most frequent sense in a given training set gives a baseline accuracy of 76.1%. The baseline is somewhat lower, at 69.1%, if we decide which sense is the most common by processing the entire text of the Bible, instead of only examining the Quechua verses that align with the Spanish verses in question. This suggests that the Spanish sentences that align with the Quechua text in question have a different lexical distribution than

classifier	features	disagree	correctly disagree	accuracy
baseline	MFS in training instances			76.1
	MFS, corpus			69.1
	MFS, other stories			61.7
	uniform guess			38.9
Simplified Lesk		21.3	19.9	65.9
naïve bayes	words	17.0	44.9	75.8
	words, wn	19.2	40.1	74.0
	words, parse	16.2	42.8	75.1
decision trees	words	6.4	52.7	76.6
	words, wn	6.5	44.0	76.0
	words, parse	7.2	56.6	77.2
KNN	words	4.8	60.0	77.6
	wn	15.8	44.3	75.3
	words, wn	6.2	52.8	77.2
	words, parse	4.0	65.2	77.6

Table 1: Classification accuracies with cross validation

the Bible as a whole. We also tried taking the most frequent sense from a smaller corpus of other Quechua-language stories, which produced better-than-chance results at 61.7% accuracy, but this is a very small corpus, at only six thousand tokens long. It does not contain many of the relevant adjectives, but the most common ones are represented.

5.2 Wordnet-based KNN

We found that our Spanish wordnet's coverage is fairly thin: out of all the verses that we would like to classify, we find entries in the ontology for words in the context in fewer than half of the relevant verses; 538 out of the 1156.

However, this approach works roughly as well as the baseline, and disagrees with it in about 15% of the training instances, although most of the time when it disagrees it gets the wrong answer. A concern about this approach is that many of the nouns present in the ontology share very abstract ancestors in the hierarchy. Nearly every noun in the network seems to have as its most abstract ancestor, *apto/capaz* ("apt/capable"), which perhaps means "this can participate in relationships of some sort". There is an accessible path, for example, from *perro* (dog) to *cariño* (kindness). Additionally there is a node in the network for "physical object", another very likely common ancestor. More clever algorithms, such as those in Wordnet::Similarity, more gracefully handle tall ontologies with nonlinear similarity functions. However, a Spanish wordnet with better coverage would reduce the need for being clever – we would be more likely to find matches with short paths through the ontology with denser coverage.

5.3 Simplified Lesk

Our cross-language version of Simplified Lesk does much better than chance, at 65.9% accuracy, but not as well as the most frequent sense baseline. Interestingly, it does much more poorly, at 55.5%, when we turn off stemming. In either case, if we found no matches between the dictionary entries and the surrounding text, we guess the most frequent sense. These backoffs occurred 24.9% of the time with stemming, and 47.1% of the time without, suggesting that the dictionary entries were often helpful, and that we might do better with broader dictionary coverage.

5.4 General-purpose Classifiers

Using only the word context features, we see accuracies slightly better than the MFS baseline, except for the naïve Bayes classifier. Adding the synsets (including hypernyms) of the words in the context does not seem to help the decision tree classifiers, which find the word features much more informative. Performance for other classifiers also went down slightly.

The best classification accuracies that we saw in these experiments were from the simple KNN classifier with the word context features (and optionally the parser features as well), at 77.6% accuracy; the decision tree classifiers did nearly as well when given the word context features and the parser features. In these cases, the classifiers found cases where they can profitably disagree with the baseline. It seems like this happened rarely (7% of cases or less), but in this particular case, it would not be helpful to disagree with the baseline more than 24% of the time.

6 Discussion and Future Work

Our work has thus far only considered adjectives; when we address other classes of content words, they will require morphological analysis, due to the inflectional richness of Quechua. As we continue to build our MT system, it may be promising to try to predict the appropriate inflection for a given lemma using CLWSD techniques. It may also be appropriate to expand to disambiguation over translations of entire phrases, as has been done in (Carpuat and Wu, 2007a); we currently only predict one word at a time.

While the version of the Lesk algorithm that we explored in our work so far has not been very effective, the entries in our dictionary for the adjectives are quite short, and we could try different dictionaries, or expand the technique to make use of source-language corpora instead of just dictionaries, similar to the LESK-CORPUS method described in (Kilgarriff and Rosenzweig, 2000). There are several other machine-readable dictionaries available, including the small but presumably expanding Quechua Wiktionary.

In the fairly near term, our goal is to integrate our CLWSD software into a translation system, such that we can show candidate translations to Quechua speakers and get their feedback. So far, our accuracy for predicting Quechua adjectives is only slightly better than the baseline performance, but we will continue developing the system, along with the rest of our MT tools for under-resourced languages.

References

Steven Bird, Ewan Klein, and Edward Loper. 2009. *Natural Language Processing with Python*. O'Reilly Media.

Peter F. Brown, Vincent J. Della Pietra, Vincent J. Della Pietra, and Robert L. Mercer. 1991. Word-sense disambiguation using statistical methods. In *In Proceedings of the 29th Annual Meeting of the Association for Computational Linguistics*, pages 264–270.

Marine Carpuat and Dekai Wu. 2007a. How phrase sense disambiguation outperforms word sense disambiguation for statistical machine translation. In *11th Conference on Theoretical and Methodological Issues in Machine Translation*.

Marine Carpuat and Dekai Wu. 2007b. Improving statistical machine translation using word sense disambiguation. In *Proceedings of the 2007 Joint Conference on Empirical Methods in Natural Language Processing and Computational Natural Language Learning*. ACL.

Academia Mayor de La Lengua Quechua. 2005. *Diccionario: Queçhua - Español - Quechua, Qheswa - Español - Qheswa: Simi Taqe, 2da ed.* Cusco, Perú.

Georgiana Dinu and Sandra Kübler. 2007. Sometimes less is more: Romanian word sense disambiguation revisited. In *Proceedings of the International Conference on Recent Advances in Natural Language Processing*. ACL.

Adam Kilgarriff and Joseph Rosenzweig. 2000. English framework and results. In *Computers and the Humanities 34 (1-2), Special Issue on SENSEVAL.*

Els Lefever and Véronique Hoste. 2010. Semeval-2010 task 3: Cross-lingual word sense disambiguation. In *Proceedings of the 5th International Workshop on Semantic Evaluation*, pages 15–20, Uppsala, Sweden, July. Association for Computational Linguistics.

Els Lefever, Véronique Hoste, and Martine De Cock. 2011. Parasense or how to use parallel corpora for word sense disambiguation. In *Proceedings of the 49th Annual Meeting of the Association for Computational Linguistics: Human Language Technologies*, pages 317–322, Portland, Oregon, USA, June. Association for Computational Linguistics.

Michael Lesk. 1986. Automatic sense disambiguation using machine readable dictionaries: how to tell a pine cone from an ice cream cone. In *Proceedings of the 5th Annual International Conference on Systems Documentation, SIGDOC '86*, pages 24–26, New York, NY. ACM.

Christian Monson, Ariadna Font Llitjos, Roberto Aranovich, Lori Levin, Ralf Brown, Eric Peterson, Jaime Carbonell, and Alon Lavie. 2006. Building nlp systems for two resource-scarce indigenous languages: Mapudungun and quechua. In *LREC 2006: Fifth International Conference on Language Resources and Evaluation*.

Lluís Padró, Miquel Collado, Samuel Reese, Marina Lloberes, and Irene Castellón. 2010. Freeling 2.1: Five years of open-source language processing tools. In *Proceedings of 7th Language Resources and Evaluation Conference (LREC 2010),*, La Valletta, Malta.

Annotating Negation and Speculation: the Case of the Review Domain

Natalia Konstantinova and **Sheila C. M. de Sousa**
Research Group in Computational Linguistics
University of Wolverhampton
Stafford Street, Wolverhampton, WV1 1SB, UK
{n.konstantinova, sheila.castilhomonteirodesousa}@wlv.ac.uk

Abstract

The paper presents the annotation of negation and speculation which is important for many NLP applications. Unlike previous research focusing on the medical domain, we investigate the review domain and attempt to annotate the SFU Review Corpus. In order to guarantee consistent annotation, we develop specific guidelines. Given the lack of research into annotation in the review domain, we explore the possibility of adapting the existing BioScope guidelines for the domain of interest. In order to reveal cases that need additional investigation, initially a small part of the corpus was annotated and this information was used for developing the guidelines. The paper describes the general principles our guidelines are based on and discusses differences with those in BioScope. It discusses the cases which were difficult to annotate. We include some insight into future work in order to improve the annotation process as well.

1 Introduction

Identification of negation and speculation is a very important problem for a wide range of NLP applications, including but not limited to information extraction, text mining, opinion mining and textual entailment. For all of these tasks it is crucial to know when a part of the text should get e.g. the opposite meaning (in the case of negation) or should be treated as subjective and non-factual (in the case of speculation).

Speculation and negation are important aspects of language. Speculation is related to the broader concept of "modality" which has been extensively studied both in linguistics and philosophy (Saurí, 2008). Various classifications of modality can be found in literature (Morante and Daelemans, 2009). Related terms like "hedging", "evidentiality", "uncertainty", and "factuality" are also used when talking about different aspects of modality. Saurí et al. (2006) state that modality "expresses the speaker's degree of commitment to the events being referred to in a text".

Negation is part of the broader concept of "polarity", which indicates whether a statement is presented as positive or negative (Saurí, 2008). In simple propositional logic, negation is an operator that reverses the truth value of a proposition (Miestamo, 2007).

In defining speculation and negation we follow the definitions introduced by Vincze (2010): "speculation is understood as the possible existence of a thing is claimed – neither its existence nor its non-existence is known for sure", so there is not enough evidence in the text to say whether information is true or not. Whereas "negation is seen as the implication of nonexistence of something".

These two phenomena are interrelated (de Haan, 1997) and have similar characteristics in the text: they both have scope, so affect part of the text which is denoted by the presence of negation or speculation cue words.

The problem of treatment of negation and speculation is quite recent, but it is becoming more popular (more details can be found in Section 2). A large scale corpus is needed for training statistical algorithms to identify of these aspects of the language. However most of the work is done for the biomedical domain and general domain texts have not received much attention (Morante et al., 2011). To our knowledge there is no big corpus from the review domain annotated with negation and speculation. This motivated our work of annotation of the SFU Review Corpus (Taboada et al., 2006) which is widely used in the domain of sentiment analysis and opinion mining. Identification of speculation in reviews can help by providing a measure of the reliability of the opinion contained and can be used for opinion mining (e.g. as suggested in (Wilson et al., 2005)). Also there is no doubt that negation is important for this task as well, because the phrase "this movie is good" has completely different polarity from "this movie is not good", even though they both contain the positive word "good".

It was decided to use the currently available guidelines for the BioScope corpus (Vincze et al., 2008) and attempt to adapt them to the review domain.

The structure of the paper is the following: Section 2 outlines related research, Section 3 describes the corpus used for the annotation and the annotation tool. Section 4 discusses the way the BioScope guidelines should be adapted to the review domain in order to take into account the peculiarities of another domain. The paper finishes with the conclusions and discussion of the directions of the future work (Section 5).

2 Related Work

The topic of negation and speculation became popular only recently, there are not a lot of works tackling this problem. The workshop organised at ACL 2010 (NeSp-NLP 2010)[1] was the key event to bring together researchers working on this problem. Also CoNLL-2010 Shared Task Learning to detect hedges and their scope in natural language text[2] contributed a lot to the development of this research topic.

Annotation of these phenomena was done at different levels ranging from words (Hassan and Radev, 2010) to whole events (Saurí, 2008). Just recently the idea of annotating keywords and scope was introduced by (Vincze, 2010; Kim et al., 2008).

There are several already annotated corpora: the GENIA Event corpus (Kim et al., 2008), which contains annotation of biological events with negation and two types of uncertainty. Medlock and Briscoe (2007) based their system on a corpus consisting of six papers from genomics literature, which were annotated for speculation. Settles et al. (2008) constructed a corpus where sentences were classified as either speculative or definite, however, no keywords were marked in the corpus.

The research community is trying to explore other domains and not only biomedical texts, so the CoNLL-2010 Shared Task on Hedge Detection (Farkas et al., 2010) included not only biomedical texts, but also Wikipedia articles, which were annotated for weasel words ("a word is considered to be a weasel word if it creates an impression that something important has been said, but what is really communicated is vague, misleading, evasive or ambiguous").

As can be noticed most of the work was done for the biomedical domain and there are only now some attempts to annotate general texts like in (Councill et al., 2010). Morante et al. (2011) also discuss the need for corpora which cover other domains. The authors point out that existing guidelines should be adapted to new domains and mention that they are currently annotating texts by Conan Doyle.

We are aware of only one corpus in the review domain described in (Councill et al., 2010), however it was annotated only for negation, but not speculation. Also this corpus is not big and contains only 2111 sentences in total, out of which 679 sentences contain negation.

There are several guidelines available for this task: guidelines for annotation of speculation in the biomedical domain can be found in (Light et al., 2004; Medlock, 2006) (however no cues are annotated there); partial guidelines for annotation of speculation and its keywords are presented in (Farkas et al., 2010). As mentioned earlier (Councill et al., 2010) provide some guidelines for annotation of negation. However the most detailed guidelines for both negation and speculation can be found for the BioScope corpus and are freely available online[3].

3 Annotation Process

The aim of this research was to further study the problem of negation and speculation and to adapt the BioScope guidelines for the annotation of texts from the review domain. A small part of the corpus was initially annotated to provide a comparison of the domains and reveal cases that need to be treated differently in the review domain. The following sections will provide more information about the corpus and the annotation tool used for the task.

3.1 Corpus Description

The SFU Review corpus (Taboada et al., 2006) was chosen for our annotation of negation and speculation. As mentioned earlier, the choice of the corpus was motivated by the lack of annotated corpora for the review domain and also by the need for identification of these phenomena in this domain. This corpus consists of 400 reviews from the website Epinions.com. All the texts are split into several sections such as movies, music, books, hotels etc. Each text gets a label based on whether it is a positive or negative review. All the texts differ in size and are written by different people (more information about the size of the corpus can be found in Table 1).

The BioScope corpus (Vincze et al., 2008) consists of three different types of texts, which is done to ensure the heterogeneity of language used in the biomedical domain. It includes abstracts of the GENIA corpus, 9 full scientific articles and clinical free-texts (more information is provided in Table 2).

As can be seen from Tables 1 and 2 the amount of sentences in the SFU Review corpus is 16,705 and therefore the corpus is of comparable size with BioScope, which consists of more than 20,000 annotated sentences altogether (Vincze et al., 2008).

In the first stage of our work reported here we annotated 20% of the SFU Review corpus using the

[1] Proceedings of the workshop can be found at: http://aclweb.org/anthology-new/W/W10/#3100

[2] Website: http://www.inf.u-szeged.hu/rgai/conll2010st/

[3] Website: http://www.inf.u-szeged.hu/rgai/bioscope

Domain	#Sentences
Books	1,596
Cars	2,960
Computers	2,972
Cookware	1,473
Hotels	2,129
Movies	1,722
Music	2,817
Phones	1,036
Total	**16,705**

Table 1: Statistics of the SFU Review corpus

Subcorpora	#Documents	#Sentences
GENIA Abstracts	1,273	11,872
Full papers	9	2,624
Clinical free-texts	1,954	6,383
Total	3,236	**20,879**

Table 2: Statistics of three BioScope subcorpora

BioScope guidelines. 10 texts were taken from each of 8 domains described in Table 1 to ensure different kinds of texts are studied. This initial step of annotation was used to understand what cases cannot be covered by the BioScope guidelines and how these guidelines should be adapted to the review domain (more detailed discussion of this is presented in Section 4).

The next section will present the annotation tool which was used for our task.

3.2 Annotation Tool

To speed up annotation and ensure its consistency the annotation tool PALinkA (Orăsan, 2003) was used. It is a language- and task-independent tool which allows you to define your own link types. Users can benefit from its intuitive graphical interface which does not require complicated training and is easy to use. The output of this program is a valid xml document, which makes the following processing easier. And the users do not need any technical education, the tool itself prevents them from introducing mistakes into the xml file structure.

The tool allowed us to select keywords and annotate them as negation or speculation. Afterwards the scope was marked in the text and then linked to the cue it belonged to. Graphical interface does not show xml tags in the texts, but uses colours to denote the keywords and scope, which makes annotation representative and easy to analyse and correct if needed. When complex keywords, such as "either...or", "neither...nor" were annotated, there was a possibility to link the scope to both keywords. The use of this annotation tool made us introduce some additional changes to the annotation guidelines described in the next section.

4 Adaptation of Guidelines

Consistent and detailed guidelines are needed when annotating a corpus in order to avoid mistakes and to ensure consistency of the annotation. We attempted to adapt the existing BioScope guidelines in order to fit the needs of the review domain. The BioScope guidelines consist of two parts: speculation and negation. Each part provides information about the marking schemes, the keywords used and the scopes to be annotated. The authors attempted to provide an extensive description of all different cases and also give examples illustrating their rules.

To illustrate examples of the annotation process we use the keywords in bold and their types in subscript; we use () to indicate the scope of speculative keywords; and [] to indicate the scope of negative keywords.

4.1 Main Principles

The BioScope guidelines are based on four main principles (Vincze, 2010):

- Each keyword has a scope.
- The scope must include its keyword.
- Min-max strategy.
  - The minimal unit expressing hedge/negation is marked as the keyword.
  - The scope is extended to the maximal syntactic unit.
- No intersecting scopes are allowed.

There are several principles we also try to follow in order to make annotation consistent:

Min-max strategy: We follow the min-max strategy suggested before in (Vincze, 2010; Farkas et al., 2010). When annotating cues, we try to choose the minimal unit which expresses negation or speculation. In this situation special attention should be paid to distinguishing complex cues and sequences of several keywords. However when annotating scope we try to annotate the maximum words affected by the phenomenon:

They ended up hitting me in the nuts, which, to say the least, was ***probably***$_{spec}$*(better than what the director of this film did to the memory of Dr.Seuss).*

Negation scope: Similar to the BioScope guidelines for the negation scope, only the words that are modified by the negation cue are included in the scope:

It ***isn't***$_{neg}$ *[scary], but it is enthralling.*

Elliptic sentences: For elliptic sentences the keyword is marked and the scope is neglected:

The Bioscope guidelines provide an example of such a case:

This decrease was seen in patients who responded to the therapy as well as in those who did ***not***$_{neg}$.

When annotating the SFU Review corpus we follow the strategy suggested in the BioScope guidelines:

I later discovered that my 11 year old understood all of them. I wish he ***hadn't***$_{neg}$.

Complex keywords: We also follow the principles of the Bioscope guidelines when annotating complex keywords. When speculation or negation is expressed through a phrase rather than a single word and these words cannot express speculation separately, they are annotated as complex keywords:

I ***have a feeling***$_{spec}$ *(that many readers would have given up before the end due to boredom, frustration or the maddening feeling of ' What the hell is Patterson thinking when he wrote this?').*

In this case, *have a feeling* could be substituted by (I) *think* which clearly expresses uncertainty. However the words *have, a, feeling, that* cannot express uncertainty on their own.

4.2 Differences with BioScope

Some differences between the BioScope guidelines and ours are presented in this Section.

Keywords: Unlike the Bioscope corpus, where the cue words are annotated as part of the scope, for the SFU corpus we decided not to include the cue words in the scope.

The choice of the annotation tool was one of the reasons why the keywords were not included in the scope. When using PALinkA the annotation is done more easily and more intuitively if instead of including the keywords in the scope, we link the scope to the keyword it belongs to, while making it possible to have embedded scopes for different keywords. Therefore the resulting xml file is easier to read as one could have the same scope linked to different keyword IDs.

Scope: When the annotator is unsure of the scope of a keyword only the keyword should be annotated.

Type of keyword: When the annotator is unsure what type the keyword should be assigned to (whether it expresses negation or speculation), nothing should be annotated.

For these last cases we set up an 'undecided' category. Those cases will additionally discussed and annotated at the next stage.

Coordination: The Bioscope guidelines suggest extending the scope for speculation and negation keywords to all members of the coordination. However in the case of the review domain as the keywords were not included in the scope, the scopes were annotated separately and then linked to the keywords:

As far as I remember , vacation with accommodation in (Rio), (Golden Nugget),(Excalibur) ***or***$_{spec}$ *(Las Vegas Hilton) were available for cheaper rates than what I paid for Riviera.*

Embedded scopes: Although keywords are not included in their own scope, a keyword can be included in the scope of other keywords and situations of embedded scopes are possible:

I'm ***not sure***$_{spec}$ *(****if***$_{spec}$ *(he* ***should***$_{spec}$ *((be angrier at his widow for giving studios the rights to his stories),* ***or***$_{spec}$ *(to the studios for stabbing his widow in the back when she trusted them)))).*

There were also cases when the combination of different types of keywords (ie. negation and speculation ones) resulted in the embedded scopes:

It **isn't**$_{neg}$ [(vulgar) **or**$_{spec}$ (sexual)]

It should be noted that while the scope for the keyword **or**$_{spec}$ should include (vulgar) and (sexual), the scope for the keyword **isn't**$_{neg}$ should include [vulgar or sexual]. It is explained by the fact that *isn't* modifies both coordinations, and should be understood as 'it isn't vulgar and it isn't sexual either'.

No scope: Unlike the BioScope guidelines which mention only the cases of negation keywords without scope, situations where speculation keywords had no scope were encountered as well in the review domain:

This movie didn't have anything to do with a children's movie as it ***should***$_{spec}$.

4.3 Problematic Cases

While annotating the review domain using the BioScope guidelines we had to face some problematic cases of annotation that had to be discussed additionally.

Differences of the domains: First of all, we had to consider the differences between both domains (biomedical and review) to be able to adapt the guidelines properly. While the BioScope corpus consists of professional biomedical writings and thus a reliable source of texts, in the review domain we are likely to find ungrammatical sentences and misspellings. In the review domain it is not uncommon to find words such as 'ain't', 'whatcha',etc. Also the vocabulary of the domains is different and therefore different words can be considered as cues of negation or speculation. We had to take these peculiarities into account both when developing the guidelines and annotating the corpus.

Titles: As we are dealing with review texts, a great number of them include titles of the books or songs or even quotations from them which authors were referring to. Therefore it was not unusual to find sentences which contain the name of a song/book such as:

Ludacris spits fluidly on "it wasn't us"

and

When ya came in the party and you saw the crowd shoulda read the sign, 'no suckas allowed'

We believe that even when these sentences contain a cue word they should not be annotated because they do not express the writer's uncertainty or negation.

Keyword sequences: The presence of the sequences of the keywords created additional difficulties for the annotation. We feel that the nature of the review domain texts introduces a greater possibility of encountering such cases than in the biomedical domain. Therefore special care should be taken when distinguishing several keywords that go one after another. Although some examples of two or more keywords in a sequence could be also considered as complex keywords they should be annotated separately if they can express hedge on their own:

I ***didn't***$_{neg}$ *[**think**$_{spec}$ (it **would**$_{spec}$ (be **possible**$_{spec}$ (for anyone to rip the heart out of a Dr. Seuss book)))].*

In this example the keywords *didn't* and *think* may seem complex keywords but they should be annotated as separate keywords since *didn't* negates *think* which is the leading cue of the whole idea of speculation.

Not sure: Also it was noted that the case of the keyword *not sure* can be difficult for annotation as its scope should include all the elements it modifies, for instance, it should include all the elements on the right in the following example:

not sure$_{spec}$ *(if he should be angrier at his widow for giving studios the rights to his stories, or to the studios for stabbing his widow in the back when she trusted them).*

Great number of keywords: Close attention should be paid to sentences with a great number of keywords, which can lead the annotator to make mistakes. One of these difficult cases is presented below as an illustration:

*This creative re-engineering draws (the viewer)^1 **or**$_{1spec}$ (reader)^1 into a parallel universe where age-old lessons **can**$_{spec}$ ((be taught)^2 **or**$_{2spec}$ (re-taught)^2) **without**$_{neg}$ [(the obstructions created in the minds)^{3,4,5}, **or**$_{3spec}$ (interferences)^{3,4,5}, **or**$_{4spec}$ (misconceptions)^{3,4,5} **if**$_{spec}$ (you prefer), **or**$_{5spec}$ even (pre-concepts)^{3,4,5}] that **may**$_{spec}$ (**probably**$_{spec}$ (lead to misunderstandings)).*

While for the keywords **or**$_{1spec}$ and **or**$_{2spec}$ the scopes are easily identified, for the **or**$_{3,4,5spec}$ the scopes are tricky since they should include all the members modified by the keyword *not* even if these members are syntactically distant from the keywords.

Passive voice: The case of the passive voice turned out to be a difficult one and generated a lot of discussions. As Morante et al. (2011) noticed there are some inconsistencies in the way the BioScope guidelines describe this problem. Therefore additional discussions and more studies are needed to decide how to mark the scope in sentences containing the passive voice. Therefore at the initial stage of annotation it was decided to mark these cases with a special label 'undecided'. However in the final version of the guidelines we are planning to describe the ways to treat the passive voice and also correct the annotation accordingly.

As can be noted, the examples of the difficult cases of the annotation presented in this Section reveal once again the need for more detailed and specific guidelines for the review domain.

5 Conclusions and Future Work

A lot of work in the field of negation and speculation was done for the biomedical domain, but there is a need for studies in other domains. In this work we attempted to study the review domain and the ways the BioScope guidelines can be adapted to this domain. The research showed the need for detailed guidelines, however we understand that they cannot account for all possible cases in the corpus and therefore difficult cases should be discussed by several annotators.

We made an initial attempt of annotation of the SFU Review Corpus and annotated 20% of the corpus, this information was used for studying the differences of the review and biomedical domains and developing the guidelines for the review domain. We provided analysis of the ways the BioScope guidelines can be adopted to the review domain and what cases should be additionally discussed. We are planning to use the created guidelines to annotate the whole SFU Review Corpus. Also several annotators will be involved in this process and that will allow us to calculate the inter-annotator agreement. Based on this information we will refine the guidelines if needed and correct the annotation. Once this is done, we are planning to make both corpus and guidelines publicly available. We hope that this corpus will be helpful for further development of negation and speculation detection.

We are also planning to analyse the differences of speculation and negation cues in different domains and get more insight into the differences of the review domain and that of biomedical texts.

Acknowledgements

We would like to thank the reviewers for their valuable comments, which helped us a lot in improving the paper. We are also grateful to Prof. Maite Taboada and Prof. Ruslan Mitkov for their support of our research. We wish to thank our colleagues Alison Carminke, Noa P. Cruz Díaz, Dr. Constantin Orăsan and Wilker Aziz for their help with various aspects of our work.

References

Isaac Councill, Ryan McDonald, and Leonid Velikovich. 2010. What's great and what's not: learning to classify the scope of negation for improved sentiment analysis. In *Proceedings of the Workshop on Negation and Speculation in Natural Language Processing*, pages 51–59, Uppsala, Sweden, July. University of Antwerp.

Ferdinand de Haan. 1997. *The interaction of modality and negation: a typological study*. Garland Publishing, New York, USA.

Richárd Farkas, Veronika Vincze, György Móra, János Csirik, and György Szarvas. 2010. The CoNLL-2010 shared task: learning to detect hedges and their scope in natural language text. In *Proceedings of the Fourteenth Conference on Computational Natural Language Learning — Shared Task*, CoNLL '10: Shared Task, pages 1–12, Stroudsburg, PA, USA. Association for Computational Linguistics.

Ahmed Hassan and Dragomir R. Radev. 2010. Identifying text polarity using random walks. In *Proceedings of the 48th Annual Meeting of the Association for Computational Linguistics*, pages 395–403, Uppsala, Sweden, July. Association for Computational Linguistics.

Jin-Dong Kim, Tomoko Ohta, and Jun'ichi Tsujii. 2008. Corpus annotation for mining biomedical events from literature. *BMC Bioinformatics*, 9.

Marc Light, Xin Ying Qiu, and Padmini Srinivasan. 2004. The language of bioscience: Facts, speculations, and statements in between. In Lynette Hirschman and James Pustejovsky, editors, *HLT-NAACL 2004 Workshop: BioLINK 2004, Linking Biological Literature, Ontologies and Databases*, pages 17–24, Boston, Massachusetts, USA, May 6. Association for Computational Linguistics.

Ben Medlock and Ted Briscoe. 2007. Weakly supervised learning for hedge classification in scientific literature. In *Proceedings of the ACL*, pages 992–999, Prague, Czech Republic, June.

Ben Medlock. 2006. Guidelines for speculative sentence annotation.

Matti Miestamo. 2007. Negation an overview of typological research. *Language and Linguistics Compass*, 1(5):552–570, September.

Roser Morante and Walter Daelemans. 2009. Learning the scope of hedge cues in biomedical texts. In *Proceedings of the Workshop on Current Trends in Biomedical Natural Language Processing*, BioNLP '09, pages 28–36, Stroudsburg, PA, USA. Association for Computational Linguistics.

Roser Morante, Sarah Schrauwen, and Walter Daelemans. 2011. Corpus-based approaches to processing the scope of negation cues: an evaluation of the state of the art. In *Proceedings of the Ninth International Conference on Computational Semantics*, IWCS '11, pages 350–354, Stroudsburg, PA, USA. Association for Computational Linguistics.

Constantin Orăsan. 2003. PALinkA: a highly customizable tool for discourse annotation. In *Proceedings of the 4th SIGdial Workshop on Discourse and Dialog*, pages 39 – 43, Sapporo, Japan, July, 5 -6.

Roser Saurí, Marc Verhagen, and James Pustejovsky. 2006. Annotating and recognizing event modality in text. In *In The 19th International FLAIRS Conference, FLAIRS 2006*.

Roser Saurí. 2008. *A factuality profiler for eventualities in text*. Ph.D. thesis, Waltham, MA, USA.

Burr Settles, Mark Craven, and Lewis Friedland. 2008. Active learning with real annotation costs. In *Proceedings of the NIPS Workshop on Cost-Sensitive Learning*, pages 1–10.

Maite Taboada, Caroline Anthony, and Kimberly Voll. 2006. Methods for creating semantic orientation dictionaries. In *Proceedings of 5th International Conference on Language Resources and Evaluation (LREC)*, pages 427–432, Genoa, Italy, May.

Veronika Vincze, György Szarvas, Richárd Farkas, György Móra, and János Csirik. 2008. The BioScope corpus: biomedical texts annotated for uncertainty, negation and their scopes. *BMC Bioinformatics*, 9(Suppl 11):S9+.

Veronika Vincze. 2010. Speculation and negation annotation in natural language texts: what the case of BioScope might (not) reveal. In *Proceedings of the Workshop on Negation and Speculation in Natural Language Processing*, pages 28–31, Uppsala, Sweden, July. University of Antwerp.

Theresa Wilson, Janyce Wiebe, and Paul Hoffmann. 2005. Recognizing contextual polarity in phrase-level sentiment analysis. In *Proceedings of the conference on Human Language Technology and Empirical Methods in Natural Language Processing*, HLT '05, pages 347–354, Stroudsburg, PA, USA. Association for Computational Linguistics.

N-gram Based Text Classification According To Authorship

Anđelka Zečević
Faculty of Mathematics, University of Belgrade, Serbia
andjelkaz@matf.bg.ac.rs

Abstract

Authorship attribution studies consider author's identification of an anonymous text. This is a long history problem with a great number of various approaches. Those ones based on n-grams single out by their performances and good results. A n-gram approach is language independent but the selection of a number *n* is actually not. The focus of this paper is determination of a set of optimal values for number *n* for specific task of classification of newspaper articles written in Serbian according to authorship. We combine two different algorithms: the first one is based on counting common n-grams and the another one is based on relative frequency of n-grams. Experimental results are obtained for pairs of n-gram and profile sizes and it can be concluded that for all profile sizes the best results are obtained for $3 \leq n \leq 7$.

1 Introduction

Language is just one of many possible ways for expressing individuality. For researchers in the field of authorship attribution the focus of interests is how this uniqueness enacts on writing and how it can be measured. During the period of nontraditional approach to this problem the variety of features for quantifying the writing style are considered – from lexical to application-specific (Stamatatos, 2009). N-grams are treated as character features and they are widely used in statistical natural language processing.

From a machine learning point of view, the authorship attribution problem can be viewed as text classification task: automatically sorting a set of texts into classes from a predefined set (Sebastiani, 2001). Here, each class represents a concrete author.

A goal of this paper is to identify authors of anonymous articles from the local daily newspapers using n-gram based algorithm. The articles discuss similar topics, all are written in Serbian and published in the same period of time.

The scheme of our algorithm is depicted in Figure 1 and represents a classical profile-based algorithm:

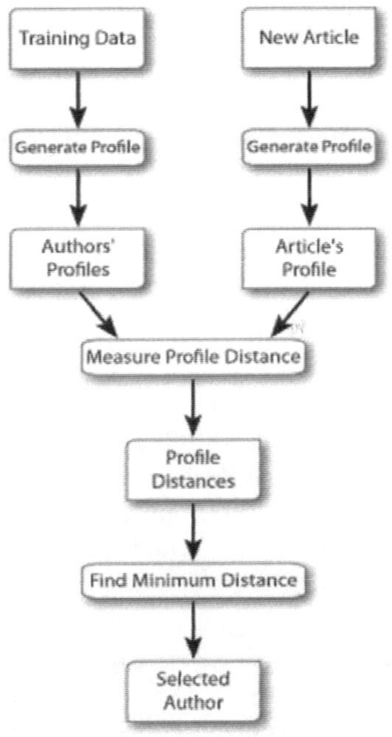

Figure 1: The algorithm schema

the training data set is used for generating authors profiles, authors profiles are laid aside until a new article arrives. Then, the article profile is generated and compared to all authors' profiles. The system selects the author whose profile has the smallest distance to the article's profile.

The remainder of the paper is organized as follows. In Section 2 we define a byte level n-gram, in Section 3 we discuss n-gram generation and propose a data structure for storing all relevant information. A text profile is defined in Section 4 while Section 5 introduces a distance measure between two profiles. Section 6 discusses measures for estimation of classification effectiveness. Section 7 summarizes obtained results and finally, Section 8 presents some conclusions and future directions.

2 N-grams

A n-gram is a continuous sequence of *n* bytes or *n* characters or *n* words of a longer portion of a text. Therefore, we distinguish *byte level*, *character level* and *word level* n-grams. For example, for portion of a text *green tee* all character level 5-grams are: *green*, *reen_*, *een_t*, *en_te* and *n_tee* where the underscore character (_) represents a blank and all word level 1-grams are: *green* and *tee*.

In this paper we will focus on byte level n-grams. Character byte representation depends on character encoding. We will consider only UTF-8 encoding. For example, for the English word *day* the appropriate sequence of bytes is 01100100 01100001 01111001 and for the Serbian word *šta* (English *what*) the sequence is 11000101 10100001 01110100 01100001. These two representations differ in size because there are a few Serbian letters (š, ž, ć, č, đ) which are two bytes long. That means we can split them in two meaningless parts if we use byte level n-grams. Despite the fact that a great number of n-grams will contain both bytes we can benefit from this approach in aspect of more efficient memory usage.

In general, n-grams afford language independent processing, tracking of lexical and contextual information, more robust behaviour in the presence of different kinds of textual errors because errors affect only a limited number of n-grams (Cavnar and Trenkle, 1994) and automatic detection of words that share the same root form (Stamatatos, 2009).

3 N-gram Generation

The computational requirements of byte level n-grams extraction are minimal – a single pass through the text is sufficient and requires no special tools. Some text preprocessing such as character selection or conversion of letters to uppercase or lowercase can be done, but it is not the case in our approach.

Adjacent n-grams overlap and contain redundant information so the memory requirements are more intensive in comparison to methods that store only words. If the portion of a text is *K* byte length the number of n-grams is $K+1-N$ so the total size of the memory is $(K+1-N)*N$ bytes.

We decided to store all n-grams in a data structure called a trie or prefix tree (Aho et al., 1983; Sedgewick, 2002). A node of a trie (Figure 2) contains a single byte value and from the node position we discover the value of the corresponding n-gram - picking up one by one byte on the path from the root of the trie to that node. Besides the field *byte* containing the byte value, each node contains the field *count* with the number of occurrences. The field *isEnd* determines if the *byte* is the end byte of the n-gram or not and it is obilagatory field because we work with n-grams of fixed size. Two additional link fields are included - one to its children named *children* and one to the next node in the trie named *nextTrieNode*.

```
struct TrieNode{
    char byte;
    unsigned int count;
    int isEnd;
    struct TrieNode* children[SIZE];
    struct TrieNode* nextTrieNode;
}
```

Figure 2: The node definition

The main advantage of using tries over using other data structures such as trees or hash tables is effective retrieval (looking up a n-gram takes worst case O(n) time) and the time for the operations insert, find and delete a node is almost indentical.

4 Text Profile

A text profile is a set of M most frequent n-grams. Precisely, it is a set of pairs

$\{(x_1, f_1), \ldots, (x_{M-1}, f_{M-1})\}$ (Kešelj et al., 2003)

where x_i denotes a n-gram value and f_i its relative frequency. The number M is called profile size.

For the purpose of classification we need text profile generation in the following steps: when we define authors' profiles and when a new article arrives for classification.

Single author's profile is generated from its training data set. For each text in the training data set all n-grams are extracted and added to the author's trie. Every time a n-gram is added to the author's trie the number of its occurrences is increased by one. When done, all n-grams are put in the array and sorted into descending order by the number of occurrences. Only the first M n-grams are kept and their numbers of occurrences are divided by the total number of n-grams in training data set to obtain relative frequencies.

The process of generating a new article's profile is the same as above except there is no training data set but only the given article.

5 Distance Measure

A distance measure used in this paper is

$$d(A, a) = \sum_{x \in A} \left(\frac{2 \cdot (f_A(x) - f_a(x))}{f_A(x) + f_a(x)} \right)^2$$

where A is an author profile, a is an article profile, x is byte level n-gram and $f_A(x)$ and $f_a(x)$ are the relative frequencies of that n-gram in author and article profile. The same distance values are obtained if condition *x in A* is replaced with *x in a* cause only common n-grams are taken into account.

This measure combines two measures originally proposed by Keselj et al. (2003) and Frantzeskou et al. (2006). The first one is *dissimilarity measure* and takes into account all n-grams of author's profile and article's profile. In case where at least one author's profile is shorter then profile size M, this function favors that author. The second measure is called *simplified profile intersection* and takes into account only the common n-grams of author's and article's profile. In case where one of the author's profile is longer then others, this function favors that author. In our case the first problem is avoided by using profiles intersection, while the second problem is avoided by calculating relative frequencies of n-grams.

When a new article arrives for classification, the distance among article's profile and each of the author's profile is calculated. The system applies 1-nearest neighbour algorithm (Mitchell, 1997), picks the minimal distance and assigns the article to the winning author.

6 Classification Effectiveness

For estimating the effectiveness of a single class classification we use F_1 measure:

$$F_1 = \frac{P \cdot R}{P + R}$$

which attributes equal importance to precision P and recall R:

$$P = \frac{TP}{TP+FP}, \quad R = \frac{TP}{TP+FN}$$

Another measure we use is accuracy:

$$accuracy = \frac{TP+TN}{TP+TN+FP+FN}$$

Values TP, TN, FP and FN are values from the contingency table: number of yes-yes, no-no, yes-no and no-yes labeled articles.

For overall estimation of effectiveness we used macroaverage of individual values (Sebastiani, 2001):

$$F_1 = \frac{\sum_{i=1}^{c} F_{1i}}{c}, \quad accuracy = \frac{\sum_{i=1}^{c} accuracy_i}{c}$$

where c is the total number of authors.

7 Results

We tried to classify anonymous articles of three authors[1]. A training data set for each author is approximately 100KB in size and contains respectively 20, 17 and 27 articles available on the Internet archive[2]. The program is tested on two test data sets – the first one sizes approximately 220KB and consists of 45 articles (15 for each author) and the second one sizes approximately 330KB and consist of 60 articles (20 for each author). Table 1 and Table 2 represent obtained values in respect to accuracy and F1 measure for the second test set.

The system achieves accuracy over 80% for all n-gram sizes greater then 2 and the profile sizes greater then 500 n-grams. Accuracy increases with the size of the profile and the best results are obtained for $3 \leq n \leq 7$.

The similar conclusion can be drawn from the Table 2. F_1 measure values are over 80% for all n-gram sizes greater then 4 and the profile sizes greater then 1000.

1 Authors names are: S. Biševac, Z. Panović and A. Roknić

2 http://www.danas.rs

8 Conclusions and Future Directions

The presented method is not novel but it gives some insights into results referring to Serbian. The algorithm has demonstrated good performance, but it should be applied to other languages to see how it works. Also a threshold existence should be examined in order to achieve precise and more effective classification according to authorship.

Profile size	N-gram size									
	1	2	3	4	5	6	7	8	9	10
20	0.7	0.68	0.62	0.64	0.71	0.7	0.62	0.63	0.54	0.58
50	0.75	0.82	0.68	0.68	0.67	0.71	0.67	0.62	0.58	0.6
100	0.56	0.66	0.71	0.72	0.71	0.75	0.7	0.7	0.64	0.67
500	0.56	0.84	0.87	0.86	0.85	0.91	0.9	0.88	0.84	0.84
1000	0.56	0.55	0.87	0.86	0.86	0.92	0.88	0.88	0.82	0.82
1500	0.56	0.55	0.91	0.93	0.93	0.95	0.91	0.91	0.88	0.91
2000	0.56	0.55	0.92	0.92	0.9	0.92	0.9	0.9	0.88	0.91
3000	0.56	0.55	0.91	0.93	0.94	0.93	0.96	0.91	0.91	0.9
4000	0.56	0.55	0.81	0.92	0.93	0.92	0.95	0.88	0.88	0.91
5000	0.56	0.55	0.82	0.92	0.94	0.92	0.88	0.92	0.92	0.84

Table 1: Accuracy

Profile size	N-gram size									
	1	2	3	4	5	6	7	8	9	10
20	0.53	0.54	0.44	0.46	0.57	0.53	0.38	0.42	0.28	0.35
50	0.61	0.72	0.53	0.53	0.5	0.53	0.5	0.39	0.35	0.37
100	0	0.5	0.56	0.59	0.56	0.61	0.51	0.53	0.41	0.48
500	0	0.75	0.81	0.8	0.78	0.86	0.84	0.79	0.78	0.76
1000	0	0	0.81	0.8	0.8	0.88	0.82	0.82	0.7	0.71
1500	0	0	0.86	0.9	0.9	0.93	0.86	0.86	0.83	0.86
2000	0	0	0.88	0.88	0.85	0.88	0.85	0.84	0.83	0.86
3000	0	0	0.86	0.9	0.91	0.89	0.94	0.86	0.86	0.85
4000	0	0	0.71	0.88	0.89	0.88	0.93	0.83	0.83	0.86
5000	0	0	0.73	0.88	0.91	0.88	0.83	0.88	0.88	0.76

Table2: F_1 measure
in our calculation when TP=FP=FN=0, F_1 measure is defined as 0

9 References

A. Aho, J. Hopcroft and D. Ulman. 1983. *Data Structures and Algorithms.* Pearson. Addison-Wesley. Paperback

A. Rahmoun and Z. Elberrichi. 2007. *Experimenting n-grams in Text Categorization.* Issue of International Arab Journal of Information Technology, Vol 4, N°.4 : 377-385.

E. Stamatatos. 2009. *A Survey of Modern Authorship Attribution Methods.* Journal of the American Society for Information Science and Technology, 60(3): 538-556. Wiley.

F. Sebastiani. 2001. *Machine Learning in Automated Text Categorization.* ACM Computing Surveys, 34(1):147.

G. Frantzeskou, E. Stamatatos, S. Gritzalis and S. Katsikas. 2006. *Effective identification of source code authors using byte-level information.* In Proceedings of the 28th International Conference on Software Engineering, 893-896. ACM Press.

R. Sedgewick. 2002. *Algorithms in C.* Adison-Wesley.

T. Mitchell. 1997. *Machine Learning*. McGraw Hill.

V. Kešelj, F. Peng, N. Cercone and C. Thomas. 2003. *N-gram based author profiles for authorship attribution.* Pacific Association for Computational Linguistics, 255–264, Halifax, Canada.

W. Cavnar and J. Trenkle. 1994. *N-gram-Based Text Categorization.* Proceedings of SDAIR-94, 3rd Annual Symposium on Document Analysis and Information Retrieval.

Instance Sampling for Multilingual Coreference Resolution

Desislava Zhekova
University of Bremen
zhekova@uni-bremen.de

Abstract

In this paper we investigate the effect of downsampling negative training instances on a multilingual memory-based coreference resolution approach. We report results on the SemEval-2010 task 1 data sets for six different languages (Catalan, Dutch, English, German, Italian and Spanish) and for four evaluation metrics (MUC, B^3, CEAF, BLANC). Our experiments show that downsampling negative training examples does not improve the overall system performance for most targeted languages and that the various evaluation metrics do not show a significantly distinct behavior across the different samples.

1 Introduction

In the last decade the research in the area of Computational Linguistics (CL) has been directed to new, flexible, efficient and most importantly automated methods for Natural Language Processing. The latter has motivated a shift from rule-based to machine-learning (ML) methods in the hope that those will lead to more robust and efficient solutions. Thus, the previously used rule-based approaches (cf. e.g. (Mitkov, 1998; Poesio et al., 2002)) to anaphora and coreference resolution (CR) have been followed by machine-learning techniques (cf. e.g. (Soon et al., 2001; Ng and Cardie, 2002b)). In general, one of the biggest disadvantages of the rule-based approaches is the fact that the created coreference resolution systems must be constantly extended in order to provide rules for yet unseen cases. Thus, whenever a new language is considered, a distinct set of rules needs to be assembled, which can hardly be completed in a reasonable time frame. Yet, approaching the CR task on a multilingual level means that the resulting coreference procedure needs to be robust and general enough to lead to good results in an unseen environment. This provides a reasonable motivation for the use of ML methods, since only those can be designed with the required flexibility by keeping efficiency in mind.

Previous work in the area (Zhekova and Kübler, 2010) developed such a robust multilingual machine-learning based CR system, UBIU (see section 3.1), which we use in our work and which is not specifically fine tuned to any of the languages it is applied to. However, achieving good and linguistically motivated results in a multilingual environment is not an easy task. For this reason, the general performance of the system must be maximally optimized so that it is able to efficiently use the little but relevant information that it is provided with.

Based on their complexity and flexibility, ML methods, as the ones used in UBIU, offer various possibilities to optimize the system performance to the given task. Such an optimization is, for example, instance sampling. Since there are contradictory opinions on whether the latter has a positive or rather negative effect on the overall coreference system performance (see section 2) and since by now there is no work on its application to a multilingual CR approach, we apply instance sampling on UBIU in this paper. We first present various approaches related to our work (section 2), further in section 3, we describe the experimental setup by introducing the CR system that we used for our experiments (section 3.1) as well as the approached investigation (section 3.2). In section 4, we present our results and, in section 5, we draw some conclusive remarks and outline a reasonable continuation and investigation of the multilingual coreference resolution approach.

2 Previous Work

In her work, Uryupina (2004) reports that in the MUC-7 (Hirschman, 1997) corpus only about 1-2% (approximate ratio of 1:48) of the instances are positive (coreferent). The same was also reported for the MUC-6 data by Ng and Cardie (2002a).

Such extremely skewed distribution of positive vs. negative examples in the training data is believed to cause difficulties for the classification process. This happens since ML approaches are influenced by the unbalanced assembly of training instances and approach a classification system that intends to partially keep the ratio that is already distorted. Hoste (2005) also comments that standard classification algorithms may show poor performance when applied to an unbalanced data set since minority classes are completely ignored by some algorithms. The latter are then not applicable on data such as the one assembled in a state-of-the-art CR tasks. However, other algorithms are able to find a reasonable trade-off between the correctly and wrongly identified minority class labels.

In order to account for the disproportionate data, multiple approaches to coreference resolution have employed instance sampling techniques (Ng and Cardie, 2002a; Uryupina, 2004; Zhao and Ng, 2007; Wunsch et al., 2009; Recasens and Hovy, 2009). One possibility for this is instead of keeping all possible instances in the training data, to randomly remove negative vectors. The latter can be also excluded via a statistically or linguistically motivated algorithm that is applied until an optimal ratio for the task is reached. Once this is done, the data can be used by the classifier. Another possibility to reach a normalized ratio is by mining more positive instances in the data such as the approach presented by Ng and Cardie (2002a).

In their work, Wunsch et al. (2009) compare different instance sampling techniques with different classifiers on the task of anaphora resolution on a single language – German. They report that all applied methods lead to an improvement of the overall system performance independently of the type of the classifier (memory-based learner, decision trees, maximum entropy learner). Better system performance from the use of instance sampling is also reported by Uryupina (2004). However, both improvements, as the authors discuss, are a result of increased recall and drastically decreased precision. In her PhD thesis, Hoste (2005) shows that downsampling negative examples leads to an unacceptable trade-off between recall and precision. The latter was recently confirmed in (Recasens and Hovy, 2009) where the authors conclude that while using a memory-based classifier, downsampling negative instances for training does not lead to an improvement of the overall performance.

All distinct methods for instance sampling were employed in different CR systems. Some of them were completely ML based, others used a hybrid approach to the task. Moreover, none of the systems was able to test the exact same sampling technique on more than one language and on more than one evaluation metric. This makes it hard to gain an objective overview of when and how instance sampling, and specifically downsampling of negative examples in the training data, influences the overall performance of a CR system. If we consider the findings as in (Wunsch et al., 2009; Ng and Cardie, 2002a; Uryupina, 2004) we can expect that using downsampling will significantly increase the performance of a multilingual memory-based coreference resolution system. However, if we favor the theories in (Hoste, 2005; Recasens and Hovy, 2009) we can only expect a change in the overall system performance gained by an unacceptable trade-off between system precision and recall.

Our assumption is that instance sampling can lead to a significant and well balanced improvement in the overall performance for systems that use hybrid approaches and are thus highly tuned for specific languages. Such systems make use of explicit rules that are language specific and often hand-crafted (in various stages of the CR process, e.g. preprocessing, postprocessing, etc.). Those rules are generally accurate on their own and lead to good performance overall. Thus, systems that make use of such rules can only benefit if the ML component favors a classification system with a higher rate for positive answers. The system that we use for our experiments is exclusively ML based and constructed in an exceptionally general way such that it can be easily applied to diverse new languages without much additional effort.

3 Experimental Setup

In order to evaluate the influence of instance sampling on a multilingual CR approach, which to our knowledge has not yet been attempted, we investigated its effect in the setting defined by the SemEval-2010 task 1 (Recasens et al., 2010). In the following section, we will first shortly introduce the employed coreference resolution system (see section 3.1) and then present the design of the experiments that we conducted (see section 3.2).

3.1 UBIU

The coreference resolution system, UBIU (Zhekova and Kübler, 2010), that we used in our work was initially designed for the multilingual CR task (Recasens et al., 2010). The prevailing purpose for the use and further development of UBIU is to gain more insight into the problems that occur when the CR task is extended from the use of only one language to multiple ones. For this reason, UBIU is structured in a way that allows for a quick and easy integration of a new language, given that the provided data is formatted in the style used by SemEval-2010 (Recasens et al., 2010).

The coreference resolution pipeline in UBIU starts with a basic preprocessing step of the data in which only insignificant formatting and restructuring of the data is conducted. Further, an important step is approached – mention identification. During this step, the relevant UBIU module extracts the nominal/pronominal phrases that are further considered in the coreference process. The system stores the mention boundaries and extracts the syntactic heads of the phrases, which are further passed to the next system module responsible for the feature extraction. The latter follows the mention-pair model that uses a subset of the features presented by Rahman and Ng (2009) (as listed in (Zhekova and Kübler, 2010)) to create feature vectors that are passed to the next module in the system. The same process is executed for both the training and the test set, which leads to their transformation from the original data format to a format represented by feature vectors. Both training and tests sets are then further used by the next module in the UBIU pipeline.

For the actual coreference classification, UBIU implements a ML approach and is thus structured around the idea of memory-based learning (MBL) (Daelemans and van den Bosch, 2005). The MBL learner that is used for classification is TiMBL (Daelemans et al., 2007). In general, a MBL classifier makes use of a similarity metric in order to identify the most similar examples (the k nearest neighbors (k-nn)) in the training data to the example that has been currently classified in the test data. Based on the classes that those k-nn instances have, a decision for the yet unlabeled vector can be made. Once labeled, the references between the syntactic heads of the phrases and the actual boundaries of the phrases is restored in a postprocessing step and the final coreference chains of clustered coreferent phrases are created.

3.2 Experiments

We conduct six different experiments on all six languages (Catalan, Dutch, English, German, Italian and Spanish) and show the results for all four evaluation metrics (MUC (Vilain et al., 1995), B^3 (Bagga and Baldwin, 1998), CEAF (Luo, 2005), BLANC (Recasens and Hovy, 2011)). For each language, we used as training data the development set provided by the SemEval-2011 task 1 corpora. As test data we employed the official test set from the task. The system performance that we report is different from the one that was reported during UBIU's participation in the task (Recasens et al., 2010) as a result of various improvements on the system and the use of a subset of the actual training data. For scoring, we employed the software provided by task 1. Each separate run of the system used different ratio between the positive and negative examples in the training process. The base ratio for all languages that was observed in the development set when derived in a context window of three sentences is as follows: Catalan – 1:25; Dutch – 1:14; English – 1:26; German – 1:31; Italian – 1:45; Spanish – 1:24. We further explored the following five ratios: 1:10, 1:7, 1:5, 1:4, 1:2. In order to achieve the downsampled sets we use an approach based on random removal of negative instances.

4 Results

In the current section, we discuss the final results of the system (listed in table 1) that the multilingual coreference resolution system UBIU achieved for all six experimental runs. In order to gain more insight into the actual effect of the sampling approach on the classification system, in section 4.1, we also report the distribution of positive vs. negative examples in the test sets that have already been classified. We then divide and report our observations in three different classes: differences in system performance across the various evaluation metrics (presented in section 4.2), differences in system performance across the various languages (introduced in section 4.3) and differences in system performance across both language families (accounted for in section 4.4).

		MUC			B^3			CEAF-M			CEAF-E			BLANC		
	train ratio	R	P	F_1	R	P	F_1	R	P	F_1	R	P	F_1	R	P	Blanc
C	1:25	14.14	**30.78**	**19.38**	53.31	**69.12**	**60.20**	**54.44**	**49.20**	**51.69**	**70.23**	46.31	**55.81**	50.65	**62.19**	49.15
D	1:14	02.65	04.48	03.33	23.71	**20.58**	**22.04**	28.75	09.35	14.11	**49.71**	06.39	11.33	**50.00**	50.21	27.71
E	1:26	11.76	**32.06**	17.21	62.79	**75.32**	**68.49**	**62.70**	**57.98**	**60.25**	**76.50**	**55.81**	**64.54**	50.41	**61.87**	49.30
G	1:31	14.04	**26.65**	**18.39**	50.67	**51.31**	**50.99**	**52.80**	**44.24**	**48.14**	**59.88**	42.47	**49.70**	**50.06**	**56.02**	44.19
I	1:45	04.31	**24.06**	**07.31**	35.70	**56.86**	**43.86**	**37.89**	**41.16**	**39.46**	**46.80**	**38.29**	**42.12**	**50.02**	**59.00**	42.98
S	1:24	15.00	**30.49**	**20.11**	54.82	**70.32**	**61.61**	**55.72**	**52.71**	**54.17**	**70.93**	50.65	**59.10**	50.71	**60.71**	49.74
C	1:10	17.25	16.73	16.99	53.87	53.20	53.53	48.16	43.52	45.73	55.93	48.44	51.92	50.59	52.89	49.64
D		04.35	04.32	04.33	24.13	18.30	20.81	28.58	09.30	14.03	45.96	06.57	11.50	49.99	49.72	27.98
E		19.54	15.84	17.50	64.01	56.86	60.22	53.27	49.26	51.19	58.23	57.09	57.66	50.68	53.09	50.25
G		**17.29**	14.16	15.57	**51.16**	42.60	46.49	48.77	40.86	44.47	51.05	**43.10**	46.74	50.01	50.52	44.36
I		05.39	10.18	07.05	35.80	50.21	41.80	34.98	37.99	36.42	41.17	38.12	39.58	49.98	49.38	43.13
S		18.18	20.36	19.21	55.51	59.09	57.24	52.22	49.40	50.77	61.55	53.21	57.07	50.95	56.17	50.42
C	1:7	17.77	15.71	16.68	53.99	50.73	52.31	47.02	42.49	44.64	53.29	48.84	50.97	50.64	52.84	49.78
D		05.87	04.89	05.34	24.45	17.33	20.28	28.82	09.38	14.15	44.43	06.70	11.65	49.99	49.84	28.13
E		20.78	15.34	**17.65**	64.13	54.37	58.85	52.05	48.13	50.01	55.44	57.12	56.27	50.82	53.66	50.48
G		16.17	11.95	13.74	51.03	40.70	45.28	47.15	39.51	43.00	48.78	42.73	45.55	49.99	49.76	44.41
I		**05.42**	08.58	06.64	35.78	48.48	41.17	34.03	36.97	35.44	39.49	38.03	38.75	50.00	50.24	43.27
S		20.26	18.54	19.36	56.01	53.28	54.61	50.32	47.61	48.93	56.47	54.54	55.49	**51.12**	55.28	50.82
C	1:5	18.91	15.45	17.00	54.23	47.94	50.89	46.14	41.69	43.80	50.84	**49.26**	50.04	**50.66**	52.78	49.86
D		09.09	**05.57**	06.91	25.40	15.24	19.05	**30.52**	**09.93**	**14.99**	43.08	07.42	12.66	**50.00**	**50.32**	28.07
E		19.90	15.57	17.47	63.95	55.68	59.53	53.42	49.40	51.33	57.34	**57.24**	57.29	50.76	54.03	50.32
G		16.29	10.93	13.08	51.05	39.06	44.25	46.05	38.59	41.99	46.82	42.66	44.64	49.99	49.80	44.49
I		05.21	07.21	06.05	35.79	46.66	40.51	33.22	36.08	34.59	37.81	37.77	37.79	49.99	49.67	43.28
S		18.80	14.62	16.45	55.68	47.30	51.15	46.21	43.71	44.92	49.19	53.60	51.30	51.04	53.83	50.79
C	1:4	18.70	13.67	15.79	54.14	43.93	48.50	43.64	39.43	41.43	46.21	49.12	47.62	**50.66**	52.33	50.00
D		09.71	05.40	**06.94**	25.45	14.36	18.36	30.43	09.90	14.94	41.33	**07.53**	**12.73**	**50.00**	50.28	28.11
E		22.08	14.56	17.55	64.35	50.60	56.65	49.64	45.91	47.70	51.44	56.82	54.00	50.78	52.98	50.48
G		16.44	10.09	12.50	51.10	37.12	43.00	44.48	37.27	40.55	44.14	41.96	43.02	49.96	49.32	44.53
I		05.36	07.26	06.17	**35.82**	46.32	40.40	32.98	35.82	34.34	37.43	37.63	37.53	49.98	49.58	43.29
S		20.86	15.67	17.90	56.08	45.83	50.44	45.53	43.07	44.26	47.87	53.76	50.64	51.08	53.64	50.88
C	1:2	**20.71**	12.23	15.38	**54.65**	34.36	42.19	37.54	33.93	35.64	34.84	47.42	40.16	50.60	51.55	**50.13**
D		**11.72**	04.52	06.52	**25.96**	10.18	14.63	28.84	09.38	14.16	29.86	07.49	11.98	49.98	49.69	**28.69**
E		**23.89**	12.65	16.54	**64.74**	42.09	51.01	43.55	40.28	41.85	41.57	55.10	47.39	**50.83**	52.18	**50.71**
G		16.80	08.26	11.08	51.06	31.84	39.22	39.87	33.41	36.36	37.06	40.25	38.59	49.93	49.17	**44.79**
I		04.02	03.54	03.76	35.64	38.98	37.24	28.88	31.37	30.07	29.95	35.97	32.69	50.00	50.00	**43.51**
S		**21.44**	13.09	16.26	**56.26**	36.29	44.12	39.11	37.00	38.02	36.91	52.41	43.31	51.07	52.45	**51.02**

Table 1: System performance over all languages (C(atalan), D(utch), E(nglish), G(erman), I(talian) and S(panish)) and sampling variations.

4.1 Test Set Distribution

In table 2, we list the various distributions of the positive vs. negative examples in both training and test sets of each sample. The base distribution of examples in the train data for all languages is as presented in section 3.2. The figures show that memory-based learning is highly sensitive to the distribution of positive vs. negative examples in the data. It approaches a classification system that ensures a distribution of the instances in the final outcome that is to some extent proportionate to the training ratio of both classes. Yet, this does not ensure that a positively classified instance is correctly labeled, which motivates our investigation of the system performance in the various samples.

train	test					
	Catalan	Dutch	English	German	Italian	Spanish
base	1:66.15	1:55.71	1:66.93	1:63.26	1:126.14	1:67.66
1:10	1:18.85	1:36.48	1:13.06	1:16.77	1:36.12	1:23.78
1:7	1:15.04	1:27.58	1:11.28	1:13.97	1:28.31	1:15.92
1:5	1:12.30	1:17.51	1:12.42	1:11.26	1:23.06	1:12.22
1:4	1:9.49	1:13.52	1:8.88	1:9.65	1:21.95	1:10.50
1:2	1:4.35	1:4.71	1:5.11	1:5.82	1:9.09	1:5.43

Table 2: Distribution of positive vs. negative examples in the train and already classified test set.

4.2 Differences Across Metrics

Considering the results displayed in table 1 there are several significant differences in system performance across the samples in respect to the evaluation metrics that were used to evaluate it.

From all four metrics only MUC and B^3 show a distinctive change in recall when the sample of negative examples in the training set reduces and in particular when it reaches a ratio of 1:2. The differences for B^3 are not surprisingly high, but the MUC metric shows an exceedingly boosted performance. The latter, we assume, is due to one of MUC's most important shortcomings, namely the fact that overmerged entities are not punished but rather rewarded by the metric. In a training setting, in which only 2 negative examples are used for each positive one, the classifier is bound to return a high number of positive instances, thus leading to highly overmerged coreference chains. Both variants of the CEAF metric do not show an improvement in recall for all different samples apart from the CEAF-M variant with respect to Dutch, which has best recall in a sample 1:5. Similar to CEAF, the BLANC metric also reaches best recall

train	Catalan	Dutch	English	German	Italian	Spanish
base	47.25	15.70	51.96	42.28	35.15	48.95
1:10	43.57	15.73	47.36	39.47	33.60	46.94
1:7	42.88	15.91	46.65	38.40	33.05	45.84
1:5	42.32	16.34	47.19	37.69	32.44	42.92
1:4	40.67	16.22	47.28	36.72	32.35	42.82
1:2	36.70	15.20	41.50	34.01	29.45	38.55

Table 3: Average system performance over all languages and sampling variations.

train	Romance	Germanic
base	43.78	36.65
1:10	41.37	34.19
1:7	40.59	33.65
1:5	39.22	33.74
1:4	38.61	33.41
1:2	34.90	30.24

Table 4: Average system performance over both language families and sampling variations.

values for most of the languages in the original examples ratio. Moreover, the differences in scores for which different ratios performed better are relatively small.

With respect to precision, the behavior of most metrics is quite similar. Apart from CEAF-E, for which precision does not show a clear pattern, all metrics reach the highest precision scores for all languages in the base example distribution.

From the given precision and recall figures, it is not surprising that the final F-scores of most metrics are also highest for the original distribution of positive vs. negative training examples. What is surprising here is that the BLANC metric reaches highest scores in the 1:2 train ratio for which neither the precision nor the recall perform best. This, we assume, is due to the more complex way of calculating BLANC's final score, which as Recasens and Hovy (2011) discuss puts equal emphasis on coreference and non-coreference links. Yet, the improvement in scores is, as an average over all languages, less than 1%, which we do not consider noteworthy.

On the basis of those observations, we can conclude that instance sampling does not lead to a considerable improvement of the CR system performance for most of the four evaluation metrics. The only relatively higher figures were reached by MUC's and B^3's recall as well as for BLANC's final scores. Our assumption is that the high concentration of positively labeled examples lead to overmerged entities for which the evaluation metrics reach better recall, but this does not necessarily lead to an overall better performance.

4.3 Differences Across Languages

Since in this evaluation approach we are more interested into how the given change in the training ratio influences the overall performance of the system per language and not each separate metric, we use the scores (listed in table 3) that are achieved by the average calculation of the F-score for each separate language. It is surprising to see that for all languages, apart from Dutch, there is no improvement on the overall performance of the system for any of the artificially created samples. For Dutch, the averaged F-score rises slightly but gradually for the samples 1:10, 1:7 and 1:5, where for the latter sample the classifier reaches an averaged performance of 16.34% as compared to its performance in the base distribution – 15.70%. Again, this is not an exceedingly high improvement of system performance. However, a possible explanation for the fact that instance sampling reaches better results only for Dutch might be triggered by its outlier nature and considerably low overall performance. On the basis of that, we can assume that instance sampling can be more advantageous for less efficient memory-based classifiers than for the high performance ones. Yet, the change in scores might also be based on the variations across the annotation schemes of the different languages. In order to determine the exact reason, further investigation on the topic is needed.

4.4 Differences Across Language Families

A multilingual coreference resolution system as UBIU is hard to design in a way in which it will be able to perform optimally for each newly introduced language. Thus, it is reasonable to assume that system generalizations and respectively optimizations will be more sensible if based around the concept of the language family and not the separate language. Accordingly, we attempt a further generalization of the system performance that allows us to note the differences in the classification output for the Romance and Germanic language families. In table 4, we report the averaged results. Yet, the classifier performance curves across the samples formed on the basis of the two language families and not on the separate languages again do not show a significant variation from one another. Both performance types gradually decrease for each sample, which shows that there are no specific differences among language families that can be captured by an instance sampling approach.

5 Conclusion and Future Work

In the current paper, we presented our results from an instance sampling approach applied on a memory-based coreference resolution system. The novelty of our work lies in the investigation and employment of the sampling procedure in a multilingual environment that, to our knowledge, has not yet been explored. We show that despite the intermediate differences in precision and recall over the four evaluation metrics their overall F-scores are highest for the base sample distribution. Our hypothesis is that when trained on a sample with high concentration of positive examples, classifiers attempt the classification process in a way that keeps the ratio of positive vs. negative examples proportionate in their output. This leads to overmerged entities for which some metrics reach better recall, yet this does not necessarily lead to a boosted overall performance because of the generally lower precision. However, the increase of performance for one of the languages, Dutch, shows that instance sampling can be advantageous to some languages. Based on the language family we did not observe a considerable variation in the system performance. On account of our results, we believe that coreference resolution approaches should further concentrate more on the integration of new and novel linguistic information as well as world knowledge rather than on technical and statistical system optimization.

Acknowledgment

We gratefully acknowledge the support of the Deutsche Forschungsgemeinschaft (DFG) through the Collaborative Research Center SFB/TR 8 Spatial Cognition (Project I5-DiaSpace).

References

Amit Bagga and Breck Baldwin. 1998. Algorithms for Scoring Coreference Chains. In *The First International Conference on Language Resources and Evaluation Workshop on Linguistics Coreference*.

Walter Daelemans and Antal van den Bosch. 2005. *Memory Based Language Processing*. Cambridge University Press.

Walter Daelemans, Jakub Zavrel, Ko van der Sloot, and Antal van den Bosch. 2007. TiMBL: Tilburg Memory Based Learner – version 6.1 – Reference Guide. Technical Report ILK 07-07, Induction of Linguistic Knowledge, Computational Linguistics, Tilburg University.

Lynette Hirschman. 1997. MUC-7 Coreference Task Definition.

Véronique Hoste. 2005. *Optimization Issues in Machine Learning of Coreference Resolution*. Ph.D. thesis, University of Antwerp.

Xiaoqiang Luo. 2005. On coreference resolution performance metrics. In *HLT '05*, Morristown, USA.

Ruslan Mitkov. 1998. Robust Pronoun Resolution with Limited Knowledge. In *Proceedings of ACL/COLING 1998*, Montreal, Canada.

Vincent Ng and Claire Cardie. 2002a. Combining Sample Selection and Error-Driven Pruning for Machine Learning of Coreference Rules. In *Proceedings of EMNLP 2002*.

Vincent Ng and Claire Cardie. 2002b. Improving Machine Learning Approaches to Coreference Resolution. In *Proceedings of ACL 2002*, Philadelphia, PA.

Massimo Poesio, Tomonori Ishikawa, Sabine Schulte im Walde, and Renata Vieira. 2002. Acquiring Lexical Knowledge For Anaphora Resolution. In *Proceedings of LREC 2002*, Las Palmas, Gran Canaria.

Altaf Rahman and Vincent Ng. 2009. Supervised Models for Coreference Resolution. In *Proceedings of EMNLP 2009*, Singapore.

Marta Recasens and Eduard Hovy. 2009. A Deeper Look into Features for Coreference Resolution. In *Proceedings of DAARC 2009*.

Marta Recasens and Eduard Hovy. 2011. BLANC: Implementing the Rand Index for Coreference Evaluation. *Natural Language Engineering*.

Marta Recasens, Lluís Màrquez, Emili Sapena, M.Antònia Martí, Mariona Taulé, Véronique Hoste, Massimo Poesio, and Yannick Versley. 2010. SemEval-2010 Task 1: Coreference resolution in multiple languages. In *Proceedings of SemEval 2010*, Uppsala, Sweden.

Wee Meng Soon, Hwee Tou Ng, and Daniel Chung Yong Lim. 2001. A Machine Learning Approach to Coreference Resolution of Noun Phrases. *Computational Linguistics*, 27(4).

Olga Uryupina. 2004. Linguistically Motivated Sample Selection for Coreference Resolution. In *Proceedings of DAARC 2004*, Sao Miguel, Portugal.

Marc Vilain, John Burger, John Aberdeen, Dennis Connolly, and Lynette Hirschman. 1995. A Model-Theoretic Coreference Scoring Scheme. In *Proceedings MUC 1995*, Columbia, MD.

Holger Wunsch, Sandra Kübler, and Rachael Cantrell. 2009. Instance Sampling Methods for Pronoun Resolution. In *Proceedings of RANLP 2009*, Borovets, Bulgaria.

Shanheng Zhao and Hwee Tou Ng. 2007. Identification and Resolution of Chinese Zero Pronouns: A Machine Learning Approach. In *Proceedings of EMNLP-CoNLL 2007*, Prague, Czech Republic.

Desislava Zhekova and Sandra Kübler. 2010. UBIU: A Language-Independent System for Coreference Resolution. In *Proceedings of SemEval 2010*, Uppsala, Sweden.

Author Index